T0238486

Working Around Disruptions
of Network Infrastructures

Amro Al-Akkad

Working Around Disruptions of Network Infrastructures

Mobile Ad-Hoc Systems for Resilient Communication in Disasters

 **Springer** Vieweg

Amro Al-Akkad
Sankt Augustin, Germany

Dissertation an der RWTH Aachen, 2015

ISBN 978-3-658-12615-5   ISBN 978-3-658-12616-2 (eBook)
DOI 10.1007/978-3-658-12616-2

Library of Congress Control Number: 2016930404

Springer Vieweg

© Springer Fachmedien Wiesbaden 2016
This work is subject to copyright. All rights are reserved by the Publisher, whether the whole or part of the material is concerned, specifically the rights of translation, reprinting, reuse of illustrations, recitation, broadcasting, reproduction on microfilms or in any other physical way, and transmission or information storage and retrieval, electronic adaptation, computer software, or by similar or dissimilar methodology now known or hereafter developed.
The use of general descriptive names, registered names, trademarks, service marks, etc. in this publication does not imply, even in the absence of a specific statement, that such names are exempt from the relevant protective laws and regulations and therefore free for general use.
The publisher, the authors and the editors are safe to assume that the advice and information in this book are believed to be true and accurate at the date of publication. Neither the publisher nor the authors or the editors give a warranty, express or implied, with respect to the material contained herein or for any errors or omissions that may have been made.

Printed on acid-free paper

Springer Vieweg is a brand of Springer Fachmedien Wiesbaden
Springer Fachmedien Wiesbaden GmbH is part of Springer Science+Business Media
(www.springer.com)

Abstract

The use of information and communication technology services can be constrained in disaster situations, when it is important for affected persons to receive and send up-to-date information on current incidents and their evolution. Previous studies have shown the importance of propagating disaster-relevant information over the World Wide Web. In such situations, users without Internet access find themselves in an "information vacuum" until the network infrastructure is restored.

This thesis addresses the exploitation of cell phones in disaster situations which cause the disruption of network infrastructure. The first part of this thesis collects empirical material on how people creatively use remnants of technology to communicate in disasters. The empirical data is drawn from primary and secondary sources: interviews with domain experts and people who have experienced a disaster situation, as well as external reports and scientific literature. Based on this empirical foundation, this work develops a conceptual framework that comprises a collection of quality attributes. When exploiting cell phones to create ad-hoc systems in disaster situations, the implementation of such quality attributes can potentially support the resilience of mobile ad-hoc systems.

The second part of this thesis focuses on the iterative design and evaluation of two such mobile ad-hoc systems, showing how these quality attributes can be implemented. To explore the feasibility of the systems and their implications for the work practices in the emergency response domain, they are deployed under close-to-real disaster conditions. The developed systems distinguish themselves from the state of the art in two essential aspects: first, they are independent from preexisting network infrastructure, and second, they run on off-the-shelf devices. Thus, this work addresses the following research questions:

- How do people creatively use remnants of technology in disaster situations?
- Which quality attributes for ubiquitous computing systems can support resilience in such situations?
- How can such quality attributes be implemented for smartphones?

Zusammenfassung

Die Nutzung von netzwerkbasierten Informations- und Kommunikationsdiensten kann in Krisensituationen eingeschränkt sein, wenn es für Betroffene wichtig ist Informationen zu aktuellen Ereignissen und deren Entwicklung zu erhalten zu verbreiten. Vorhergehende Studien haben gezeigt, dass Informationen zu Krisen häufig über das Internet verbreitet werden. Nutzer ohne Internet-Zugriff befinden sich dadurch in einem 'Informationsvakuum', bis die Netzwerkinfrastruktur wiederhergestellt ist.

Diese Arbeit erforscht den Einsatz von Mobiltelefonen für Krisensituationen, in denen Störungen in der Kommunikationsinfrastruktur auftreten. Hierfür wird empirisches Material gesammelt, welches beschreibt, wie Personen kreativ noch funktionierende Teile der IKT einsetzen, um in Krisensituationen zu kommunizieren in denen die Infrastruktur gestört ist. Das empirische Material setzt sich aus primären und sekundären Quellen zusammen: Es wurden Nutzer-Interviews mit Experten des Krisenmanagements und Personen, welche unmittelbar eine Krisensituation erlebt haben oder anderweitig betroffen waren, geführt. Des Weiteren wurden externe Berichte in den Medien sowie die Forschungsliteratur untersucht. Auf der Grundlage dieser Empirie wird ein konzeptionelles Rahmenwerk erstellt, welches sich auf einer Sammlung von Qualitätsattributen stützt. Wenn Mobiltelefone dafür genutzt werden um in Krisensituation ad-hoc Systeme aufzubauen, kann die Umsetzung dieser Qualitätsattribute potentiell die Resilienz mobiler ad-hoc Systeme unterstützen.

Der zweite Teil dieser Arbeit widmet sich der iterativen Entwicklung zweier mobiler ad-hoc Systeme mit dem Ziel, exemplarisch Gestaltungsansätze für die konzipierten Qualitätsattribute aufzuzeigen. Um die technische Machbarkeit beider Systeme sowie deren Wechselwirkungen mit bestehenden Arbeitspraktiken der Domäne des Krisenmanagements zu untersuchen, wird deren Einsatz in krisenähnlichen Szenarien erprobt. Die entwickelten Systeme unterscheiden sich vom Stand der Technik in zwei wesentlichen Aspekten: a) ermöglichen sie Kommunikation ohne bestehende Kommunikationsinfrastruktur und b) lassen sie sich auf handelsüblichen Smartphones installieren. Diese Arbeit trägt damit zur Beantwortung folgender Forschungsfragen bei:

- Wie setzen Personen in Krisensituationen kreativ noch funktionierende Technologie ein?
- Welche Qualitätsattribute für allgegenwärtige Systeme können Resilienz in solchen Situationen unterstützen?
- Wie können solche Qualitätsattribute für Smartphones umgesetzt werden?

Acknowledgements

First and foremost, I would like to thank my beloved family for their support and encouragement all these years. Especially, I am grateful to my wife and son for their love and patience—it has been a long road.

I would like to acknowledge and thank my principal supervisor Professor Matthias Jarke for the guidance and support that was essential for the completion of this thesis. I would also like to express my gratitude to my second supervisor Professor Volker Wulf for making helpful suggestions how to consolidate my research.

Leonardo Ramirez Zúñiga was an invaluable mentor who inspired me to frame my research subject. I am incredibly thankful to him, not only for setting me on this path, but especially for his habit of daring to disagree and challenging me by asking the difficult questions. I am also extremely thankful to Alexander Boden for helping me with arranging my ideas and pointing out key aspects. Further, I would like to express my thanks to Sebastian Denef and Dave Randall for supporting me in publishing my work in order to discuss it with the research community.

My employment at the Fraunhofer Institute for Applied Information Technology provided me a creative space to develop and to reflect on my ideas. I would like to thank Markus Eisenhauer, head of the user-centered computing group, for his high degree of trust. Of course, I am grateful to Andrea Bernards for supporting me to cope with the workaday hurdles. I would also like to give my special thanks to Andreas Zimmermann for giving me the encouragement to implement my ideas. Further, I would like to thank Mark Vinkovits, Erion Elmasllari, and Jonathan Simon for advising me on aspects of my research. Many other colleagues, students, and persons of the IT infrastructure and the administration assisted me with the preparation of this thesis, both directly and indirectly. However, instead of making a long list of names I simply like to say from the bottom of my heart—thanks!

My research was funded by the European Union as part of the BRIDGE project (FP7SEC-2010-1). In the project I have collaborated with a lot of partners. I would particularly like to express my gratitude to Christian Raffelsberger for all the discussions on complex technical aspects and an ideal way of cooperating. I would also like to thank Thomas Kulbe, Lisa Woods, Monika Büscher, Peeter Kool, and Friedrich Steinhäusler for their support before and during the user studies.

Doing a PhD in mobile computing for disaster situations meant that I had the possibility to meet with many great persons. This ranged from professional first responders to casualties who immediately have faced a disaster. I would like to express my gratitude for their generosity in telling me about their experiences and their good will to participate in the user studies. Without their support this research would have not been possible.

Contents

List of Figures

List of Tables

Abbreviations

3G	Third Generation (of mobile telecommunications technology)
AP	Access Point
API	Application Programming Interface
ARP	Address Resolution Protocol
ASCII	American Standard Code for Information Interchange
App	Mobile Application
BRIDGE	Project acronym. Full title: "Bridging resources and agencies in large-scale emergency management"
BSSID	Basic Service Set Identifier
CSCW	Computer-supported cooperated work
dBm	decibel milli-Watts
FO	Front-line Officer
GO	Group Owner
GPS	Global Positioning System
GSM	Global System for Mobile Communications
HCI	Human-Computer Interaction
HTTP	Hypertext Transfer Protocol
ICT	Information and Communication Technology
ID	Identifier
IDE	Integrated Development Environment
IEC	International Electrotechnical Commission
IEEE	Institute of Electrical and Electronics Engineers
IMEI	International Mobile Equipment Identifier
IP	Internet Protocol
ISM	Industrial, scientific and medical
ISO	International Organization for Standardization
LTE	Long Term Evolution
MAC	Medium Access Control
MANET	Mobile Ad-Hoc Network
Mbps	Megabit per second
MD5	Message-Digest Algorithm 5
N/A	Not Applicable, Not Available
NGO	Non-Governmental Organization
NFC	Near Field Communication
QR	Quick Response

QUAT	Quality Attribute
P2P	Peer-to-Peer
RFID	Radio-Frequency Identification
RQ	Research question defined in the scope of this thesis
SARS	Severe acute respiratory syndrome
SIG	Special Interest Group
SMS	Short Message Service
SOS	Save our soules
SQL	Structured Query Language
SSID	Service Set Identifier
STA	Station
TCP	Transmission Control Protocol
Ubicomp	Ubiquitous Computing
UDP	User Datagram Protocol
UI	User Interface
UMTS	Universal Mobile Telecommunications System
URL	Uniform Resource Locator
VPN	Virtual Private Network
WiFi	A local wireless area network that is based on IEEE 802.11 standards
WLAN	Wireless Local Area Network
WPS	WiFi Protected Setup
XML	Extensible Markup Language

Conventions

For the sake of readability the thesis uses the following conventions:

- The "s/he" expression refers to neutral persons.

- Quotes are put *italicized*.

- Due to privacy issues images depicting persons have been reworked. Except the author of this work, the faces of persons have been retouched.

- Code fragments and other technical constructs are set in `Courier` font.

- If no author was indicated for a referenced article/report/standard, the name of the institution/publisher/organization is instead enlisted as the author.

1 Introduction

This thesis examines opportunities for facilitating communication in the aftermath of disasters despite challenges arising from disrupted infrastructures. The thesis presents a study of ad-hoc created wireless networks in the field of ubiquitous computing (ubicomp) using smartphones as the central communication platform.

Various forms of ICT services have found their way into the everyday world. People have become, for instance, accustomed to use ICT services such as blogs, Wikis, texting services, such as SMS and Whatsapp, map-based services such as Google Maps, social networks such as Facebook, or microblogging services such as Sina Weibo or Twitter. Dourish and Bell (2011) point out that as a result of this omnipresence of ICT services, ubicomp technologies have become embedded in social structures. They are increasingly used to support complex social actions, such as social engagement, domestic regulation, or civic protest. From a technical perspective this 'embrace of technology' has mainly been driven by two intertwined movements: the increasing roll-out of broadband coverage, such as UMTS / LTE or public WiFi hotspots, and the proliferation of portable wireless devices like smartphones and tablet computers.

While people are more and more relying on technology in their everyday routine, having access to ICT services can equally be crucial in disaster (Coyle & Meier 2009) situations, when it is important to obtain and send up-to-date information on the current emergency. What people need to communicate can be very diverse. For example, people want to inform family members or friends about their state of health, to ask for shelter, or to request medical support and nutrition. Related to this, a relatively new research field called *crisis informatics* (Hagar & Haythornthwaite 2005; Palen et al. 2009) evolved from the broader research areas of human-computer interaction (HCI) and computer-supported cooperative work (CSCW). The research field of crisis informatics examines sociotechnical concerns in disasters and how to address those with technology design. A large set of studies (cf. Palen & Liu 2007; Palen & Vieweg 2008; Shklovski et al. 2008; Qu et al. 2011; Starbird & Palen 2012; Perng et al. 2013) examined how people in distress or affected people near or far away from the impact zone of a disaster use ICT services in order to convey their needs. These studies focused mainly on the use of ICT services while the underlying technological structures are still working.

However, the availability of ICT services can be severely disrupted in disaster situations where the ability to communicate emergency needs can be critical. These disruptions can result from damage to or congestion in preexisting network structures, or from large-scale outages. Analyzing the challenges that people experienced in the aftermath of the February 2011 Christchurch earthquake (see section 2.2), Sutton (2012) framed this phenomenon as "online is off". She points out that, while there are people who are propagating information on the World Wide Web, at the same time there are people who do not have Internet access, and are left in an "information vacuum" until network structures can be restored. A few studies have focused on the use of remnants of technology in the aftermath of a disaster. For example, some studies (Mark & Semaan 2008; Mark et al. 2009; Semaan & Mark 2011) analyzed the use of technology in ongoing, lingering war zones. Also, Palen et al. (2011) investigated how people re-appropriate discarded resources, such as a power generator in response to a large-scale outage caused by a hurricane.

At first glance, disrupted infrastructure in these circumstances introduces severe and unanticipated challenges. On the other hand, as disruptions cause changes in the technological landscape, new opportunities to combine remnants of technology into ad-hoc assemblages become apparent. Therefore, this thesis investigates how people creatively use remnants of technology to deal with the adverse effects arising from disruptions of infrastructure. To 'use' in conjunction with remnants of technology, means: to repurpose, reconfigure, improvise, or combine surviving portions of technology, adopt discarded resources, or share access to still working ICT services. Building on the analysis of the collected empirical material this thesis further proposes eight quality attributes that potentially can support the ad-hoc creation of network infrastructures. Furthermore, it examines the state-of-the-art for ad-hoc communication and contributes to this stream of research by designing and evaluating smartphone-based prototypes in iterative cycles.

1.1 Research Questions and Approach

The work being presented in the thesis can be framed by three research questions, as follows:

RQ1 How do people creatively use remnants of technology in disaster situations?

RQ2 Which quality attributes for ubiquitous computing systems can support resilience in such situations?

RQ3 How can such quality attributes be implemented for smartphones?

To answer RQ1 this thesis will examine empirical material from primary and secondary sources, which describes how people creatively use remnants of technology to restore their ability to communicate despite disruptions of preexisting networks.

To tackle RQ2 the author proposes a set of quality attributes that are inspired by the findings that resulted from answering RQ1 as well as, by a thorough review of the state of the art of wireless communication technologies. In doing so, this thesis examines research approaches pursuing mobile ad-hoc communication by examining the extent to which these technologies meet the suggested set of quality attributes.

RQ3 will be addressed by the iterative design and evaluation of two systems that implement the suggested set of quality attributes resulting from tackling RQ2. To get a better understanding of the degree to which these systems may foster the ad-hoc creation of resilient network infrastructure, the evaluations are conducted in close-to-real disaster situations.

1.2 Contributions

In answering the three research questions identified in the previous section, this work makes three contributions as illustrated in Figure 1.

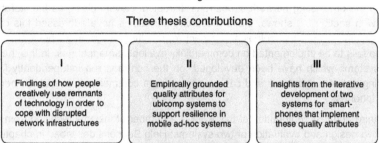

Figure 1 Contributions made by the thesis

The first contribution is an investigation into how people creatively use remnants of technology in the light of disrupted network infrastructures. Orienting to the methodology of grounded theory, the work has taken an exploratory stance while collecting a variety of materials on how people communicate their needs in disaster situations without making upfront a definitive statement about the underlying form of network structures. The purpose of this research was to open up new opportunities for the design of systems enabling communication in disaster situations. Having positioned the focus on situations of disrupted network infrastructure, three categories relating to how people creatively use remnants of technologies have been identified. The empirical material has been drawn from primary and secondary sources (see also section 3.3 for details). *Primary sources* cover several interviews with professionals of the emergency response domain and people who either witnessed an emergency or a disaster, or were affected by one. Furthermore, *secondary sources* comprise a review of the scientific literature and also reports, describing how people creatively use technology to cope with a disaster situation.

The second contribution of this work reflects a set of quality attributes, grounded in the analysis of the empirical findings. The purpose of suggesting these quality attributes, or shortly qualities, is to consider them for the design of ubicomp systems to support resilience in network infrastructures. Proposing empirically grounded qualities for the design of technology facilitating communications despite disruptions is a novel approach to the best of the author's knowledge. The author does not claim that having implemented these empirically grounded qualities would have helped to avoid communication hurdles in all of the incidents that inspired the formulation of one or more of the qualities. Instead, the author argues that implementing these qualities in ubicomp systems can potentially support resilience in network infrastructures. Of course, a number of emergency systems (see section 2.5) that enable people to communicate their needs when being immediately inside the impact zone of a disaster or from remote locations already exist. However, these solutions require the functioning of the preexisting underlying network structures. Furthermore, a lot of research has tackled the challenge of enabling ad-hoc communications for situations where the preexisting network structure is disrupted. Nevertheless, as the literature review in section 6.3 shows, these research approaches have addressed this challenge mainly from a technological perspective, resulting in systems whose practical usage fails to be implemented on commercially available smartphones. In this thesis, the systems which have been developed, on the contrary, run independently from existing network structures and can be deployed on commercially available Android smartphones.

The third and last contribution of this work is a number of insights resulting from the iterative design and evaluation of two systems: Help Beacons described in chapter 7 and Local Cloud described in chapter 8. Both systems exemplify how the suggested qualities can be implemented for smartphone-based systems. In order to explore the technical feasibility of the developed prototypes, the author evaluated both systems in situations as close to a *real* disaster situation as one can get. For instance, the first prototype of the Help Beacons system has been evaluated in a real-world exercise that was organized inside an underground tunnel, where curves, a high amount of steel, and vapor weakened the strength of signals. The author considered this strategy as very important in identifying benefits and limitations of the prototypes. Moreover, to understand the implications and practicality of the systems for the domain of emergency response, the author let professional first responders and members of the public gain first-hand experiences with the prototypes during these real-world exercises. For the scope of this work, the author had to look into two aspects of implementation. At first, he conducted, in section 6.2, a thorough review of wireless communication technologies for smartphones, and based on this review he argues, in section 6.4, for using WiFi in infrastructure mode, i.e. the most widespread form of WiFi networks, as the baseline technology to enable ad-hoc communications in the frame of this work. Based on this selection, the author examined to which extent the two most widespread mobile platforms, iOS and Android, support the development of systems using WiFi in infrastructure mode as the main backbone for communication, before he decided to build the systems on top of the Android platform.

1.3 Thesis Walkthrough

The following chapter 2 provides the background for this work. The relevant disaster terminology and disaster situations are explained. Subsequently, this chapter dis-

4

cusses the notion of infrastructure, and it underlines the importance of the research field of crisis informatics. Finally, this chapter summarizes available mobile emergency systems.

Chapter 3 firstly presents the user groups focused on in the thesis, and it explains how the data was collected and by which methodology it has been analyzed. It also explains how prototypes have iteratively been developed in the frame of this work.

Chapter 4 provides the empirical foundation for this work. The focus is set on three categories of how people creatively use remnants of technology to communicate their needs despite disruptions of the network infrastructure.

Chapter 5 presents the conceptual framework developed in this work. Inspired by the empirical data presented in the previous chapter, eight quality attributes are defined whose implementation potentially can support resilience in the design of mobile ad-hoc systems.

Chapter 6 to begin with recaps technological foundations of wireless communication technologies that are commonly available in smartphones. And then presents research approaches that aim towards the opportunistic construction of mobile ad-hoc networks.

Chapter 7 presents the Help Beacons system as the first of the two prototypes which were developed in the course of this thesis. In order to provide an account for the quality attributes that were previously defined in chapter 5, the qualities are incrementally implemented in the Help Beacons system.

Chapter 8 describes the development of the Local Cloud system. As in chapter 7, the Local Cloud system exemplifies how the quality attributes, which were previously defined in chapter 5, can be implemented, and thus what benefits can be gained from such implementation.

Finally, chapter 9 concludes the thesis by explaining how its contributions helped to address the research questions raised in the introduction. Moreover, this chapter describes potential aspects which could be explored in future work.

2 Background

This chapter elaborates on the background of this thesis. First, it defines the body of terms when referring to disaster and the domain of emergency response. Subsequently, core information is summarized on all disasters, which are relevant for the presented work. Moreover, this chapter introduces the notion of infrastructure, which forms of infrastructure can emerge in the aftermath of disasters, and how people creatively engage in critical situations to form new infrastructures. Then, it presents crisis informatics as an emerging field of research, and highlights its importance by outlining disaster situations in which people have exploited different mediums of ICT. Finally, this chapter closes with a review of existing mobile emergency systems.

2.1 Terminology

This section introduces relevant terms with regard to the application domain of emergency response.

2.1.1 Emergency and Disaster

An **emergency** is an unexpected situation of danger. Examples of an emergency are a car accident, a coal fire, or a power outage. Most emergencies can be handled through routine procedures by one or more agencies. However, when emergency response fails, emergencies can turn into disasters.

A **disaster** is similar to an emergency, but on a much bigger scale. Compared to an emergency it usually involves several agencies of emergency response, which requires response organizations to carefully coordinate their efforts. Disaster situations can comprise either man-made or natural disasters. A natural disaster, for example, is an earthquake, a flooding, a hurricane, a wildfire, and further natural hazards. Examples of man-made disasters are terroristic attacks such as bombings, industrial accidents such as nuclear explosions, or transport accidents such as train crashes.

Several definitions have been developed for the term disaster (Kreps 1984; Gilbert 1998; Perry 1998). Lots of those studies, such as (Gilbert 1998), focus on the destructive nature of a disaster. For instance, how many people lost their lives or homes. Other disaster researchers have developed models to systematically frame the process of how society recovers from a disaster. Most models define time stages where key social processes emerge before, during, and after a disaster (Powell 1954; Dynes 1970; Mileti et al. 1975). The most widely known model is the one of Powell (1954). Powell's model proposes to divide a disaster into eight stages (depicted in Table 1). First, there is the stage of *pre-disaster* that denotes the period of time before the disaster emerges. Then, in the *warning* stage the potentially affected community is informed about the threat; though, in many cases there might be no warning. The third stage of *threat* is when people perceive changed conditions and take preventive actions, such as evacuating people at risk. The *impact* stage denotes the climax of a disaster. At this stage the whole community understands the adverse effects and begins to think about contingency plans. Afterwards, in the *inventory* stage individuals take stock of disruptions. People adapt to what happened and collectively agree on a course of action. For instance, people agree on the resources, which should be protected first of all or which places to go for shelter. In the *rescue* stage people help themselves and people who are nearby. Such help arises in a spontaneous and unofficial manner. Finally, in the stage of remedy professional first responders enter the disaster zone. In the final *recovery* stage the community restores its properties. Often, this stage is referred to as the post-disaster phase. Depending on the destructiveness of a disaster the recovery stage can be of different length.

Stage 0: PRE-DISASTER
State of social system preceding point of impact
Stage 1: WARNING
Precautionary activity includes consultation with members of own social network
Stage 2: THREAT
Perception of change of conditions that prompts survival action
Stage 3: IMPACT
Stage of "holding on" where recognition shifts from individual to community affect and involvement
Stage 4: INVENTORY
Individual takes stock, and begins to move into a collective inventory of what happened
Stage 5: RESCUE
Spontaneous, local, unorganized extrication and first aid; some preventive measures
Stage 6: REMEDY
Organized and professional relief arrive; medical care, preventive and security measures present
Stage 7: RECOVERY
Individual rehabilitation and readjustment; community restoration of property; organizational preventative measures against recurrence; community evaluation

Table 1 Eight socio-temporal stages of disaster

Source: (Powell 1954)

Some research points out that disasters do not take place across specific stages of time. For instance, Neal (1997) shows that the actions occurring in the stages described in Powell's model may overlap and that the recovery process might be long and complex. Further, Palen et al. (2009) argue that the boundaries between the stages are fuzzy and that different groups of people may experience different stages at different times.

2.1.2 Crisis, Crisis Management, and Emergency Response

A typical definition for the term *crisis* is that of a "larger" disaster, i.e. a situation in which societies suffer from damage or unavailability of routine infrastructure (Kreps 1984). Due to their similarity, both terms are often used synonymously. However, the latter term covers way more than the former one. Besides man-made or natural disasters, a crisis can refer to severe physical disease, economic decrease, starvation, inadequate housing and further. All these examples show that the term crisis can refer to situations that can last for a significantly longer time than the term disaster encompasses.

The terms crisis management, disaster management or emergency management are used to express nearly the same thing, as the boundaries between all notions are not clear-cut. Similarly, the terms crisis response or emergency response are utilized to describe the same thing. Nevertheless, the author likes to use the terms crisis management and emergency response in the remainder of this work to express the following. *Crisis management* refers to the whole process of sub processes involving humans and systems to deal with an unexpected disaster situation. And, *emergency response* is rather used in the context when referring to the application domain and the organizations and agencies being involved in crisis management.

2.1.3 First Responders

A common misconception of the meaning of the term first responders is that this only encloses trained professionals that are commanded to enter a disaster zone, such as fire fighters or paramedics. However, in many situations victims either help themselves or are assisted by people who are nearby and have the courage to help spontaneously and in an unofficial manner, as it was already underlined in the rescue stage of Powell's (1954) model. This is why Palen and Liu (2010) point out that first responders are often not professionals, but people from the local communities or volunteers. In fact, in the light of disruptions those people emerge into groups of responders before professional response is ready to take action. Examples of such actions were observed during the recent 2011 Norway attacks (see section 2.2). It has been reported that people in the surrounding area of Utoya island noticed gunfire and observed people requesting to being picked up with nearby boats (Rosenberg 2011). Some people who made these observations used their private boats to rescue people from the island before the gunman would shoot them.

Further, volunteers' actions might be performed when the stage of 'remedy' has already taken place. At this stage, professional response necessitates the support of amateur first responders. Again, during the 2011 Norway attacks volunteers transported policemen with their private boats from the mainland to Utoya island, as previously the police boat had suffered from an engine failure due to being loaded too heavily. In retrospective on their investigations on the 2011 Norway attacks, Perng et al. (2013) framed such phenomenon as 'peripheral response'.

Summarizing, professional first responders are those people belonging to formal response units (fire brigade, ambulance, police, etc.), and amateur first responders are members of the public, that often are the first one to arrive at the incident site taking action to help people in need.

2.1.4 Resilience

Originally, the concept of resilience has been developed in the fields of ecology and psychology. In the field of ecology Holling (1973) points out that resilience defines the persistence of relationships within a system. It reflects to which degree a system is able to deal with *"changes of state variables, driving variables, and parameters"* and still survive. In Hollings' definition resilience is a property of a system and its persistence is the result. In the field of psychology mainly studies, such as (Benight et al. 2000; Galea et al. 2002), have looked into how people retain a positive stance despite experiencing a disaster or war. Manyena (2006) gives a detailed literature review on resilience while taking a stance of psychology. However, to sustain the scope of this thesis, the author prefers not to discuss ecological or psychological views on resilience. Rather, the goal is to view resilience from a disaster and system perspective.

Examining the effects of the World Trade Center attacks in 2001 Kendra and Wachtendorf (2003) define resilience as the ability of an individual or organization to adapt to or to 'bounce back' from unanticipated disruptions of technological systems. In general, resilience reflects how people deal with a situation in order to regain an acceptable state (Wildavsky 1989; Comfort 1999). Similarly, from a system perspective Hollnagel et al. (2011) indicate that the ability to respond to unforeseen events, such as disasters, is one of the four key abilities of resilient systems. Further, Urken et al. (2012) describe resilience as the ability of a system to mobilize still functioning elements of the system in order to restore the stability of a system. And if restoration might not be possible, the system shall try to degrade gracefully in order to minimize the adverse effects and "survive" in a temporally acceptable state. And, from a network perspective Sterbenz et al. (2010) define resilience as *"the ability of the network to provide and maintain an acceptable level of service in the face of various faults and challenges to normal operation"*.

This work defines resilience as the ability of humans and systems to regain a state that is temporarily acceptable.

10

2.2 Relevant Disasters

This section summarizes the basic information about man-made and natural disaster situations, which the presented work will refer to.

The 9/11 attacks were a series of four coordinated terroristic attacks that struck New York City and the Washington, D.C., metropolitan area, on 11 September 2001. It was reported that this man-made disaster was organized by the terror group al-Qaeda. The attacks killed 2996 people and caused at least $10 billion due to the destruction of property and infrastructure (IAGS 2004).

The **SARS epidemic** broke out on November 16th, 2002. The severe acute respiratory syndrome (SARS) probably took its course in the Guangdong providence of China (WHO 2003). The epidemic had a wide reach on China's population with low information from official sources on the epidemic per se and how to protect oneself from it (Palen & Liu 2007). Inconveniently, people were living and working in affected areas, helping the epidemic to rage across the region. In total, SARS caused the infection of 8.096 persons and 774 persons died (Smith 2006).

The **2005 London bombings** occurred on 7th July 2005. A series of attacks were undertaken to harm people using London's public transfer system during rush hour in the morning; these bombings are often referred to as 7/7. Four suicide attackers detonated four bombs—three bombs were placed in the London underground and the fourth bomb was placed on a double-decker bus. Besides the four bombers, 52 people were killed and over 700 persons were injured (Storey & Addley 2010).

Hurricane Katrina formed on 25 August 2005. It was the deadliest and most destructive tropical storm. In detail, this disaster killed at least 1883 people and resulted in an economical damage of $108 billion. Hurricane Katrina came with an advanced forewarning. Many people evacuated in preparation of a serious tropical storm. However, they could not return back as early as expected. The most damage emerged from the levee breaches of the lake Pontchartrain causing city-wide flooding (Knabb et al. 2005).

The **2007 Virginia Tech shooting** happened on 16th April 2007. A student of the Virginia Tech University ran amok and shot 32 persons and himself. Further, 17 others were wounded in two separate attacks (Kelman 2014).

The **2008 Hurricane Gustav** was the second most destructive tropical storm of the Hurricane season in the Atlantic in 2008. Several countries were affected, for example Cuba, Jamaica or US Southern States (Beven & Kimberlain 2009). Hurricane Gustav caused the death of 153 people and an economic damage of $6.5 billion (Rogers et al. 2013).

The **2009 L'Aquila earthquake** struck central Italy on 6 April 2009 with a magnitude of 6.3. It was reported that in L'Aquila, which is located in the Abruzzo region, 3.000 to 10.000 buildings have been damaged. The earthquake caused the death of 308 people and approximately 1500 people were injured. Several buildings collapsed and around 65.000 lost their home. The earthquake was felt throughout Abruzzo, as far away as Rome or Umbria (Kennedy 2009).

The **2010 Haiti earthquake** came about a 7.0-magnitude near its Port-au-Prince capitol on 12 January 2010. Due to the earthquake's intensity, as well as the vulnerable infrastructure of Haiti, the earthquake caused severe destructions over the island. By 24 January, at least 52 aftershocks were recorded. Nearly, three million people were affected by the quake (Millar 2010). Between 200.000 and 250.000 people died. In the aftermath of the earthquake, thousands were trapped beneath collapsed structures, which included hospitals and transport facilities.

The **2010 Chile earthquake** occurred off the coast of central Chile on Saturday, 27 February 2010. The earthquake had a magnitude of 8.8 on the moment magnitude scale, with intense shaking lasting for about three minutes (Saavedra 2010). It ranks as the sixth largest earthquake ever to be recorded by a seismograph. It was felt strongly in six Chilean regions, which together make up about 80 percent of the country's population. Tremors were felt in many Argentine cities (Pallardy 2014), and as well in the far north as the city of Ica in southern Peru (approximately 2.400 km). The earthquake's intensity was stronger than the 2010 Haiti earthquake that happened nearly one month before. But, as Chile's infrastructure was more resilient, the effects of the earthquake were relatively 'weak' compared to the 2010 Haiti earthquake.

On 24 July 2010, a stampede happened in the **2010 Love Parade** event in Duisburg, Germany. The Love Parade was an electronic dance music festival, which was carried out annually. The stampede caused the death of 21 people, and at least 500 persons were injured (Helbing & Mukerji 2012). As a consequence of this tragedy, the organizer of the festival announced the permanent end of this music festival.

The **2010/11 Tunisian Revolution** was an intensive campaign of civil resistance. This resistance included a series of demonstrations, which took place in several Tunisian cities, such as Tunis, the capital, but also other towns such as Sidi Bouzid. The resistance started on 18 December 2010 and achieved on 14 January 2011 the suppression of the longtime president Zine El Abidine Ben Ali. Ben Ali's attempt to suppress public protests resulted in over 300 dead and 2000 injured people (Lamont & Boujneh 2012).

In the course of the **2011 Egyptian Revolution**, i.e. in the late January 2011, many Egyptians protested against the current regime by occupying public places all over the country, such as the famous Tahir Square in Cairo. Eventually, the military took sides with the crowd, which resulted in the resignation of the former president Hosni Mubarak. Clashes between security forces of the Egyptian government and protesters resulted in at least 846 persons were killed and over 6.000 persons were injured (BBC News 2011).

The **February 2011 Christchurch earthquake** came about 22 February 2011. It was a powerful natural disaster that severely damaged Christchurch—the second-largest city of New Zealand located in the Canterbury region. The earthquake's intensity was measured to have a magnitude of 6.3. This killed about 185 people and between 1.500-2.000 persons got injured (McSaveney 2014). Further, the earthquake caused widespread damage, in particular to the central part of the city and eastern suburbs. In fact, this earthquake was part of the aftershock sequence of the previous 2010 Canterbury earthquake, which occurred on 4 September 2010. Moreover, this earthquake caused as an aftershock the June 2011 Christchurch earthquake.

The **2011 Norway attacks** occurred on 22nd July 2011. Two sequential lone wolf terrorist attacks caused in total 77 casualties in the Oslo region (CNN Wire Staff 2011). The first attack was a car bomb explosion in the government quarter of the city of Oslo. The second attack occurred nearly two hours later on Utoya—an island located 38km northwest of Oslo city—where the same perpetrator, dressed as a policeman, shot members of the youth division of the Norwegian Labor Party.

Hurricane Sandy was a tropical storm that came about 22 October 2012. It killed several people (148 direct, 138 indirect) and caused a huge economic damage. Estimates assess a damage of $68 billion, at total surpassed only by Hurricane Katrina. Sandy killed at least 286 people in seven countries; for instance, the Bahamas, Cuba, Jamaica, most of the eastern United States, and eastern Canada (Blake et al. 2013).

The **2013 Boston bombings** happened on 15 April 2013. Two pressure cook bombs, i.e. improvised explosive devices, exploded during the Boston Marathon. The explosions killed 3 people and injured circa 264 persons (Kotz 2013). The blasts occurred near the finish line of the marathon and blew out windows on adjacent buildings, though did not cause any structural damage.

The **Syrian civil war** (also known as the Syrian uprising) is an ongoing, armed conflict that started in the early spring of 2011. Inspired by the Arab spring dream a peaceful uprising took place in March 2011. Nationwide demonstrations against President Bashar al-Assad's government spread out spontaneously. However, the governmental forces responded with violent crackdowns. The conflict gradually morphed from peaceful protests to an armed rebellion after months of military conflicts. So far, this war has caused the death of about 200.000 people (Smith-Spark 2014) and about 5 million people have been displaced (Charron & Arnaud 2012).

2.3 Infrastructure

This section summarizes the meaning of the term infrastructure, what forms of infrastructure can emerge in disaster situations, and how people creatively use infrastructural elements in the light of disruptions

2.3.1 Disambiguation of 'Infrastructure'

This thesis draws on Susan Leigh Star's (1999) ethnographical fieldwork to examine the notion of 'infrastructure'. The essential point that resulted from Star's longitudinal fieldwork is that infrastructure is never a thing, but a relation between humans and systems. This means how people interpret and take action towards the availability of infrastructural elements creates infrastructure.

Star (1999, p.380) underlines that infrastructure is commonly understood as a "system of substrates", such as railroads, wires, pipes or plumbing. These are elements that usually become only visible in the presence of failure or disruption. For example, when people look at the signal strength icon of their mobile phone as a result of entering spaces with low or no network coverage. Or when people cannot access remotely persisted data, as cloud services temporarily become unavailable.

According to Star (1999), infrastructure is a fundamental "relational concept", and not solely a system. She points out that certain groups (e.g. residents) can take a technology for granted, such as the functioning of the plumbing system, while another group (e.g. a plumber) can regard such technology as an object of common analysis or challenge. Elements like streets are not per se "infrastructure", but can be regarded as infrastructure based on the relation people establish to the streets. Streets become an element of infrastructure for people who drive cars on them. Infrastructure denotes rather an ongoing process of interpretation of the relations humans have with things they engage with, than referring to an enclosed element being a part of these relations (Star & Ruhleder 1996).

Dourish and Bell (2011) stress, that it is important not to consider "infrastructure" as being quiescent and stable. Infrastructures must rather be actively maintained, and relationships to them must be continually negotiated. Following the above example, due to the wear of streets, streets need to be restored from potholes. Furthermore, the way people use streets requires continuous regulations depending on how and to what extend they can be used. Similarly, in terms of ICT people consider elements like telecommunication networks or email servers not as their immediate infrastructure. Rather, they experience it as an integral part to perform common tasks (Pipek & Wulf 2009), such as composing emails or replying to emails.

With regard to the technical context of this thesis services and network require continuous re-interpretation in order to find new opportunities. The following section details what this notion of infrastructure can imply for the relationship people lose, build and appropriate with technology in the light of disasters.

Immediately, one critical question arises: If infrastructure is a "relation", but not a thing or system, then how can humans appropriate infrastructure? In the scope of emergency response, this thesis proposes that it is the effects of a disaster that are appropriated. This means, in response to disaster situations, people with different contexts come together to form new relationships, which can be appropriated to exploit new opportunities.

Palen and Liu (2007) exemplify this by how people appropriated in the aftermath of the terroristic 9/11 attacks sidewalks as a notice board for missing persons. People placed photographs of missing persons on sidewalks, so that other people can look at them. The whole of all elements, i.e. *"the gaze of concerned others, with eyes, ears and social connections"* creates a potential to trace missing persons (Al-Akkad et al. 2013). All these elements brought together create an infrastructure. In that particular case a notice board where family members or friends could look for help in finding missing persons. Coming back to Star's (1999) definition of infrastructure, parts of a pavement are temporarily borrowed from its normal purpose of being a pedestrian thoroughfare in order to be used as a fundament to place photographs displaying missing persons.

It is important to note here that the pavement per se does not define the infrastructure. The heterogeneous relations that people establish to the photographs placed on parts of the pavement, making it work as a notice board, form the infrastructure. In fact, when relations with elements break down, which is often the case in disaster situations, infrastructural elements become disrupted and remain in this state until they are re-appropriated or incorporated into new arrangements. What this thesis pursues, is to examine how surviving technological elements of infrastructure, shortly *remnants of technology*, can be brought together in order to create new relations forming new infrastructure(s).

Such 'opportunistic' infrastructures might be formed by elements, which are not explicitly meant to support the work of emergency response. Though people affected by a disaster may appropriate elements in unforeseen ways to support their immediate needs, as section 2.4 will explain by some real-world examples.

The author uses the term infrastructure to describe the whole of the relations humans form with technological structures lying beneath applications and the interactions they enable. Throughout this work the author sets the focus on network infrastructures, mostly with smartphones as the central technological infrastructural element.

2.3.2 Forms of Network Structures during Emergency Response

During an emergency response operation, available forms of network structures can be classified through three possible forms of deployment depicted in Figure 2.

Existing structures refers to network structures already present in the impact zone of a disaster. Portions of preexisting infrastructure, which survived the adverse effects of a (large-scale) disaster, may to some extent be operable. For instance, cell towers providing GSM/UMTS, or access points offering WiFi networks might still constitute a resource for communication, which is available inside the disaster impact zone.

These everyday communication elements are, for example similar to fire hoses being a central element for fire fighters to extinguish a fire.

Additionally, fire fighters or other professional first responders may carry with them elements that are *deployable*, i.e. elements that can be used for in-situ deployment of networks. For instance, Ramirez et al. (2012) describe the Landmarke platform that enables the deployment of a mesh network. Fire fighters usually carry door jams with them. These door jams are enhanced with networking technology and used to establish the mesh network. Real-world evaluations of the Landmarke platform have proven a potential to support indoor navigation inside smoke-filled buildings. Although, such a form of network structures might connect to existing network structures, its deployment is carried out in an ad-hoc manner.

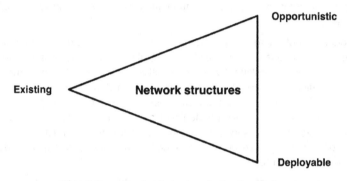

Figure 2 Forms of network structures in disaster situations

The third and last form of network structures is *opportunistic*. Opportunistic refers to the co-incidental use of resources being at hand. For instance, cell phones or tablet computers, which people usually carry with them, can be exploited opportunistically as a resource to communicate in disaster situations. People might use these elements to form new network structures in an improvised manner. Analogue, in the aftermath of a disaster that caused a power outage, a reconstruction engineer may re-appropriate obsolete power generators, as described above in section 2.1.

The last two forms of network structures, i.e. deployable and opportunistic, can be classified into ad-hoc constructed networks. In this regard, Manoj and Baker (2007) point out that it is more challenging to deploy elements in an ad-hoc manner in situations where portions of preexisting infrastructure have survived the effects of a disaster, which is the usual case. A common challenging factor is the interference between surviving elements of existing network structures and elements of ad-hoc constructed network structures.

This thesis focuses on the design and evaluation of systems leveraging opportunistically network structures in an ad-hoc manner. In particular, this thesis

will look into creative use of infrastructural elements in order to create mobile ad-hoc communication systems.

2.3.3 Creative Use of Infrastructural Elements

The improvisation entailed in creating new network infrastructures clearly introduces challenges. But, viewing it from the opposite angle it creates at the same time a new potential that can help to identify new opportunities to deal with technological break-downs. A disaster denotes a state of being unprepared. However, this incomplete-ness creates the need that people look quickly for new plans. In fact, plans that exist before a disaster are often modified or not used at all (Quarantelli 1994; Wachtendorf & Kendra 2004), but people will look for new ways in order to cope with the severe situation. In terms of assembling remnants of technology, *improvisation* means the bringing together of elements such as cell phones (see also next section), tablet PCs, laptops, digital cameras, cloud services like Google maps or dropbox, or social net-works like Facebook. These elements can be used and combined to create unfore-seen arrangements.

In this context, a common misconception is that people in distress are too nervous to act properly. In fact, practitioners, such as (Auf der Heide 2004), and also research studies (Dynes 1970; Quarantelli 1994) have shown the opposite. People creatively use everyday infrastructural elements to deal with particular disaster situations (Kreps & Bosworth 1994). Weick (1993; 1998) coined the process of creatively using at hand infrastructural elements as *bricolage*. This process is sparked off due to the lack of resources, and therefore people create infrastructure out of whatever ele-ments are available to them (Webb, 2004). For instance, during the ongoing civil war in Syria, it was reported that due to the lack of anesthesia medics use metal bars to make patients incautious before performing surgery (Wilson 2014).

Also, people can learn from previous negative experiences and keep 'back up' ele-ments to deal with recurring challenges. For instance, to deal with the flooding caused by the damage of the 2005 Hurricane Katrina a lot of poor African Americans saved themselves in New Orleans by the use of axes which they used to cut a hole in the roof of their attics (CNN News & Lionheart Books Ltd. 2005; Marable & Clarke 2007). Families kept axes in their attics, in the event there was another hurricane that forced them into the attic. In an earlier flooding no one came to rescue people and as they got forced up the stairs into the attic many drowned, as they could not get out onto the roof. Besides, the repurposing of routine infrastructural elements or keeping 'back up' elements, people might adapt new or obsolete elements as exemplified in the empirical material below in section 4.2.3.

Concluding, disruptions trigger the unfolding of natural processes in which people are very well capable of using technology. In this context *use* can con-

note, to repurpose or combine remnants of preexisting technology, adopt discarded resources, or share access to still working ICT services.

2.3.4 Smartphones as a Ubicomp Device Fostering Infrastructure

The availability of broadband communication technologies, such as UMTS or LTE, and wireless communication technologies, such as Bluetooth or WiFi, has significantly increased over the last decade (Whitbeck et al. 2012). Along this development the cell phone has become a ubiquitous device. This resulted in an omnipresence of mobile ICT services. For example, map-based services such as Google Maps or OpenStreetMap, or social networks such as Facebook or Twitter.

People take the cell phone with them nearly everywhere they go. It has become a common practice to take, besides the keys and wallet, the cell phone before leaving the house. In the notion of Weiser (1999), in the present world cell phones are woven into the fabric of everyday life and thus increasingly affect the spaces people enter. The cell phone is the ubicomp device of the last decade. People use cell phones to interact with their immediate environment and their social network.

De Souza e Silva and Frith (2012) allude that cell phones constitute interfaces to the world and the immediate environments around humans. While Weiser's ubicomp vision was that smart objects would dissolve in the environment, cell phones as computing devices are highly visible and can be used to accomplish many and varied tasks. Cell phones are the most mainstream of actual implementation of Weiser's ubicomp vision. The research community has appropriated the cell phone as, if not the primary, platform for the design of ubicomp systems (Kwok 2009).

It has been shown that people are commonly using their cell phone to communicate their needs in emergency or disaster situations (Al-Akkad & Zimmermann 2011; Al-Akkad & Zimmermann 2012). For example, investigations of the relief work for Hurricane Katrina indicated that cell phones were the first ICT devices becoming operational in the aftermath of the hurricane (Farnham et al. 2006). Landgren and Nulden (2007) point out that cell phones can be a very useful tool for emergency response work. Cell phones can help to negotiate and establish communications between professionals in order to collectively tackle the challenges imposed by a disaster.

Due to its strong proliferation, the smartphone is the ubicomp device of the present. To benefit from this fact, this thesis will build prototypes for smartphone-based systems.

2.4 Crisis Informatics

In the light of a disaster people face situations in which routine procedures and practices might not be applicable anymore (Quarantelli 2005). Many studies have looked at how affected communities deal with disruptions, and how people appropriate new forms of procedures to deal with unanticipated conditions (Dynes 1970; Mileti et al.

1975). Given the ubiquity of ICT in their everyday life, people tend to depend on ICT services in disaster situations, too. Also, professional response units deploy ICT in order to support the coordination of response efforts. The importance of ICT in disaster situations led to the emergency of a relatively new field of research in CSCW and HCI called *crisis informatics*. The goal of crisis informatics is to examine sociotechnical aspects of a crisis and how to address those with the design of technology. The term itself was coined in 2005 by Hagar and Haythornthwaite (2005). Besides the formal response, the research field of crisis informatics also sets the focus on the practices of members of the public to use technology in order to deal with the contingent needs created by a disaster, which is commonly understood as informal response (Hagar & Haythornthwaite 2005; Palen et al. 2010).

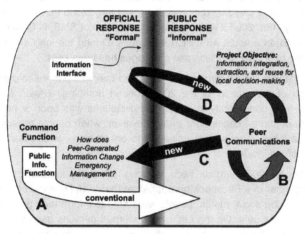

Figure 3 Schematic of ICT-enabled information pathways

Source: (Palen et al. 2010)

In particular, Palen et al. (2010) call out for a vision that considers a bidirectional flow of information between formal and informal responders. Figure 3 illustrates four types of information flows. The white arrow (A) shows that traditionally the management of public information goes from the formal into the informal spheres. The dark gray arrow (B) indicates that communication among peers of informal response occur and are proliferating due to the emergence of pervasive ICT systems. This evolution has two consequences being depicted by the two remaining black arrows (C and D). While arrow C shows that publicly-generated data can flow into the spheres of formal response and be used there, arrow D highlights that this data, after some processing, can also be sent back to the informal spheres. In fact, official formal response organizations have considered to follow such a vision, as stated in the words of the FEMA Chief Fugate: *"we have to look at the public as a resource, not as a liability"* (O'Keefe 2009). However, to let such a vision become reality requires not only a rethinking of conservative attitudes, but new regulations and tools that help to assess out which data sources are trustworthy and which not (Palen et al. 2011). Also, in the light of emerging social media technologies, it requires a continuous assessment of available tools in order to understand which systems are appropriate for which information pathway (Reuter et al. 2012).

For instance, there have been reports about a grassroots approach of people starting to share information about the locality of apparently infected persons during the SARS epidemic. For this form of peer-to-peer (P2P) communication, people mainly used the well-known short message service (SMS). People literally confined themselves at home or at the hospital in order to avoid cross-infections of SARS. Yu (2004) explains that in the event of the SARS epidemic, *"mobile phones became a powerful anti-SARS medium, and SMS the people's weapon for fighting the highly contagious virus"*. On January 10th, 2003 it was reported that the flow of SMS, in Guangdong province added up to an amount 45 million messages. During the long aftermath of the crisis, a volume of up to 120 million text messages has been sent.

Furthermore, people in underground stations used their cell phones to capture images and videos of the attacks of the 2005 London bombings (Palen & Liu 2007). Since, at this time connectivity in underground stations was poor or not available, people could not share images right away. However, when people regained Internet access later, a lot of images were uploaded to online blogs, which were helpful for post-analysis of the incident.

Moreover, after the 2007 Virginia Tech shooting, affected people and their beloved ones came together in a Facebook group, before the official release of victim names and numbers. Using social media, people were able to inform their beloved ones directly that they were safe. On the other hand worried persons used social media to investigate the well being of potentially affected friends or relatives. In at least one case, an unresponsive person was found among the 33 victims. In their investigations of the event, Vieweg et al. (2007) conclude that this allowed to assume the person was probably affected with some certainty, before any official information has been released.

Also, during the uprising of the 2010/11 Tunisian Revolution social media played an important role. Looking into how the resistance was formed around the town of Sidi Bouzid, (2013) found that the activists intensively used Facebook as a communication medium. For instance, activists posted messages (including photos) conveying a picture of what was going on. The intention behind these posts was to inform their friends who were living in other towns. Also, Facebook was used to organize the resistance inside the city. This included the planning of demonstrations, building of barricades, or advice on how to deal with attacks by the police.

Not least, Starbird and Palen (2012) indicate the intensive use of Twitter as a communication medium during the 2011 Egyptian Revolution. Twitter was used to coordinate meetings of protesters, and many times people abroad re-posted, i.e. to 're-tweet', original messages of people in Egypt to spread the word. Furthermore, these retweeted messages express some sort of social loyalty that has also been acknowledged by local activists.

The exemplified disaster situations described in the previous section underline the benefit of using ICT for establishing communication in order to coordinate efforts in response to a disaster. However, most of these crisis informatics related studies and further related work (cf. Shklovski et al. 2008; Vieweg et al. 2010; Qu et al. 2011; Starbird & Palen 2011; Lotan et al. 2011; Olaore 2011; Sarcevic et al. 2012; Kavanaugh et al. 2012; Al-Ani et al. 2012; Denef et al. 2013; Perng et al. 2013; Reuter et al. 2013; Wulf, Aal, et al. 2013) investigated disaster scenarios in which the underlying technological structures were still functioning. Few studies (Mark & Semaan 2008; Mark et al. 2009; Semaan & Mark 2011) examined the use of technology in situations where the communication networks are not available anymore, such as in ongoing, lingering war zones like Iraq, and how ICT can help in such situations to enable communication by repairing or creating new infrastructures.

This thesis contributes to this stream of research by investigating into how people use remnants of technology in order to create new network infrastructures.

2.5 Mobile Emergency Systems

In the course of the emergence of the crisis informatics phenomenon a lot of ICT systems have been developed whose purpose is to support people to communicate in the aftermath of an emergency or a disaster. The following paragraphs outline a series of related systems.

M-Urgency[1] enables users to stream live audio and video reports over the cellular network to a local public-safety answering point. In order to support the dispatcher and responders in making time-critical decisions, M-Urgency provides, besides audio and video, contextual data. For instance, the real-time position through GPS, WiFi fingerprint, or cell tower triangulation, disability or gender, to prepare aid accordingly, or information relevant to approach the incident scene such as weather or traffic (Krishnamoorthy & Agrawala 2012). Currently, the application is private and only available to students and employees of the University of Maryland, United States.

The Federal Emergency Management Agency (**FEMA**) provides an application[2] that enables people in distress to receive shelter information and allows them to submit images with a short description to the FEMA website. These images will be placed on a map for public viewing. Before images become available online, the images need

---

[1] The M-Urgency App, http://m-urgency.umd.edu/

[2] FEMA App, http://1.usa.gov/P8V5sf

to go through a basic approval process. This guarantees that they are relevant and do not disclose any personal information.

A similar system is **SafeCity**[1] that allows the reception of live video streams from mobile devices reporting crimes or other distress situations. Professional responders use a dedicated app to stream video and their GPS position to the command center or to other professional responders in the field. Users can install a free application called Bambuser[2], which enables them to view and stream live videos. In order to report live video to authorities, users need to register in advance for specific "shares", such as "Crime stoppers" or "Public Officials".

Zello is a walkie-talkie application that enables PC and smartphone users to exchange short voice messages. Messages are sent over channels that support to talk to one person or to a group up to 100 persons. Recently, some people in Ukraine and Venezuela have leveraged this application to organize their protests (see section 4.2.2.5). Zello runs over cellular networks providing EDGE, GPRS, and 3G and also works via WiFi.

NowForce[3] enables communication over 3G/4G or WiFi in an enclosed system between people on site, who are either professional responders or members of the public, and a remotely located private security organization. In order to receive messages members of the public need to register as volunteers a priori of events. In response to the recent kidnapping events of three Jewish teenagers in Israel (Goldman 2014), NowForce launched a mobile SOS application that enables users to send a distress call and their GPS position to a dispatch center.

Similarly, **HELP! App**[4] is an application that involves via the cellular network a dispatch center and registered volunteers to respond to emergencies. For instance, if a volunteer observes how an elderly person collapses while having a walk, s/he can trigger to send out a help message, which informs the dispatch center and other nearby volunteers. The help can be categorized such as a fire, heart attack, physical injury, poisoning or allergy, violence and more.

Also, Google provides a web-based application called **Google Person Finder**[5]. It enables users either to announce via a message board that they are looking for someone or that they have information about a missing person. The Google Person Finder was deployed successfully in a range of events, such as the 2010 Haiti and Chile earthquakes, 2013 Boston bombings, or the 2013 Typhoon Haiyan that hit the Philippines. When users report information they are asked to indicate an expiration

---

[1] The SafeCity Project, http://www.safecity-project.eu/

[2] Bambuser, http://bambuser.com/

[3] NowForce Inc. http://www.nowforce.com/

[4] HELP App, http://enviu.org/our-work/help-app/

[5] Google Person Finder, https://google.org/personfinder

time, and then the records are persisted in an online database by the use of an open standard called People Finder Interchange Format (**PFIF**[1]). PFIF was set up in the Katrina PeopleFinder project in order to support the reallocation of separated families and friends being separated from each other due to the outbreak of Hurricane Katrina in 2005. Emergency response agencies and NGOs can contribute to the database and receive updates by the use of PFIF.

Ping[2] is a check-in tool for groups. Its use originated from the disaster need to "ping" family members or friends in order to tell them a sort of "I'm OK". Before a disaster strikes, users can create a list of relevant contacts, such as beloved ones or coworkers. In the light of a disaster users can then send out a request for everyone to check-in. This request triggers the administrative server to send out a 120 characters message that always appends as a specific suffix ("are you OK?"). The message is sent via the texting service or email to the registered contacts. If there is a response within five minutes the relevant person is considered to be fine. Otherwise, further confirmation requests are sent out.

Similar to Ping, the **I Am Alive**[3] application supports people in distress to notify their beloved ones of their well-being. The design of the application resulted from the that fact that Lebanese citizens living abroad were worried about their family and friends in Lebanon when bombing attacks hit places in Lebanon. To inform affected people users only need to tap a button that will trigger the posting of a standardized message ("I am still alive!") to Facebook and Twitter accounts. In case of Twitter the message also contains two default hash tags (#Lebanon #IAmAlive).

In contrast to the previously described applications, **Refugee Finder**[4] expects disruptions of network infrastructures. When affected people arrive at aid stations (hospitals, Red Cross center, etc.) workers register the victims by using the camera embedded in their cell phones. Figure 4 shows that besides an image, basic personal details, time and place of registration, are stored in an internal system. Afterwards, this information is synchronized between other aid stations, the Internet or TV broadcasts. Finally, people can find out if their friends or relatives are safe. While this approach lacks a significant delay in sending data from point A to point B, it presents a good example of how to work around disrupted infrastructures.

---

[1] PFIF Format, http://zesty.ca/pfif/

[2] Ushahidi Ping, http://www.ushahidi.com/product/ping/

[3] I Am Alive, https://play.google.com/store/apps/details?id=hassan.sandra.iamalivevip

[4] RefugeeFinder, http://www.fysisk.dk/275-2/ciid-projects/refugee-finder/

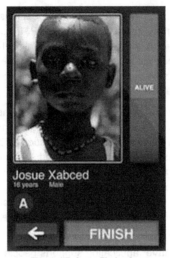

Figure 4 Refugee Finder App

While the presented systems appear to be promising solutions, their usage is constrained to situations in which the preexisting network infrastructure, such as mobile networks or public WiFi hotspots, is still working.

2.6 Summary

In many of the analyzed disaster situations the use of ICT systems proved to be helpful for communicating needs such as requests for food, electricity, or shelter, as well as for finding missing persons or to inform relatives or friends about the well-being of affected persons. It can be concluded that people who already use ICT systems in everyday scenarios are also eager to use them in disaster situations. This finding is underlined by approaches from the field of crisis informatics that work towards a paradigm shift of traditional information pathways between crisis management authorities and members of the public. Nevertheless, the mobile emergency systems that have been investigated in this context are constrained to disaster situations in which preexisting network structures are still functioning. Several studies (Palen & Liu 2007; Jennex 2012; Al-Akkad et al. 2013) have indicated that in the aftermath of a disaster, it can take hours to weeks until the preexisting network infrastructure can be restored. In order to address this research gap, this thesis investigates into approaches enabling communication that is independent from existing networks.

3 Methodology

This chapter explains the methodological choices that have been made to tackle the different challenges. First, it presents the project in whose context this work has been conducted. Then, this chapter describes how and from which sources, empirical data has been collected. Subsequently, it explains how the empirical data has been analyzed. Finally, this chapter concerns the approach of iteratively developing prototypes in the frame of this thesis.

3.1 The Role of BRIDGE

The presented work has mainly been undertaken in the scope of the BRIDGE project. Among others, BRIDGE aims to provide new forms of communication in situations of disrupted network infrastructures. One essential pillar in the BRIDGE project is to explore strategies allowing for the use of opportunistic elements (see Figure 5). Those opportunistic elements may facilitate the creation of networks in ad-hoc manner in order to support communications between people themselves and with professional first responders.

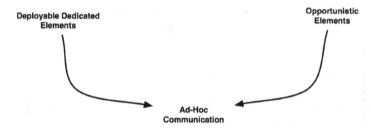

Figure 5 BRIDGE approach towards ad-hoc communication

As emergency response is a domain with high stakes, the BRIDGE project also aims to strengthen the involvement of end-users. From the outset, an end-user advisory board has been built, which comprises an international circle of experienced professionals of emergency response. The end-user advisory board includes members of the three main response forces: ambulance, fire brigade, and police. The concepts developed have been evaluated in workshops with members of the end-user advisory board and/or external end-users on a regular base (see Figure 6). Workshop participants were asked to sign a declaration of consent (see Figure 7).

Figure 6 Involvement of domain experts

European Commission
Seventh Framework Programme (FP7-SEC-2010-1)
SEC-2010.4.2-1: Interoperability of data,
systems, tools and equipment

www.sec-bridge.eu
www.bridgeproject.eu

BRIDGE

Bridging Resources and Agencies in Large-Scale Emergency Management

Informed consent to participate in EU research project Bridge

Your signature on this form will signify that you have received information about the procedures, possible risks, and benefits of this research project, that you have received an adequate opportunity to consider this information, and that you voluntarily agree to participate in the project. You will be given a copy of this consent form

I confirm that I have read and understood the Participant information sheet August 2011 for the above research. ☐

I have had the opportunity to consider the information, ask questions about the research and have had these answered satisfactorily. ☐

I agree to take part in the research and understand that my participation is voluntary. ☐

I understand that I have the right to withdraw from the research process, without giving reasons for this, at any point during the research process. ☐

I am satisfied that the information I provide will be treated confidentially by the researchers. ☐

I agree for my contributions to be recorded. ☐

I agree that records can be shared with Bridge project team members and used in multimedia reports, workshops and in other presentations and publications. ☐

I understand that my data will be used anonymously, under the pseudonym I have chosen, unless I wish to be named. ☐

I understand that I may obtain copies of the results of this study, and register any complaint I might have about the project with the researchers named in the Participant Information Sheet. ☐

I wish to have my identity remain anonymous and choose the following pseudonym ☐

_____

Copy for your own records. No need to return.

Please turn over

Figure 7 Informed consent form of the BRIDGE project

3.2 User Groups

This work focuses on two user groups.

Mobile users. In the first instance, any person who is carrying a cell phone and is unable to connect to existing network structures belongs to the first user group. Those mobile users can be ordinary members of the public; this group includes also professionals of emergency response who are not in service. In many cases, mobile users are the first one to respond immediately after a disaster took place as already described in section 2.1.3. Recent research (Palen et al. 2010) has prompted the vision that the wide population should not be considered as an aggrieved party anymore, but as active actors in preparing against and responding to disasters. Another point to recall is the common misconception that people in distress would be too nervous to act properly, so that designing technology for them would overstrain their needs (see also section 2.3.3).

While much research (cf. Starbird & Palen 2011) has tried to make use of data generated from people being rather on-/off-site the disaster site, this thesis looks into ways of supporting people being immediately on-site but disconnected from everyday ICT services.

Professionals. The second user group encompasses professionals around the domain of emergency response. Professionals such as fire fighters, paramedics, police officers, and mountain rescuers, or people operating *in the remote*, such as incident commanders, logistic engineers, members from non-governmental organizations, experts for explosion and consultants. However, in terms of technology design this work concerns only professionals acting in the field. As previous studies have shown this can be a quite challenging task. Traditionally, the information flow between formal and informal response is unidirectional (see section 2.4). However, recent developments have started to investigate into bi-directional flows of information.

This thesis provokes the unfolding of new tasks beyond existing work practices, which includes communication between mobile users and professionals.

3.3 Data Sources

To create a foundation for design data has been collected from primary and secondary sources. *Primary sources* were interviews with professionals from the emergency response domain. This involved various professions, such as professional first responders, experts and consultants for crisis management, as well as post-disaster psychologists. Furthermore, ordinary members of the public were interviewed. These people had either experienced a disaster themselves in the past or were affected indirectly as friends or family members were in distress. To approach both groups of people either separate meetings were arranged or workshops were organized. *Secondary sources* comprised a set of external reports on how people creatively use remnants of ICT to cope with the challenges introduced in the aftermath of a disaster. Furthermore, a review of the scientific literature, in particular studies of crisis informatics (see also section 2.1), was conducted to trace relevant aspects.

3.4 Interviews

In order to get a common understanding of work practices of professionals and the complexity of the emergency response domain, the author engaged professionals in guideline-based interviews. The guideline comprises a list of sample probe questions that were developed by Hoffmann et al. (1998) and which are enlisted in Table 2. The interviews lasted from 30 to 120 minutes. Interviews were audio or video recorded and later transcribed using the software *f4 & f5* (audiotranskription.de 2014). Interviews were also translated into English, if necessary, for instance, from German or Norwegian.

Probe Type	Probe Content
Cues	What were you seeing, hearing, smelling?
Standard scenarios	Does this case fit standard or typical scenario? Does it fit a scenario you were trained to deal with?
Goals	What were your specific goals and objectives at the time?
Options	What other courses of action were considered or available?
Basis of choice	How was this option selected/other options rejected? What rule was being followed?
Experience	What specific training or experience was necessary or helpful in making this decision? What training, knowledge, or information might have helped?
Decision making	How much time pressure was involved in making this decision? How long did it take to actually make this decision?
Aiding	If the decision was not the best, what training, knowledge, or information could have helped?
Situation Assessment	If you were asked to describe the situation to a relief officer at this point, how would you summarize the situation?
Errors	What mistakes are likely at this point? Did you acknowledge if your situation assessment or option selection were incorrect? How might a novice have behaved differently?
Hypotheticals	If a key feature of the situation had been different, what difference would it have made in your decision?

Table 2 Sample Critical Decision Method Probe Questions

Kahn and Cannell (1957) point out that interviews can be considered as a "conversation with a purpose". How the conversation evolves and what will be its content depends on the types of questions raised and the interview technique being used. Based on the degree an interviewer follows a set of prepared questions, Fontana and Frey (1994) divide interviews into three categories: *unstructured, structured, semi-structured*. There is no 'right' or 'wrong' technique for conducting interviews. Rather, it depends on the research questions and scope of the study. For example, if the goal is to gain first impressions on what users think of a new feature or an idea for a system, unstructured interviews might be more appropriate. However, if the goal is to evaluate a particular feature, such as the usability of a search bar inside a web browser, a structured interview usually makes more sense. As a rule of thumb: the more the researcher knows about the field of interest, and the more specific his research question is, the more it makes sense to apply formal, structured methods for interviewing. As this work tackles a rather novel field of research the author decided to conduct semi-structured and unstructured interviews.

Semi-structured interviews comprise a set of prepared questions and questions that arise spontaneously[1] during the course of an interview. Due to this flexibility semi-structured interviews can help to gain a thorough understanding of complex contexts (Wood 1997). The overall goal is to understand the interviewees' subjective point of view on different aspects rather than collecting generic statements. In general, semi-structured interviews may contain closed and open questions. The use of open-ended questions (*"Could you please tell me about..."*) allows respondents to respond to questions by their own words and be less biased in their answers.

Unstructured interviews are interviews in which questions have not been predetermined (Minichiello et al. 1992). This allows the interview to emerge in any direction, as the interviewer and interviewee can control the themes of the conversation. This interview technique can bring interviewees to talk more open and freely about several aspects. Because of that in the literature this technique is also called *informal conversation*. Since, those interviews occurred spontaneously, such as in coffee breaks during workshops, the author made manual notes and sketches instead of recording audio/video.

The author either interviewed one person or a (rather small) group of people. The latter form is often referred to as *group interviews*, in which the interviewer guides the group in order to discuss a specified set of topics. For this the author organized workshops with professionals (for example, see section 7.4.3).

---

[1] Spontaneous questions usually are responses to previous statements, such as asking the interviewee about something new (*"You mentioned previously that, so is it..."*) or to elaborate an aspect (*"Could you tell me more about..."*)

3.5 Grounded Theory and the Constant Comparative Method

Grounded theory is a method that helps to systematically develop theories on the basis of analyzing a set of data (Glaser & Strauss 1967). In their seminal book 'Awareness of Dying' two sociologists called Glaser and Strauss (1966) laid the foundation for the grounded theory approach. Their book presents findings based on studying the process of dying and how the medical personnel and family or friends get along with such situations in different hospitals. Today, grounded theory is a well-established approach for research in fields such as HCI and CSCW.

When applying grounded theory, researchers do not define a theory a priori, but let it evolve in the course of their investigation. The rationale for such a methodology is to stay open minded for unforeseen and important aspects of the investigated practices. An upfront-framed theory can result in having a biased view when approaching the field. Today, there are several approaches of grounded theory in use (Glaser & Strauss 1967; Charmaz 2006; Corbin & Strauss 2008).

The presented work follows Glaser and Strauss approach (1967). The author collected data from primary and secondary sources (see section 3.3) and analyzed the data by the use of the *constant comparative method*. According to Glaser and Strauss the constant comparative method is an ongoing method for analyzing data in order to frame a grounded theory, which incorporates four steps being listed in Table 3.

Step	Description
1	Comparing incidents applicable to each category
2	Integrating categories (and their properties)
3	Delimiting the theory
4	Writing the theory

Table 3 Constant comparative method towards a grounded theory

Using the constant comparative method, the author initially coded each disaster situation in the data into as many categories as possible (Step 1). Then, the focus was changed to comparing disaster situations from newly collected to previously identified disaster situations (Step 2). In order to increase the integrity of the data analysis, the author either aggregated identified categories into more abstract categories or discarded some categories (Step 3). The latter implies, that the empirical findings presented below in section 4.1 only present an extracted portion of the actual collected data. A lot of meaningful and interesting observations were finally cast aside in order to sustain a sharp focus.

As this work did not develop a theory (Step 4), it only oriented itself to the constant comparative method. This helped to identify categories of how people use remnants of technology in situations of disrupted network infrastructure.

The reflection on these categories helped to frame a conceptual framework described in chapter 5, which in turn informed the design of two systems presented in chapter 7 and 8.

3.6 Iterative System Development

Mogensen (1992) points out that prototyping reflects three characteristics:

- Prototyping triggers *the construction of the future*. When prototyping one creates prototypes that may result in a more mature ICT system.

- The need for *iteration* is an elementary part of the design process, potential solutions are sketched, and then partly implemented, tested, and on this basis new designs are generated, whereupon the process can start again.

- Users are encouraged to make *concrete experiences* with prototypes representing prospective ICT products. In order to evaluate the usefulness of an app somebody must use it in a given context—getting hands on. While traditional models imply that the product first needs to be finished before assessing, prototyping as an approach pursues to overcome this contradiction by continuously making the future more visible.

Technology designers often use prototypes as proof-of-concepts, because prototypes allow them to communicate the ideas behind their concepts. Therefore, prototypes stimulate critical and constructive reflections on design decisions or strategies, and are sometimes regarded as "materialized" hypotheses. Thus, they can be the practical tools for framing or refining a new idea, avoid an unfortunate decision, or to discover new possibilities in a given design space.

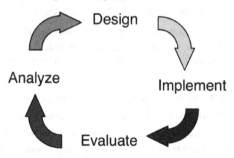

Figure 8 Iterative cycles of system development

This work presents two systems: Help Beacons (see chapter 7) and Local Cloud (see chapter 8). Applying two to three iterations (see Figure 8), initial primitive prototypes were refined into enhanced prototypes. On the one hand, prototypes served to evaluate the feasibility of technical core features. On the other hand, prototypes served to let users make concrete experiences, i.e. to allow for hands on experiences with the prospective system (Bødker & Grønbaek 1991).

The author followed the approach of Edwards et al. (2003) to identify benefits and constraints of 'core system functionalities'[1] of the implementation of both concepts at an early stage of design. In summary, Edwards et al. (2003) suggest seven lessons which they should be considered as guidelines for designing core system features. For the presented work, in particular, the following four lessons were guiding:

- Lesson 1 - Prioritize core system features

- Lesson 2 - Build prototypes that expose the core system features

- Lesson 4 -Initial proof-of-concept applications should be lightweight

- Lesson 8 - Do not fake data and components for testing user experience

As the Help Beacons system (see chapter 7) has been applied as part of real-world emergency response exercises, some feasibility tests were conducted at the premises before the actual exercise took place. These feasibility tests helped to identify constraints in order to enhance the design of the prototypes helping the author to improve their robustness. Therefore, strictly speaking inside some evaluation phase (see Figure 8) little sub cycles of "(re-) design-implement-evaluate-analyze" emerged.

In order to identify at early stage benefits and constraints of ideas and core features the author followed the approach of Edwards et al. (2003). This means, that tests have been conducted in environments in which communication signals were hampered, e.g. due to high amount of steel weakening communication signals. Based on the analysis of these tests the author took corrective actions.

An evaluation of the developed systems in real disaster situations is problematic (Turoff 2002; Lukowicz et al. 2010). Thanks to the BRIDGE project (see also section 3.1), there were possibilities to evaluate the systems in close-to-real disaster conditions as described in detail in chapters 7 and 8.

Prototypes foster reflections on designs, and thus can help to frame or refine ide-as, to revert unfortunate decisions, or to discover new opportunities in the design space. Prototypes can be a valuable tool for experimenting with the benefits and constraints of technologies in an early stage of development.

---

[1] In detail, Edwards et al. (2003) focus on 'software infrastructures'. A software infrastructure *"comprises system-level software providing functions, capabilities, or services to other software"*. This is a constrained view on the term of infrastructure and more important compared to the definition provided in section 2.3.1, this definition views infrastructure rather as a 'thing' than a relation between humans and systems. Therefore, the author replaces the term infrastructure with system.

3.7 Summary

To approach the complex domain of emergency response, the author decided to use semi structured/unstructured interviews with open-ended questions. The aim was to get a detailed understanding of the needs of possible user groups, without biasing the research with assumptions about the targeted application domain. The empirical findings will be used to lay the ground for defining a collection of quality attributes whose implementation can foster resilience in the design of ad-hoc communication systems (see chapter 5). Through several iterations of prototypes, this work will further (re-) design and evaluate the potential of the developed systems.

4 Empirical Findings

Analyzing the empirically collected data by means of the constant comparative method, this chapter presents three identified categories. Those categories exemplify how people creatively use remnants of technology to cope with disrupted network infrastructures. In the end, this chapter bridges to chapter 5 by arguing that the findings can inspire quality attributes supporting resilience in the design of ad-hoc communication systems. The empirical findings described in this chapter have been originally published in (Al-Akkad et al. 2013), but have been edited and enhanced by new findings along the work on this thesis.

4.1 Data Set

Table 4 lists disaster incidents to which this work refers in chronological order. Section 2.2 has provided general information about these incidents. The empirical data was collected from primary and secondary sources (see section 3.3). Primary sources ranged from interviews with professionals (e.g. fire fighters, policemen etc.) to members of the public that personally experienced a disaster or were affected by one. Table 5 lists the interviewees to which this work refers.

Date	Incident	Source(s)
8/25/08	Hurricane Gustav	Paper
4/6/09	L'Aquila earthquake	Interview, report
1/12/10	Haiti earthquake	Interview, report
2/27/10	Chile earthquake	Interview, report
7/24/10	Stampede at Love Parade	Interview
12/18/10	Tunisian Revolution	Paper
1/25/11	Egyptian revolution	Interview, email
2/22/11	Christchurch earthquake	Report
7/22/11	Norway attacks	Interview, report
10/22/12	Hurricane Sandy	Report
4/15/13	Boston bombings	Report
Ongoing	Syrian civil war	Interview

Table 4 Relevant disaster incidents

ID	Role and Experience
P1	Reconstruction engineer, e.g. after the 2010 Haiti earthquake
P2	Policeman who operated during the 2011 Norway attacks
P3	Well-known Dutch consultant and innovator for safety solutions[1]
P4	A civilian who survived the 2009 L'Aquila earthquake
P5	Citizen affected by the 2010 Chile earthquake
P6	Visitor who experienced the stampede at the 2010 Love Parade
P7	Citizen who experienced the 2011 Egyptian revolution
P8	Casualty and news courier during the Syrian civil war

Table 5 Interviewed Persons

4.2 Categories of Using Remnants of Technology

Using the constant comparative method, described in section 3.5, the author identified three categories of how people use remnants of technology to cope with disrupted network infrastructures.

4.2.1 Category 1 – "Islands" of Connectivity

During critical infrastructure disruptions the disturbance of services can be concentrated on specific localities, extend to a large scale, or be geographically scattered over a territory with some places intermittently allowing temporal access. This means the adverse effects of a disaster usually do not disrupt the whole technological landscape. Often, some portions of the technological structures survive and can still provide access to services in specific localities. Those surviving structures will be referred to as "islands" of connectivity in this thesis.

4.2.1.1 Localization of "Islands"

The localization of disruptions can exhibit a very fine granularity. Consider, for example the stampede that happened at the 2010 Love Parade (a music festival) in Duisburg, Germany:

P6: Immediately on site, circa 15–20 min before the stampede occurred and 1–2 hours later, calls were not possible [...] When I approached the edge of the event site my phone regained connectivity [...] on my screen a lot of missed calls and received SMS were indicated from people who knew I was there and thus were worried something had happened to me.

---

[1] Due to a non-disclosure agreement the name of the solutions cannot be named, as otherwise the name of the innovator would be easy to find out.

It was also reported that in the aftermath of the 2013 Boston bombings the cellular network was overloaded hindering people to make calls. Further, although the texting service was not working well, some people were still able to send short messages from some spots (Mattise 2013).

4.2.1.2 Calibration of "islands"

Disruptions of network infrastructures can be a result of severe damage, huge overloading, or outages. Therefore, in the early stage of the remedy of a disaster with heavy disruptions, newly deployed communication structures often require some time to calibrate.

P1: When I arrived in Haiti all data connections permanently broke down, even satellite. [...] We received guidelines to conserve the bandwidth. [...] Nevertheless, connections broke down [...] You know even if relief organizations do stick to recommended ways of consuming the bandwidth, other organizations like the media do not.

4.2.1.3 "Lands" of Non-Connectivity

In analogy to "islands" of non-connectivity, "lands" of non-connectivity can emerge due to disrupted infrastructures that can extend to a large scale and might last for a relatively long time. For example, when reflecting on events that took in the aftermath of the 2009 L'Aquila earthquake P4 reported the following:

During the first hours the mobile network was jammed [...] we waited outside for the rescue team [...] it was cold [...] we waited like 2 hours [...] hoping for them to come. To know when the rescue service is probably arriving would have calmed me down [...] after being deported to a rescue camp, this was 3-4 hours later, I finally was able to inform my parents and friends that I was not hurt.

4.2.1.4 Disappearing "clouds"

Nowadays, the Internet seems to be seamlessly accessible. This amounts in particular to modern urban areas in which ICT services are accessible via broadband technologies (UMTS, LTE) and/or publicly available WiFi hotspots. However, the physical underlying structures of the Internet still consist of a set of "boxes and wires" being delicate to break down in disaster situations.

A good example for this are the severe destructions caused by Hurricane Sandy in October 2012. The metropolis of New York and its surrounding area were cut off from the Internet and the cellular phone network, after previously suffering from an outage (Allen 2012). Besides that, Hurricane Sandy unsheathed a new phenomenon of isolation in terms of accessibility of cloud services. People use cloud services on a daily basis, including for instance file hosting services such as dropbox[1] or digital application distribution platforms such as the AppStore[2] or Google Play[3].

Although the notion of the "cloud" might obfuscate this fact, *"people have to remember the cloud lives in data centers"* (Darrow 2012). Data centers usually operate in the remote, and thus can only be accessed via (remote) cloud services. At the same time, data centers can be directly affected by disasters themselves.

4.2.1.5 Summary

In situations of disrupted infrastructures "islands" of connectivity emerge as illustrated by the effects of the stampede that occurred during the 2010 Love Parade festival. The actions fostering the creation and interconnections of "islands" may require some time for a calibration (P1), as it is challenging to maintain "islands" depending on the dimension of a disruption or the complexity of ad-hoc assemblages. Further, the Hurricane Sandy disaster underlines once more the interweaving of technological services. Moreover, the constraint in relying on a centralized approach when consuming services can be a pitfall, as the outbreak of a disaster can also affect the relation between technology and people crosstown as exemplified by the effects of Hurricane Sandy.

4.2.2 Category 2 - Degradation of Services

Aligned to the previous category, access to services is often still possible in the aftermath of disasters, though the access can be hampered compared to the status quo ante. This *degradation* of services may represent a change in quality, costs, effectiveness, or access to services may temporarily become impossible. While such degradations of services pose at the first glance challenges, they might also open up new possibilities for repurposing remnants of technology.

4.2.2.1 Combining remnants of technology

As a consequence of the 2010 Haiti earthquake the network infrastructure over the whole island got disrupted. Making phone calls only worked in rare occasions, though the texting service was still partly operable.

P1: To make calls did not work at all […] sending SMS worked well in contrast.

As Haitians had already adopted the texting service before the disaster, authorities customized it to comprise a free of charge short code (4636). This short code enabled cell phone users to send messages about various needs, such as missing persons, medicines, nutrition, electricity or water (Hersman 2012). At the same time, digital volunteers who analyzed the large amount of text-generated data and populated

---

[1] Dropbox, https://www.dropbox.com/

[2] AppStore, https://itunes.apple.com/en/genre/ios/id36?mt=8

[3] Google Play, https://play.google.com/store

crisis maps joined accordingly (Starbird & Palen 2011). These maps became a reference point for relief organizations in order to coordinate their logistic efforts efficiently all over the affected parts of the island.

4.2.2.2 Exploiting everyday services

To reach a large part of a society, P3 stressed the importance to use (or provide a link to) everyday ICT services such as text, email, or social networks. In the following, P3 describes a problem s/he faced in an ongoing project.

We designed an app that engages citizens to help in increasing safety in urban areas. [...] People launch the app, and live video is streamed to the local police. [...] By this a citizen who, for example, observes a crime can inform the police about it. [...] It's not used much. [...] The app has not been downloaded many times. [...] People prefer to use the services they use in daily life like Facebook, or Twitter.

This stresses the need to build on tools that people are familiar with in order to efficiently support communication in disaster situations.

4.2.2.3 Territorial escapes

Another way to work around the disturbance of services is to exploit being in the vicinity to another country. For example, in respect to the ongoing civil war in Syria, P8 explains:

After the first demonstrations fixed line and the Internet were shut down. [...] Within the last 7 months only once for 1 day the phone line was reopened. [...] Being near to the Jordanian border, we changed to use the Jordan mobile network. [...] We used it for SMS or to access the Web. [...] Videos you see in the news show in general something that happened 1-2 days ago. [...] Yes, we record them with our cell phones.

Again, this illustrates that people sometimes take unexpected routes for re-establishing communication channels when the usual ways of communication do not work anymore.

4.2.2.4 Bridging blocked services

Another phenomenon is the combination of two services, which are still operable, but work orthogonal to each other, in order to replace the breakdown of one specific service. In a normal situation, the service in question would be the preferred way of communication. But due to its disturbance, the combination of two orthogonal services could be the only remaining way for communication. As an example serve the following events that occurred in the aftermath of the 2010 Chile earthquake.

P5: Immediately after the earthquake stroke Chile, parents of my friends could not contact their children. [...] My friends were at that time in Spain. [...] I was at that time in Germany. [...] Their parents wanted to tell their children, according to my friends, that nothing had happened to them. [...] They found me online on a messenger. Their parents send messages to me, which I then read out to my friends [...] I contacted my friends via the fixed line network.

In the light of 2010/11 Tunisian revolution, social media played a crucial role (see also section 2.4). In particular, Facebook was used to spread information between activists and supporters outside the country. One reaction of the government was to arrest several activists whose Facebook account privacy was unfortunately set to public access (i.e. the largest possible number of users). Moreover, the government obliged local Internet service providers to manipulate the data transfer. As people experienced long upload times when trying to share multimedia files on Facebook, they looked for workarounds. One solution was to send emails to friends abroad that contained low-resolution videos and the request to upload the videos for public use (Wulf, Misaki, et al. 2013).

4.2.2.5 Foiling service blockades

Another challenge is to cope with blockades of services due to man-made disasters. During the Egyptian revolution in 2011, several actions evolved to counteract this challenge.

P7: At first the Internet was shut down and then the SMS. [...] In the end, I used my analog phone to dial via a proxy into the Internet [...] a guide how to work around proxies was sent via email.

P7 forwarded the mentioned email to the author, which was originally sent during the middle of the revolution, explaining strategies for communicating with the online world despite of blockades. S/he explained to the author that the basic content of this email was also spread via texts to many Egyptians in order to foil the blockades. Mentioned strategies were to work around DNS blockages of popular websites such as Facebook, Twitter, or doctor.org, for which three alternatives were suggested: to use open DNS servers, to use proxy servers, and to use anonymous browsing sites.

Later, when Internet access from Egypt was shut down, dial up service providers were recommended, besides one unblocked Internet service provider that was related to the Egyptian stock market.

In recent events of protests in Ukraine and Venezuela, people used a walkie-talkie app called Zello (see also section 2.5) to organize their protests (Samuel Burke 2014). However, it is apparently one of the social network apps that the Venezuelan government now has blocked. To evade governmental roadblocks, the app vendor released an update that changes the IP addresses, making it much harder to block them. Further, images and videos were blocked for the Twitter service, which led many people to install VPN software on their phones to circumvent the blockades.

4.2.2.6 Unanticipated dangers in using everyday services

In some disaster situations, using everyday services can become a risk, which contradicts with the findings described in section 4.2.2.2, and underlines the complexity that they bring with them.

For instance, in the events of the 2011 Norway attacks people on the mainland tried to contact their beloved ones being on the island. They did so by making calls or sending short messages, which proved to be less helpful.

P2: Some worried relatives and friends on the mainland tried to contact people they knew about being at the incident site on the island. [...] But, the ringtone for phones or sounds when receiving an SMS would alert the shooter to hiding persons.

Another delicate example is given by actions during the Syrian civil war when P8 need to enter dangerous zones in order to regain connectivity to the outline world.

P8: Indeed repeaters were deployed to amplify the signal of the mobile network. But due to the lack of money, only cheaper repeaters were bought. These provide lower intensity. [...] I had to stand on top of the roof of the building I used to live in to receive a sufficient signal. [...] Shots wounded me when I was standing there.

This illustrates another aspect that has to be kept in mind when designing technologies for disaster situations: that design decisions can have grave consequences for people that have to rely on them.

4.2.2.7 Summary

The exploitation of everyday services can produce interesting side effects. For instance, considering the fact that the Haitian population appropriated the SMS service before the earthquake occurred, and being able to allocate volunteers to utilize SMS generated data, cleared the way for a success story. Further, if the conventional use of services is blocked due to a man-made disaster, people try to work around those roadblocks as exemplified above by manipulated data transfers during the 2010/11 Tunisian Revolution or the nationwide Internet shutdown emerging during the 2011 Egyptian Revolution.

4.2.3 Category 3 – Usage of surviving resources

In situations of disrupted infrastructures, portions of preexisting technology may not survive and need to be replaced with other technologies.

4.2.3.1 Freeing virtual resources for the common good

Commonly, people or organizations in daily life protect or charge other people when using their communication resources such as the cellular phone network or WiFi hotspots. However, in the aftermath of disasters, attitudes of sharing resources can shift to some extent.

For instance, in response to the 2009 L'Aquila earthquake all Italian telecommunication operators sent free minutes and credits to all their pre-paid customers in the city of Abruzzo. Further, they suspended billings to all post-paid customers. Moreover, some mobile operators extended their coverage with additional mobile stations in order to cover homeless camps (Online Geography Resources 2009).

Aligned to this example, there are reports of people and/or authorities posting online requests to unlock and share private WiFi hotspots to enable Internet access or to relieve an overloaded mobile network. This means, in response to the 2010 Chile earthquake (Choney 2012) and the 2011 Utoya island shootings (Jones et al. 2011).

Moreover, in the aftermath of the 2013 Boston bombings Twitter messages were posted requesting to launch a mobile application, called Open Garden[1].

@YourAnonNews: People in Boston, open up your WiFi nodes and download OpenGarden mesh-net app for your computing device. | #OpBoston #Anonymous (7:14 PM - 15 Apr 13)

@CIApressoffice: Ppl in #Boston, open up your WiFi nodes & download OpenGarden mesh-net app for your computing device. | #bostonmarathon #OpBoston #Anonymous (7:17 PM - 15 Apr 13)

Open Garden facilitates its users to communicate via a mesh network. The public authorities and members of the public have posted similar requests during the 2010 Chile earthquake.

4.2.3.2 Re-appropriation of remnants of technology

Another recurrent phenomenon is that people re-appropriate remnants of technology to cope with the challenges introduced by a crisis. This includes exploiting resources that might have been discarded or are only rarely used, but due to disrupted infrastructures have become valuable again.

For example, in their investigation on the impact of 2008 Hurricane Gustav, Palen et al. (2011) describe that on a dedicated website information was shared to support people in acquiring help. For instance, the authorities asked local residents through an online survey, if electricity could be made available in affected areas by any means. In that particular case, one person responded to offer an old power generator.

Similarly, the February 2011 Christchurch earthquake caused power cuts affecting landline phones in multiple areas. In response to this damage, telecommunication companies collected analogue phones that do not require electricity, and distributed those phones to people in need (NZPA 2011).

---

[1] Open Garden Inc., https://opengarden.com/

4.2.3.3 Conserving remnants of technology

Announcements how to use remnants of technology efficiently can help to avoid any inadvertent usage.

In the same February 2011 Christchurch earthquake, severe outages occurred. However, as the cellular phone network was still operable, telecommunication companies asked their customers to stick to texting instead of calling in order to save the battery power of their cell phones (Pullar-Strecker 2011).

Further, in response to the outages caused by the 2010 Chile earthquake, Twitter messages were posted that asked people to conserve and share energy resources. For example, it was recommended to buy candles or batteries for flashlights. Moreover, the affected people were given the possibility to charge their mobile phones at local fire stations (Choney 2012).

4.2.3.4 Fallibility of technology

In the aftermath of disasters, resources may partly survive. However, often they cannot provide all core services anymore or might be completely defect. According to P1, relief organizations may compensate the fallibility of technology by applying systems that require no electricity.

P1: We expect in the worst case the entire breakdown of digital systems. For example, when being in the field systems can run out of battery. Therefore, we are trained to work with a pencil and a sheet of paper. You ask one person to put over a message from point A to point B, like people used to do it in the Stone Age. This approach is clear to everybody and enables us to spread messages over some distance.

This example shows that resilience of certain technologies can help to alleviate the fallibility of others, and that those can become important in cases where usually available resources are not functioning anymore.

4.2.3.5 Summary

In sum, crisis or disaster situations shift the attitudes of people to free or unlock resources such as the provision of Internet access through private WiFi hotspots. This shift occurs as the primary goal has become to provide "new" channels of communications, while at the same time common economical or privacy principles are often paid less attention in the light of the unfolding situation. Further, people look for discarded resources that have suddenly regained value, as their successors have become disrupted. Moreover, people share strategies to conserve limited resources as well as they offer sources to recharge remnants of technology.

4.3 Conclusion

The previous section presented three categories reflecting empirical material on how people creatively use remnants of technology to cope with critical situations, such as disasters or a crises (cf. Dewey 1983). From a technological stance, this thesis argues that the value of the analyzed material is, that it can be considered as a resource for informing the definition of quality attributes that can support to promote resilience for the design of ad-hoc communication systems. Figure 9 depicts the structure of this logic. The next chapter will propose a set of such quality attributes and chapter 7 and chapter 8 will each exemplify how those qualities can be implemented, and moreover evaluate their impact on the domain of emergency response.

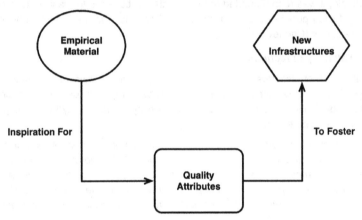

Figure 9 Approach to resilient ad-hoc communication systems

5 Conceptual Framework

This chapter constructs the conceptual framework for this thesis. In particular, it clarifies the meaning of the term quality attributes and corresponding terms. Then, this chapter suggests a set of quality attributes, whose usage can potentially foster resilience in the design of ad-hoc communication systems. For each quality attribute, its empirically grounded inspiration and a generic definition are given. Not least, a coherent scenario exemplifies the usage of the proposed set of quality attributes.

5.1 Disambiguation of Quality Attributes

While it is alright to say non-functional requirements are a synonym for quality attributes, the author preferred to use the latter term, as its meaning is less blurred due to various definitions and less biased from a technical angle (Glinz 2007). This work takes the following comprehensive definition by the Microsoft Developer Network[1] as a basis:

Quality attributes are the overall factors that affect run-time behavior, system design, and user experience. They represent areas of concern that have the potential for application wide impact across layers and tiers. Some of these attributes are related to the overall system design, while others are specific to run time, design time, or user centric issues. The extent to which the application possesses a desired combination of quality attributes such as usability, performance, reliability, and security indicates the success of the design and the overall quality of the software application.

Quality attributes per se can be classified into sub categories. The standardized ISO/EIC (2014) norm splits quality attributes into three categories: system, business, and architectural. System qualities comprise availability, performance, security, or usability. Business qualities include time to market, integration, cost and benefit, and others. And architectural qualities reflect the conceptual integrity, correctness and completeness.

Other bodies take a different stance in categorizing quality attributes. For instance, the Microsoft Developer network suggests four categories: design, run-time, system, and user qualities. Design qualities are similar to the architectural qualities provided by the ISO/EIC norm. They encompass qualities such as conceptual integrity, maintainability, and reusability. Run-time qualities are equivalent to the system qualities provided by the ISO/EIC norm, while comprising attributes such as availability, performance, security, interoperability, scalability and more. System qualities comprise supportability and testability, and, user qualities define the usability of a system.

---

[1] Microsoft Developer Network (MSDN), Library, Chapter 16: Quality Attributes,
http://msdn.microsoft.com/en-us/library/ee658094.aspx#QualityAttributeFrame

5.2 Proposal of Quality Attributes

Drawing on the empirical findings presented in chapter 4 this section proposes eight quality attributes that can potentially foster resilience in the design of ad-hoc communication systems:

QUAT-1 Prevalence

QUAT-2 Ad-hoc communication

QUAT-3 Quick connectivity

QUAT-4 Serendipity

QUAT-5 Short-lived interactions

QUAT-6 Graceful degradation

QUAT-7 Self-management

QUAT-8 Decentralized distribution

The following sections will provide one or more examples of the empirically grounded inspiration for each quality attribute, present a generic definition, and describe at least one approach for implementing it.

5.2.1 Prevalence

5.2.1.1 Inspiration

In the aftermath of the 2010 Haiti earthquake the cellular network broke down (see also section 4.2.2.1). In detail, making calls did almost not work at all, but the texting service was still working across parts of the "islands" of connectivity. Therefore, a free short SMS code was launched which people could use to send various needs, such as medicine, electricity, water and more. This approach was the way to a success story, which was enabled by the fact that the Haitian population had appropriated the texting service in their everyday life beforehand.

5.2.1.2 Definition

Prevalence denotes the potential of a system for reaching the critical mass of a population during the response to a disaster. To enable this, it is recommendable that a system design considers to be based on widespread technological protocols and standards to which many people have become familiar with before a disaster strikes.

5.2.2 Ad-Hoc Communication

5.2.2.1 Inspiration

This quality attribute is inspired by several crisis incidents in which preexisting network infrastructure got disrupted. For example, in the aftermath of Hurricane Sandy electricity broke down, which resulted in the unavailability of routine ICT services. Further, in the aftermath of the 2013 Boston bombings, making calls or sending text messages in the impact zone was nearly impossible as the cellular network was overloaded.

5.2.2.2 Definition

Ad-hoc communication refers to the quality of a system that is able to communicate data without the need of external network structures. Rather, the system is independent from existing infrastructure and might complement it.

5.2.3 Quick Connectivity

5.2.3.1 Inspiration

During critical disruptions of technology the disturbance of services can be concentrated on specific localities, extend to a large scale, or be geographically scattered over a territory with some places intermittently allowing temporal access (see section 4.2.1). For dealing with such situations, agencies are trained tools that do not require electricity. However, in general, the requirement for deploying any tools is that they can be used in a straightforward and quick manner and be easily placed into operation.

5.2.3.2 Definition

Network infrastructures might temporarily be unavailable. In order to complement "islands" of connectivity, the quality attribute of quick connectivity is suggested that underlines the need for facilitating the quick ad-hoc creation of networks without the need for cumbersome configurations. To speed up the connection process, it should only ask users for input if strongly required.

5.2.4 Serendipity

5.2.4.1 Inspiration

Section 4.2.3.4 concluded that responders have to prepare for the fallibility of humans and systems. Thus, organizations as the German Technical Relief also train their workers on procedures that are independent from tools that require electricity. Those procedures are kept simple on purpose, so that performing them is straightforward.

5.2.4.2 Definition

Aligned to the previous quality attribute this one goes beyond simply creating a network as a means of communication. Instead, it aims to look into ways for enabling serendipitous forms of communication. The overall goal is that other systems are able to discover "islands" of connectivity opportunistically. Serendipity, in general, refers to the occurrence and development of events by chance in a lucky or beneficial way. In our case, it covers the chance of connecting to peers to retrieve or share crisis information.

5.2.5 Graceful Degradation

5.2.5.1 Inspiration

In some disaster situations, certain services may still operate, although on the contrary corresponding services might not work anymore. In the aftermath of the 2010 Haiti earthquake, the texting service still worked, whereas making calls was not possible anymore (see section 4.2.2.1).

5.2.5.2 Definition

The concept of graceful degradation, often equated to fault-tolerance (Randell et al. 1978), denotes that a system may still operate to a certain degree, although some services may dissolve or cannot be provided anymore.

5.2.6 Short-lived Interactions

5.2.6.1 Inspiration

Reuter and Ludwig (2013) indicated that in the aftermath of a disaster, announcements of infrastructural disruptions as well as information about efficiently using resources that are still operating can have a strong impact on the evolution of the technical landscape in the aftermath of a disaster (see section 4.2.3.3). For example, there were several reports of outages as a result of the February 2011 Christchurch earthquake. Therefore, mobile network providers recommended their customers to preserve battery power by avoiding to make calls. (Pullar-Strecker 2011). Similar approaches were applied when power failed across Chile in 2010 as a result of a strong earthquake. The authorities used social media to ask people to buy candles or batteries for using flashlights. Further, affected people had the possibility to recharge their phones at local fire stations (Choney 2012).

5.2.6.2 Definition

The examples presented above underline that in disaster situations, valuable resources, such as electricity or bandwidth of network links, might be scarce. Therefore, the quality attribute *short -lived interactions*, pursues to use resources as efficiently as possible. The overall idea behind this concept is to maintain interactions as links between devices or processes that consume power only until a specific purpose has been accomplished. By doing so, similar to the quality attribute of graceful degradation, this approach might help to avoid bottlenecks in mobile networks.

5.2.7 Self-Management

5.2.7.1 Inspiration

During the response to a disaster, systems require a certain phase of "calibration" before they work properly again. The events in the aftermath of the 2010 Haiti earthquake exemplified such calibration phase by the establishment of a network (see section 4.2.1.2). This means, due to the ever-changing conditions, systems may require to be calibrated more than once. In detail, this means that the first trial of establishing any form of communication may fail due to wrong assumptions, as experimenting and acquiring information about the situation at hand, might be necessary to create and maintain the communication.

5.2.7.2 Definition

In computer science self-management denotes a quality of a system to adapt to unanticipated events (Bhat et al. 2006). The inspirational example underlines that in disasters connections can break down one after another. Self-management as a quality attribute anticipates these continuous changes of the underlying structures, for instance the topology of a mobile ad-hoc network (see also section 6.3.1). Thus, the author argues that resilient ad-hoc communication systems should effectively adapt to changing environments by means of self-management.

5.2.8 Decentralized Distribution

5.2.8.1 Inspiration

In the aftermath of the 2013 Boston bombings, several messages were sent over the Twitter network, which asked users for unlocking their private WiFi hotspots, in order to launch and distribute an application called OpenGarden (see section 4.2.3.1). OpenGarden enables users of adjacent devices to create via Bluetooth a mesh network. A device that can access the Internet can then share this connection with the remaining devices. Besides members of the public, authorities made the same request. The discussed examples shows that people often act for the common good and are willing to share resources in the aftermath of disasters.

5.2.8.2 Definition

Decentralized distribution denotes a quality attribute that requires a system to offer ways to distribute data or the system itself through a decentralized manner. Following such a grassroots approach can be helpful in situations of disrupted network infrastructure. In particular, it can help people who have not installed a certain system before a disaster strikes. If a system enables its dynamic deployment of systems, people may still obtain it despite the disruption of the commonly used centralized entity of distribution.

5.3 Example Scenario

The following scenario serves to exemplify the suggested set of quality attributes:

In the aftermath of an earthquake, Liz searches for members of her family. As the mobile network has become disrupted, Liz enables her phone to use wireless network radios as alternative communication channels (Prevalence, QUAT-1). By this she is able to discover a network called "island 1" (Serendipity, QUAT-4). Afterwards, she triggers her phone to connect to "island 1". The association to the network is carried out smoothly (Quick connectivity, QUAT-3). Another phone being part of "island 1" enables Liz to tether Internet connection. She receives a message from her sister that she is not hurt and currently staying at a rescue camp. "Island 1" is constructed in 1:n (one host, many clients) topology. Clients join "island 1" and disconnect as soon as information has been exchanged (Short-lived interactions, QUAT-5). Also Bob's phone joins "island 1". As the Internet connection seems to be weak and unstable the system recommends Bob to post messages only with text, but no multimedia content (Graceful degradation, QUAT-6). After some time another client device will need to create an "island 2" due to the draining battery level in the phone acting as the host device of "island 1" (Self-management, QUAT-7). In "island 2", no Internet connection can be provided, and thus attempts of Liz to access web pages or other online actions result in being redirected to a static web page. The web page indicates the distribution of an emergency app. Liz downloads and installs the app on her phone. After that, she is able to communicate with people in the same ad-hoc network (Ad-hoc communication, QUAT-2). Moreover, she is able to distribute the app in the same decentralized manner to other people in the area (Decentralized distribution, QUAT-8).

5.4 Conclusion

This chapter presented the conceptual framework for this thesis. Table 6 recaps each quality attribute, its goal and the (generically described) approach for reaching it. The overall goal of compiling such a collection of quality attributes is to relate the design of the system to the findings which resulted from the prior empirical investigation of the application domain. To the best of the author's knowledge, for the particular application domain such a collection has not yet been generated. To go beyond this hypothetical stage of research, the chapters 7 and 8 will exemplify how each quality attribute can contribute to the design of an ad-hoc communication system.

Quality	Goal	Approach
Prevalence	Reach of wide population of people	Use of widespread technologies
Ad-hoc communication	Independent from preexisting networks	Communicate in an ad-hoc manner
Quick connectivity	Smooth creation of networks	Easy configurable networks and association
Serendipity	Coincidental communication	Descriptive identifiers
Graceful degradation	Targeted use of still functioning services	Gradual restrictions of services
Short-lived interactions	Efficient use of scarce Resources	Use resources only as long as required
Self-management	Adapt to unanticipated events	Context-based (re-) configuration of the system
Decentralized distribution	Loose dependency to centralized entity	Deployment to adjacent devices

Table 6 Overview of quality attributes

6 State of the Art

This chapter summarizes the state of the art relevant to the technology that has been developed in the frame of this thesis. First, it explains the scope and delimitations of this work, before it describes the emergence of smartphones and wireless communication technologies in the context of smartphones. Against this background the chapter examines several approaches that enable mobile ad-hoc communication and reviews the extent to which the approaches meet the quality attributes described in section 5.2. Finally, this chapter concludes with the choice of the most appropriate wireless communication technology for implementing resilient mobile ad-hoc communication systems.

6.1 Scope

Communication systems for professional first responders have been addressed by many studies (Hofmann et al. 2006; Manoj & Baker 2007; Bruno et al. 2008; Dilmaghani & Rao 2008; Lien et al. 2010; Toups et al. 2011; Ley et al. 2012; Ramirez et al. 2012; Ludwig et al. 2013; Betz & Wulf 2014; Ley et al. 2014; Reuter et al. 2014). Large organizations dealing with emergency response have entered this terrain by the development of systems such as DTFR[1], MERS[2], or WISPER[3]. Further subjects that relate to ad-hoc networks, but have already been well examined, are, for example, the design of routing protocols and strategies for mobile ad-hoc created networks in order to deal with ever-changing network topologies, which may occur due to the human mobility or draining the battery (Conti & Giordano 2007a; Conti & Giordano 2007b; Cucurull et al. 2010; Luqman et al. 2011; Mehendale et al. 2011; Wu et al. 2011; Kravets 2012; Martín-Campillo et al. 2013). Combining these with the use of store-and-forward mechanisms, often referred to as delay-tolerant networking in order to work around temporary disruptions (Fall 2003; Delosieres & Nadjm-Tehrani 2012; Raffelsberger & Hellwagner 2013). Thus, the overall goal of this work is to complement the *status quo* by providing technology that supports people in distress to communicate their needs despite being disrupted from existing network infrastructure. This form of communication can be between members of the public or between the public and professional first responders.

---

[1] DTFR (Distributed Test bed for First Responders), National Institute of Standards and Technology (NIST), http://www.nist.gov/itl/antd/emntg/ps_dtb4fr.cfm

[2] MERS (Mobile Emergency Response Support), Federal Emergency Management Agency (FEMA), http://www.fema.gov/mobile-emergency-response-support

[3] WISPER (Wireless Intelligent Sensor Platform for Emergency Responders), Department of Homeland Security, https://www.sbir.gov/sbirsearch/detail/254404

This thesis concerns scenarios in which network infrastructures need to be created in an ad-hoc manner (i.e. requiring no preexisting infrastructure) using commercially available smartphones.

6.2 Wireless Communication Technologies for Smartphones

The first commercial cell phone, the Motorola DynaTAC[1], has been initially designed with the goal to enable "mobile" telephony. Since this development, cell phones have evolved into much more sophisticated *smartphone* devices. Smartphones are a relatively new class of digital devices, resulting from the confluence of cellular/wireless radio interfaces and the miniaturization of mobile computers. Smartphones are devices that enable people to do various things: organize calendar, take photos, record audio or video, listen to music, access the World Wide Web, send emails, navigate, purchase products, make electronic payments, chat with one person or in groups, and also mundane things like use the phone as a torch. These enhancements resulted from enhancing phones continuously with more sensors, actuators and communication modules.

Examples of sensors embedded into smartphones are: accelerometer, camera, fingerprint sensor, GPS, gyroscope, brightness, magnetometer, microphone, proximity, touch, vibration. In particular, the possibility to retrieve a more or less accurate location by the use of the GPS sensor or WiFi fingerprint can be highly valuable. Collecting the location and corresponding time creates a certain context, as services can track where people have been and when. Estrin (2010) points out that regarding the authenticity of the data this context is at least as important as the identity of the owner of the cell phone. One example is the approach of Wirz et al. (2010), which investigated the use of sensors embedded in cell phones (e.g. GPS, acceleration, compass, and microphone) in order to deduct places with a high density of people during music concerts to prevent stampedes.

---

[1] Motorola DynaTAC, http://en.wikipedia.org/wiki/Motorola_DynaTAC

Figure 10 Wireless radio interfaces embedded in smartphones

Besides wireless cellular radio (2G/3G/4G) for telephony, current smartphones support mainly three additional wireless communication technologies as illustrated in Figure 10: Bluetooth, IEEE 802.11 (WiFi), and Infrared (NFC). These technologies may enable communications in so called dead zones, such as cellars or subways[1] (Bassoli et al. 2007), where no mobile network services are available. Conti and Kumar (2010) point out that encounters of people carrying cell phones support for opportunistic ad-hoc communication are the norm rather than a rarity. This fact might enable social interactions that reflect serendipity (i.e. a happy accident), such as meeting friends by chance for having dinner together, or, on the contrary an opportunity people explicitly are looking for, such as encountering potential players who like to join a mobile game while being on a train ride. Converting these scenarios to situations of disrupted network infrastructures, these wireless technologies might enable serendipitous communications between nearby casualties. People in distress could explicitly request to be discovered by professional first responders or passers-by.

6.2.1 Near-Field Communication

Near Field Communication, shortly called NFC, is a standard for enabling short-range radio communication. It covers protocols for wireless communication and formats for exchanging data. NFC builds on an RFID smart card system developed by Sony in Japan called FeliCa[2] and the ISO/IEC 14443 standard (ISO/IEC 2011) concerning

---

[1] In the recent years, large modern cities as New York or Shenzhen started to provide in central parts of the city fair coverage of cellular network connectivity to their citizens while taking the subway. But, widening this service is still an ongoing progress.

[2] FeliCa, Sony Japan, http://www.sony.net/Products/felica/

proximity cards used for identification. In 2004 Nokia, Philips Semiconductors, and Sony founded the NFC Forum having now 190 members (NFC Forum 2014a). NFC as a technology holds a great potential, especially for users carrying smartphones or tablet computers. NFC operates on the 13.56 MHz frequency, with data transfers up to 424 Kbps (Ahson & Ilyas 2011). For communication NFC requires that two NFC-compatible devices are in range, usually not more than four centimeters, the theoretical maximum are ten centimeters. Like other radio interfaces NFC can be used for social networking needs, such as exchanging photos, music or video files in a secure manner. NFC is inherently secure, as one main design goal was to realize the electronic wallet replacing present credit cards. As the setup process of NFC is fairly simple and fast (0.1 ms), it can be leveraged for bootstrapping other more capable. Wireless radio interfaces such as Bluetooth or WiFi (NFC Forum 2014b). Smartphones equipped with an NFC module can be paired with NFC tags or stickers that can be implemented by the use of NFC apps. Those NFC tags can be used to let mobile users interact with posters, magazines, or products for purchase.

As NFC was designed to support very-short distance communication, it is not a suitable technology for the scope of this work.

6.2.2 Bluetooth

Bluetooth is a wireless communication standard which facilitates the exchange of data between devices in short distance to each other. For example, Bluetooth allows connecting in a wireless manner close devices, such as a laptop with a mouse, keyboard, or headset, serving as a substitute for cables. The original idea behind Bluetooth was conceived in 1994, when Ericsson Mobile Communications unit investigated the design of a low-power system for substituting the cables in short ranges of cell phones and relevant accessories (Ferro & Potortí 2005). In 1998 Ericsson, IBM, Intel, Nokia, and Toshiba formed the Bluetooth Special Interest Group (SIG), which in later years also other companies joined, such as Microsoft or Motorola. Then, in 1999 the first Bluetooth protocol was released.

The Bluetooth radio operates in the industrial, scientific and medical (ISM) band 2.4GHz, same as the IEEE 802.11 standard, which is described in the next section. In this band it leverages the frequency hopping spread spectrum (FHSS). FHSS is a method in which radio signals are transmitted by rapidly hopping from frequency channel to frequency channel upon a pseudo-random number that is known between sender and receiver. Bluetooth splits this band into 79 designated channels and usually performs 1600 hops per second between these channels. Bluetooth is currently at version 4.0 enabling data rates of 721.2 Kbps, 2.1 Mbps for Enhanced Data Rate, and high-speed operation up to 24 Mbps (Bluetooth SIG Inc. 2010), which already amounted for version 3.0. Smartphones commonly support versions upwards of Bluetooth 2.0 + EDR (Extended Inquire Response) allowing for a data rate up to 3 Mbps.

A Bluetooth device may operate either in the *master* or a *slave* mode. Bluetooth constitutes a 1:n network topology. The simplest configuration of a Bluetooth network is called a piconet, which comprises one master device and a maximum of seven active slave devices (see Figure 11). Up to 255 slaves can be put in park mode, i.e. a state in which no data exchange happens, but only maintaining synchronization with the master's transmission. A more complex configuration of Bluetooth networks is a *scatternet*, which essentially, interconnects two or more piconets. Two piconets can communicate by means of a common node, i.e. a node that belongs to both piconets. Such a node, often also called a *relay*, can be a master in one piconet at most while being a slave in several other piconets (see Figure 12); besides a relay, a node can be a slave in more than one piconet (Ferro & Potortí 2005). When a node is active inside one a piconet, it must be parked in any other network it belongs to.

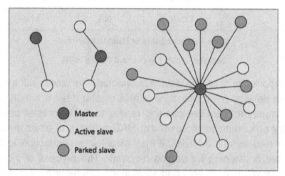

Figure 11 Piconet configurations

Source: (Ferro & Potortí 2005)

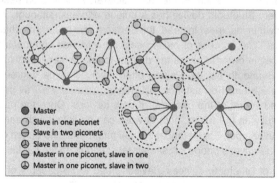

Figure 12 A complex Scatternet configuration

Source: (Ferro & Potortí 2005)

There exist three power classes for classifying Bluetooth communication. Devices that are Class 1 allow a maximal consumption of 100mW, which enable to exchange data over ranges up to 100m. Class 2 devices, most commonly found in cell phones or tablets, allow consuming a maximum of 2.5mW enabling ranges up to 10m. And not least, Class 3 devices only permit a small maximum of 1mW power facilitating ranges up to 1m. Table 7 illustrates the maximum, nominal, and minimum output power of each power class. Souissi and Meihofer (2000) evaluated that in a nominal range of 10m 20 piconets can be freely allocated without any interferences.

Power class	Maximum	Nominal	Minimum
1	100 mW	NA	1 mW
2	2.5 mW	1 mW	0.25 mW
3	1 mW	NA	NA

Table 7 Power classes of Bluetooth devices

Based on Table 5 in (Ferro & Potortí 2005)

When the Bluetooth interface of a device is enabled, the device will try to operate as one of the slave devices of an already available master device. It then starts listening for a master's inquiry for new devices and replies to it. The master performs periodically the inquiry procedure to discover the MAC address of other devices in range. Once a master retrieves an address, it may establish a connection to the slave, assuming the slave is listening for paging requests. The process of including a slave into a piconet, the whole discovery and association can require up to 9.48 seconds.

Any Bluetooth device broadcasts the device name, device class, list of services, and the technical information such as the manufacturer, specification used, clock offset and further. Every Bluetooth device has a unique address, although, this address is usually not shown in inquiries. Instead, the device name is shown, which can be configured by users. The process of *pairing* sets up a trusted communication between Bluetooth devices in order to exchange data or to enable services which allow users to control the Bluetooth device. Pairing often involves some degree of user interacttion with the system. For instance, by entering manually a PIN sequence representing a shared secret of the owner(s) of both devices. Once the pairing has completed successfully, in the future, both devices can be linked with each other requiring no manual user input. For instance, the cell phone must be paired once with a car kit, afterwards the driver's phone will seamlessly connect to the car kit.

For the pairing of Bluetooth devices, devices need to be capable of understanding specific Bluetooth profiles. Smartphones like the new iPhone devices support PAN (Personal Area Network) or HID (Human Interface Device). To this effect, Bluetooth defines not only a wireless radio interface, but also a whole communication stack allowing for the discovery of devices and the advertisement of services. For example,

PAN is a profile that has been designed to create a link on the network layer between laptops, cell phones, or other handheld devices. HID provides links with low latency requesting low power, and is designed for devices, such as keyboards or mice. There, exist many specifications of other Bluetooth profiles, such as SPP (Serial Port Profile), which is based on the widely known RFCOMM protocol for emulating a serial cable.

6.2.3 IEEE 802.11 (WiFi)

802.11 are a set of specifications residing on the MAC and physical layer in order to implement a wireless local area network (WLAN). A WLAN is a network linking two or more wireless devices with radio frequency signals.

Essentially, IEEE 802.11 (IEEE 2012) is a wireless communication standard that has been designed to support the quick establishing of longer-range connectivity between devices in a WLAN. IEEE 802.11 enables connecting to a WLAN, and thus if bandwidth is not a decisive factor, it is often used to extend or replace cabled local area networks. The 802.11 standard and its many amendments (802.11a, 802.11b, 802.11c, 802.11d, 802.11e, 802.11g, 802.11n etc.) provide the basis for products equipped with an IEEE 802.11 radio interface, which can be various: laptops, tablets, smartphones, cameras, TVs, or printers. These products use the brand name *WiFi* to indicate that they are capable to communicate inside a WLAN. In fact, only products passing successfully the complete WiFi Alliance interoperability testing may be labeled with this trademark. The brand name is referred to either as WiFi or Wi-Fi, while the latter spelling shows better the play on the audiophile term Hi-Fi. Consequently, both terms, i.e. the IEEE 802.11 standard and the WiFi trademark, are used synonymously.

WiFi radio operates in the 2.4, 3.6, 5 and 60 GHz frequency bands. Bluetooth also operates in the 2.4 GHz frequency band, but, compared to Bluetooth, WiFi has been designed for longer ranges. Depending on the explicit standard values may vary. Ferro and Portortí (2005) examined the use of 802.11g and yielded as a result a nominal range of 100m (line of sight) and usually a power consumption between 100 to 350mA. For the 2.4 GHz spectrum assignments vary worldwide. For example, while Australia and Europe allow for a spectrum of 13 channels, the US only permits a spectrum of 11 channels. A WiFi signal occupies five channels in the 2.4 GHz band. Any two numbers of channels that differ by five or more, such as 1 and 6, will not overlap.

Initially, the IEEE 802.11 standard specified devices to have a signal rate of 1-2 Mbps. In the following years, a lot of amendments followed, which have significantly increased the performance. Current smartphones support at least the 802.11n standard enabling minimum data rates of 140 Mbps for single data streams; dual data streams can allow up to 300 Mbps. Recent, flagship phones support the 802.11ac standard, which supports higher throughput.

When a WiFi device is enabled it will scan the available channels for WiFi networks transmitting beacons. When the device finds a network it will associate with it. The IEEE 802.11 standard (IEEE 2012) defines two modes of operation: *infrastructure mode* and *ad hoc*[1] *mode*.

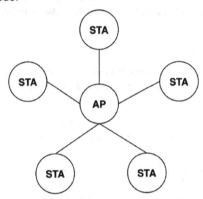

Figure 13 802.11 infrastructure network topology

Figure 13 illustrates how an infrastructure network constitutes a star topology, which consists of one mandatory AP device and zero to multiple station (STA) devices. All STAs are directly connected with the AP, which is responsible for transporting data between the STAs. In terms of WiFi, STAs that are connected with an AP are often called clients. An AP can act as a 'bridge' between its clients and other networks, for example, when an AP is at the same time a router enabling clients to access to Internet. An AP constantly broadcasts frames in order to announce its presence and maintains each client connection, although there is no actual transmission. The energy consumption of an AP varies depending on the implemented standard and the amount of operations it needs to perform. For further details the reader is asked to look into the study of Trifunovic (2011).

802.11 ad hoc mode constitutes a decentralized network topology consisting only of STAs (see Figure 14). Since no AP exists, the administration of the network is distributed between the STAs. Figure 14 illustrates that an STA is connected with other STAs through links. Since links can break down, STAs need to be able to dynamically restructure a network. In order to track if an STA joined or left the ad hoc network an STA transmits beacon frames, exposing its presence and listens to beacons from its neighbors. In ad-hoc networks the data transfer rate is often limited to 11 Mbps, which is significantly smaller than the usual rates of the infrastructure mode. In 802.11 ad hoc mode, each STA consumes in idle mode 156mA energy (Feeney &

---

[1] In conjunction with the 802.11 standard the notation "ad hoc" is used to comply with the standard. Otherwise the more readable notation "ad-hoc" is applied.

Nilsson 2001), which is significantly higher than an AP (infrastructure mode) consumes.

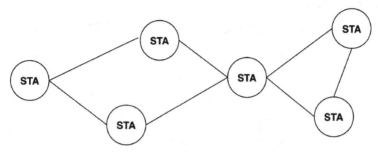

Figure 14 802.11 ad hoc network topology

After an STA has associated with an AP, the STA is considered a client of the WLAN. In order to transmit directly or indirectly packets to STAs the AP deploys a DHCP server that assigns an IP address to each STA immediately after having successfully associated with the WLAN. STAs can only be connected to one network. However, despite being connected, STAs can still scan for networks in range and disconnect from the current network in order to associate with a new network. One reason would be, if the new network transmits a stronger signal or provides enhanced security mechanisms. A STA can go into a doze/sleep mode to save power, or disconnect from a network when it finishes all its operations; the specification considers no power save mode for APs.

The base for a WiFi WLAN is a cellular architecture that calls each cell as a basic service set (BSS). The simplest BSS comprises one AP and one client. Access to the WLAN medium is managed through the distribution coordination function (DCF) being the MAC protocol. In general, once a device detects that no other device has transmitted in short time, called an interframe space (IFS), it transmits a frame. In an infrastructure mode WiFi network the AP is responsible for routing packets between devices. This implies, that an AP may act as a mediator between two clients, which are not in range to each other as displayed in Figure 15.

For 802.11 ad hoc mode, a network comprises at least, two devices interconnected in an ad-hoc manner. Also, a BSS maybe part of a wider network, which is called extended service set (ESS). Each BSS has a unique basic service set identification (BSSID), which is the MAC address of a device. Further, a network is described by an SSID, which reflects normally a human readable name, and thus commonly described as the "network name". An IBSS is an independent basic service set, which constitutes a WiFi network in ad-hoc mode. In an IBSS, the device starting the network generates the SSIDs. The BSSID and SSID are two elements of the beacon frame a WiFi network broadcasts periodically. According to the specification (IEEE

2012) a beacon frame may comprise also the frequency, the detected signal strength, capabilities as security mechanisms, the timestamp, the interval a beacon is broadcasted and more.

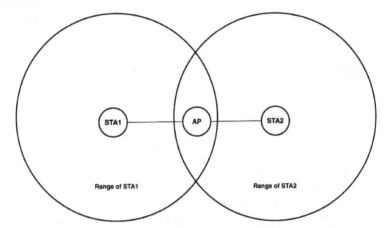

Figure 15 AP acting as mediator between STAs out of range of each other

WiFi is characterized by three procedures: scan, authentication, and association. The *scan phase* sniffs for beacons in order to identify the BSSID and other parts of beacon frames. In passive mode, the scan procedure requires nearly 50ms multiplied by the number of channels to check. In active mode, the sniffing device sends a probe request frame and waits for probe responses from the APs that received the probe request. For such procedure the minimal time of discovery requires:

`(Probe Request + DCF IFS Interval + Probe Response) x Number of Channels`

For instance, it would require 3ms at 1 Mbps or 0.45ms at 11 Mbps.

In an infrastructure mode WiFi network, once a device has scanned an AP it goes over into the *authentication phase*. In this phase, the device has to authenticate itself with the AP and then perform the association. For 802.11 ad hoc WiFi networks the authentication phase is optional. When the authentication is successful, the device sends an association request and waits for an association response. This procedure lasts as long as it takes to send a frame and receive the response, exactly as for the scan phase. The time required, but also the energy consumed in order to scan for APs or associate with an AP may vary due to different firmware (Camps-Mur & Loureiro 2014).

Since its initial release in 1997 and the release of its amendments, in particular 802.11b in the mid of 1999, the IEEE 802.11 standard yielded a tremendous market success. Several stationary and mobile devices support WiFi connectivity, besides other wireless radio interfaces. Most of this success has been built around the deployment of WiFi in infrastructure mode, which therefore is often is referred to as *common* WiFi. The reasons behind this are, in particular, that this mode allows a set of clients to share connection to the Internet through an AP. Also, WiFi in infrastructure mode enables to interconnect devices at home into a (wireless) LAN. Further, a lot of companies use it in order to provide an internal network or file access. In the course of its wide deployment the infrastructure mode has continually been revised for improvement in order to satisfy various user needs and technical difficulties. Recently, new requirements evolved due to the emergence of the Internet of Things vision, pursuing the establishment of a junction between the Internet and wireless sensor networks comprising small computers embedded into everyday objects (Gubbi et al. 2013).

6.2.4 WiFi Direct

WiFi Direct is an evolving wireless communication standard that provides an interesting potential for enabling P2P communication between devices. Thus, its goal is enhancing device-to-device communication between IEEE 802.11 capable devices. It builds upon the widespread IEEE 802.11 standard in infrastructure mode. WiFi Direct allows nearby devices to interconnect without the presence of an AP (Wi-Fi Alliance 2010). Compared to the 802.11 infrastructure mode, WiFi Direct tries to enhance WiFi connectivity for three features: device discovery, service discovery, and power management.

The author considered version 1.1 of the WiFi Direct specification (Wi-Fi Alliance 2010). The specification refers to WiFi Direct devices as *P2P Devices*. In order to uniquely refer to a P2P device, it must have one P2P Device Address complying with the format specified in the IEEE Standard 802.11-2007 (IEEE 2007), which basically is the MAC address. Communications between P2P Devices are always established inside a *P2P group*. Each group has an owner, formally known as the P2P Group Owner. Figure 16 shows, that besides the owner, a P2P group may comprise *P2P Clients* and/or *Legacy Clients* supporting only the 802.11 standard. Legacy devices will see the P2P Group Owner (GO) as a common AP and will not be able to benefit from the enhanced functionalities, as formally they will not belong to the P2P Group. For associating to an AP/P2P GO legacy device, devices must support the WiFi Protected Setup (WPS). WPS is a network security standard enabling to securely peer two devices by a entering a common PIN or pushing a button, where the former method is the baseline method any WPS capable device has to implement (Wi-Fi Alliance 2006). The role of the P2P GO cannot be handed over to another device, which implies that the remaining devices need to re-establish a group by means of the specified procedures. Same as a common AP, a P2P GO broadcasts beacons and its clients can also go into power saving mode. Further, it must provide a DHCP server in order to assign IP addresses to its P2P clients.

To enable device-to-device communication a WiFi Direct certified device has to implement both IEEE 802.11 infrastructure mode roles: client and AP. However, compared to common 802.11, the roles are not static. Indeed, the roles should rather be considered as dynamic. When two P2P devices discover each other they may negotiate their roles (P2P Client or P2P GO). The procedure of establishing a communication is called a *group formation*. The way WiFi Direct enables the formation of a P2P group is similar to the way the Local Cloud system (see chapter 8) opportunistically creates a network. Thus, section 8.4.2 summarizes the procedures WiFi Direct performs to form a P2P group and compares it with the ones the Local Cloud system performs to establish local ad-hoc networks.

The simplest configuration of a P2P topology would be a 1:1 network comprising a P2P GO and a Client (P2P or legacy client). Each client in a P2P Group may be either a P2P Client or a Legacy client (see Figure 16). The specification considers a P2P Device as a P2P Concurrent Device, if it can act simultaneously with an infrastructure mode WLAN and a P2P Group as depicted in Figure 17. Therefore, a device needs to have one MAC entity operating as an IEEE 802.11 client of an infrastructure mode WLAN and another MAC entity operating as a P2P device. A dual MAC entity may, for example, be provided by two different physical radios or by two virtual MAC entity of one physical radio. A P2P Group can operate in the same or different channel as a concurrently running infrastructure mode WLAN. The specification requires that only the P2P GO can cross connect P2P devices to external networks (e.g. a cellular network, such as LTE or an infrastructure mode WLAN).

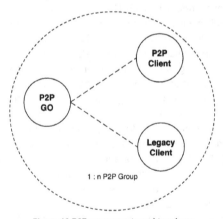

Figure 16 P2P components and topology

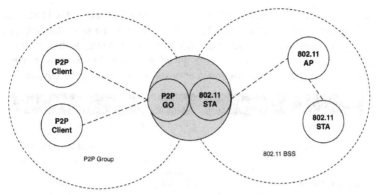

Figure 17 Device acting concurrently as P2P GO and 802.11 STA

Thanks to their logic nature of roles P2P devices can extend networks as illustrated in Figure 18. There, the middle device acts both as a P2P Client of group 1 and as the P2P GO of group 2. In order to do so Camps-Mur et al. (2013) suggest that such P2P device could switch between the two roles (GO, client) by time-sharing the physical WiFi radio. Due to the high penetration of the IEEE 802.11 standard one key design goal of WiFi Direct is to allow for a more energy efficient battery usage. P2P Clients can already benefit from power saving modes being defined in the specification of the IEEE 802.11 standard (IEEE 2012). In comparison to 802.11, WiFi Direct provides also power saving modes (OPS and NoA) for the owner of a WLAN. For further details regarding power saving strategies the reader is asked to look into the specification (Wi-Fi Alliance 2010).

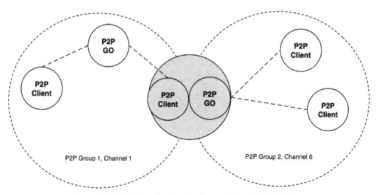

Figure 18 Extension of networks by switching the P2P roles

6.2.5 Overview

Current smartphones mostly provide two forms of wireless radio: Bluetooth or 802.11. Table 8 shows the technical contrasts between both technologies, whereby the 802.11 standard is distinguished between 802.11n and 802.11ac. Current smartphones at least implement the 802.11n standard, while some flagship phones already provide the 802.11ac standard. Besides the standard, technical properties such as range or throughput can be strongly influenced by the provided firmware or by contextual conditions as interferences or obstacles weakening the signals.

	Bluetooth	802.11n	802.11ac
Frequency band	2,4 GHz	2,4 and 5 GHz	5 GHz
Nominal Range	10 m	70 m (indoor), 250 m (outdoor)	Similar as 802.11n, but with higher signal rates
Minimum Rate	721.2 Kbps	140 Mbps	500 Mbps
Maximum Rate	24 Mbps	600 Mbps	~7 Gbps

Table 8 Comparison of Bluetooth and 802.11 (n/ac)

Table 9 illustrates from an operational perspective the differences between Bluetooth, 802.11 in ad hoc and infrastructure mode, and WiFi Direct.

	Bluetooth	802.11 Ad Hoc	802.11 Infrastructure	WiFi Direct
Operation modes	Master, Slave	STA	STA, AP	P2P GO, P2P Client
Network Topology	1 master : n slaves	1 STA : 1 STA	1 AP : n STAs	1 GO : n P2P Clients
Minimal infrastructure	Master	N/A	AP	N/A
Basic cell	Piconet	IBSS	BSS	P2P Group
Extension of basic cell	Scatternet	N/A	ESS	N/A
Network set-up	Inquiry, Paging	Scan, Authentication	Scan, Authentication, Association	Scan, Find, Provisioning
Authentication	Shared secret, pairing	N/A	Shared secret, Challenge-response	Shared Secret, Peering (PIN, Push Button)
Power save modes	Sniff, hold, park; standby	N/A	Doze	Client: Doze Go: OPS, NoA

Table 9 Operational view on wireless communication technologies

Summarizing, the main advantage of Bluetooth is the low consumption of power. This has made Bluetooth very popular among various products on the market that can communicate with each other. These communications are intended to last for a longer time, but do not require large data transfer and no long distances. Compared to Bluetooth the 802.11 infrastructure mode allows for higher bandwidth and wider ranges, but requires significantly more energy. The idea behind the 802.11 ad hoc mode was to enable P2P communication between nearby devices. It never reached any particular success because of its lack of security, high power consumption, and relatively low throughput (11 Mbps). Due to the decentralized nature every STA has to forward traffic even when unrelated to itself. As a result of this, 802.11 ad hoc WLANs suffer from security issues, transmission delays, error rates, or availability limitations. WiFi Direct is an emerging technology that aims to fill the gap left by 802.11 ad hoc mode. It builds on the success of 802.11 infrastructure mode. Its implementation is merely in software, as it can reuse existing WiFi radios. WiFi Direct provides backwards compatibility with common WiFi devices, i.e. devices operating in 802.11 infrastructure mode. In WiFi Direct networks clients are only intended to communicate with the P2P GO, while in infrastructure WLANs the AP forwards data between the clients in its network. This emphasizes that WiFi Direct is rather intended to be used for securely peering nearby devices into a temporary WLAN. In contrast, the 802.11 infrastructure mode also supports permanent networks. Due to enhancements in security, a downfall of current WiFi Direct implementations is the cumbersome pairing mechanism, similar to Bluetooth. This does not allow for quick, serendipitous connections to networks.

The last two sections provided the technical background of wireless communication technologies on which the systems and approaches described in the next two sections have built on. These technologies are therefore highly relevant to keep in mind when evaluating the state of the art of systems, which potentially can support communications in the face of disasters.

6.3 Towards Opportunistically Created Mobile Ad-Hoc Networks

The section introduces first the paradigm of mobile ad-hoc networks (MANETs). The remainder of this section examines different approaches of opportunistically creating MANETs. Besides the need for enabling ad-hoc communication in the face of disruptions of network infrastructure, these approaches emerged from the need to address the tasks of everyday life.

6.3.1 The Paradigm of Mobile Ad-Hoc Networks

"Ad-hoc network" refers to the approach to construct a network of devices that does not rely on any preexisting infrastructure. The term *ad-hoc* is Latin and means *"for a particular purpose only"*[1]. An ad-hoc system is a system whose existence lasts usually for a limited time. In ad-hoc networks, devices can reach any other device through multiple hops over nodes until the designated node is reached.

A mobile ad-hoc network (MANET) denotes a collection of mobile devices that form a wireless network in an ad-hoc manner. As the owner of mobile devices might move, the topology of a MANET is subject to continuous changes. This fact alone implies the need to revisit all of the networking paradigms that evolved around the Internet. Thus, a lot of research has explored the design of routing protocols dealing with ever-changing network topologies (Conti & Giordano 2007a; Conti & Giordano 2007b). As for MANETs the assumption of end-to-end connectivity is not suitable anymore, this research has investigated delay-tolerant networking (Fall 2003), which upfront anticipates temporal disruptions of networks. Raffelsberger and Hellwagner (2013) underline that MANETs are a promising solution for setting up temporary networks in situations of disrupted infrastructure.

---

[1] http://dictionary.reference.com/browse/ad+hoc

6.3.2 Bluetooth-based Approaches

Davies et al. (2009) developed a system that uses Bluetooth Device Name tags to enable users to spontaneously interact with public displays deployed on a university campus. For this, users need to (re-) configure the Bluetooth Device Name of their cell phone, which is then scanned by the Bluetooth Scanner attached to the public display, and then internally interpreted to display user requests upon a validation process. Their implementation is based on Bluetooth version 2.0. According to the corresponding specification (Bluetooth SIG Inc. 2004), the inquiry phase, i.e. the time Bluetooth devices need to discover neighboring devices, should be set to 10.24 seconds. Reducing the time may result in failure to detect devices in proximity. To reduce such delay O'Neill (2006) proposes to deploy multiple Bluetooth scanning devices. However, such a strategy holds the complexity in terms of installation and software to control parallel activities of the multiple devices. Turning to the discovery time of the prototype, approximately two seconds more are spent in the name resolution phase. In this phase, the scanning device needs to determine the name of a detected device. For this, the scanning device forms a communication link to the detected device and sends a request for its name. Application specific processes use up the remaining time.

Hossmann et al. (2011) designed Twimight, an application which enables Twitter users in proximity to communicate with each other despite disruptions of network links to the centralized Twitter server. For this Twimight applies opportunistic techniques of communicating through P2P, delay-tolerant messaging in disaster situation. Therefore, their Android prototype application foresees two modes of operation. First, a 'normal mode' that connects to the Internet in order to provide the usual Twitter functionality, such as viewing the timeline, tweeting, retweeting, or direct messaging. Second, a 'disaster mode' that periodically scans for the presence of Bluetooth devices in order to locate nearby Twitter users. Users can exchange messages via delay-tolerant epidemic routing (Vahdat & Becker 2000), when their devices are in range. As soon as a smartphone can connect again to the online Twitter server, all messages stored locally on the phone will be posted to the online server. Twimight employs security features (authentication, confidentiality, accountability) for the delay-tolerant epidemic spreading of tweets (Legendre 2011). Despite the constraints of Bluetooth, i.e. cumbersome pairing, short range, or limited data rate, Legendre et al. (2011) opted for using Bluetooth, because it incorporates an acceptable trade-off between the wireless communication features and battery lifetime. Another advantage is that Twimight runs on off-the-shelf Android phones.

Open Garden[1] enables sharing an Internet connection between laptops, tablet PCs and cell phones. For this Open Garden creates a mesh network of devices acting concurrently as clients consuming data over multiple hops, or as relays or gateways

---

[1] Open Garden, https://opengarden.com/

(see Figure 19). In order to share an Internet connection, it is required that at least one device has access to the Internet (via 3G or WiFi). Other devices can tether to it via Bluetooth. In the background Open Garden identifies the best Internet connections in order to increase the available bandwidth (Iosifidis et al. 2014). Besides Bluetooth, Open Garden also facilitates the interconnection between devices via WiFi Direct (see section 6.2.4).

6.3.3 Approaches based on 802.11 Ad Hoc Mode

Scott et al. (2006) and Su et al. (2007) presented the design of the Haggle platform. Haggle enables mobile users in proximity to exchange content requiring no fixed infrastructure. Haggle is the first comprehensive architecture that has been designed for facilitating opportunistic networking. Haggle enables neighboring devices to exchange content directly between themselves, when they happen to come in close

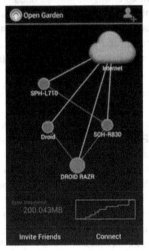

Figure 19 Open Garden: Internet Sharing

Source: Open Garden App in Google Play Store[1]

range. A reference implementation of its architecture is available[2] to the public. In order to provide seamless communication, Haggle's architecture separates the transport layer from the application layer. Through an asynchronous publish-subscribe system (Baldoni et al. 2003), users can express interests via keywords and then receive content from other peers, according to how well the available content matches their interests. Various proximity-based systems have been built on top of Haggle ranging from picture-sharing among cell phones (Nordström et al. 2009) to

---

[1] https://play.google.com/store/apps/details?id=com.opengarden.android.MeshClient&hl=en
[2] Haggle, https://code.google.com/p/haggle/

seeking friends and localization (Papandrea et al. 2009) and further systems (Borcea et al. 2007; Pietiläinen et al. 2009; Martín-Campillo et al. 2010; Martín-Campillo et al. 2011; Mokryn et al. 2012). One example is MobiClique (Pietiläinen et al. 2009), a middleware for social networking. MobiClique enables mobile users to meet by chance, in case the mobile users are in the immediate vicinity and their user profiles share some pre-defined relationships. For this, users are notified and can introduce each other, confirm to exchange content and possibly create a friendship. Another good example is the use of Haggle for implementing electronic triage tags. Their deployment requires no preexisting network structures and is targeted to be used in order to triage victims in the aftermath of disasters (Martín-Campillo et al. 2010; Martín-Campillo et al. 2011). Haggle supports connectivity via Bluetooth and 802.11 ad hoc mode. Haggle runs on Windows Mobile and Android; for the latter, users need to have root access on their devices.

Bell et al. (2006) investigated the design of the Domino framework for facilitating local wireless connections between proximate mobile devices in order to exchange data. For this, either the IEEE 802.11 ad hoc or infrastructure mode is used. In detail, Domino exchanges software modules, which are based on recommendations, and their usage histories. Communications rely upon an agreement to connect with a network, with the same SSID, until explicitly triggered to associate with another network. In the 802.11 ad hoc mode, static IP addresses are assigned, as the developers experienced that automatic addressing was slow and unreliable. Every second each peer sends a UDP broadcast in order that any nearby peers become aware of it. Such a UDP broadcast contains an IP address and a port number, which a receiving device can use in order to create a TCP connection.

Lu et al. (2011) examined the use of 802.11 ad hoc mode for opportunistically creating MANETs. A device announces its presence by broadcasting beacons filled with relevant information in the SSID field, for instance, the device ID. This allows the simultaneous discovery of multiple devices by one device, without establishing a connection. This approach shows good results in terms of energy efficiency and satisfactory connection speed between peered devices.

Gardner-Stephen and Palaniswamy (2011) initiated the Serval project, which leverages a mesh of WiFi networks consisting of laptops, Android-based smartphones and tablets, or other devices in order to build low-cost community telephony networks (Gardner-Stephen & Palaniswamy 2011). Communication mainly goes over Voice over IP (VoIP). For this, the Serval project deploys an overlay mesh network called the Serval Mesh that facilitates the conversion of dialed cell phone numbers into Serval-augmented IP addresses, so called SIPs. In detail, the caller phone broadcasts to other network peers the phone number of the phone it aims to reach (see Figure 20). When the caller phone receives a response in the form of a SIP, the call proceeds without any user interaction. The seamless communication is constructed via a mesh of 802.11 ad hoc mode devices using the B.A.T.M.A.N. (Abolhasan et al. 2009) routing protocol. To retrieve data from phones that only support communications via the IEEE 802.11 infrastructure mode, Serval also considers four operation modes in terms of WiFi: ad-hoc, client, AP, and off. If no peers are detected, a cycling strategy is applied, which spends approximately 30s in each active mode before it advances to the next.

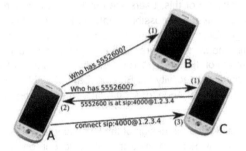

Figure 20 Call resolution using Serval numbering architecture

Source: (Gardner-Stephen & Palaniswamy 2011)

6.3.4 Approaches based on 802.11 Infrastructure Mode

Wirtz et al. (2011) explored MA-Fi (Mobile Ad-Hoc WiFi). MA-Fi is an approach that combines a set of MANETs operating in the 802.11 in infrastructure mode into a mesh of networks. In MA-Fi client devices can deploy an AP with which other STA devices can connect, and at the same time these client devices can establish connections with other APs. Although it uses common WiFi, this approach still manages to enable for multi hop communication through these interconnections. The approach configures the MAC level of a WiFi interface into virtual interfaces. Each virtual interface can be configured to run in a different operation mode, i.e. AP or client, with the restriction of using the same WiFi channel on that interface. Another way to simultaneously operate a device in AP or client mode is to use multiple network cards per device. However, current smartphones or tablets are usually equipped with a single physical network card. Due to this fact and because mobile virtualization is still in its infancy, the practicality of this approach in the early stages of emergency response is arguable.

Trifunovic et al. (2011) examined the feasibility of opportunistic communications among collocated devices by the use of IEEE 802.11 in infrastructure mode. They point out that the drawback of infrastructure mode WiFi networks is that clients connected to different APs cannot communicate with others resulting in groups of isolated "islands". To tackle this problem the developed framework, called Wifi-Opp, triggers devices to randomly swap roles between AP and client mode. Reconfiguring topologies dynamically will allow dissolving these isolated "islands" in order to disseminate content in opportunistic fashion. Alternation of nodes relies on three fixed parameters: a) the duration of time an AP can spend when no clients are associated, b) the duration of time a client can be connected to the same AP, and c) the duration of time a client scans for the presence of APs. Trifunovic et al. designed a prototype based on the mobile Android platform. To opportunistically create wireless networks, Wifi-Opp utilizes hidden functions of the Android WiFi API via JAVA reflection. Thus, their solution runs on commercially available Android smartphones. Evaluations conducted in a lab environment show that Wifi-Opp has a significantly lower energy footprint than the 802.11 ad hoc mode. From a technical perspective, this approach comes the closest to the networking approach developed in this thesis. The same hidden functionality of the API is used, which per se represents a risk, as this functionality is "officially" not supported and therefore might be removed from future releases. According to this[1] mailing list, there exists no open source distribution, which made it difficult for the author to evaluate the functioning of the Wifi-Opp framework.

Dubois et al. (2013) investigated the possibilities of re-configuring opportunistically created WiFi networks operating in the 802.11 infrastructure mode. Their goal is to allow for the spontaneous opportunistic creation of WiFi networks in order to store and exchange data between different mobile devices; for instance, smartphones, tablets, TVs, printers, cameras or recently available FlashAir SD cards. For this they propose the use of a self-organizing policy, which considers that devices change their roles, i.e. a device can turn from a client device into AP and vice versa. As changing of the roles implies that the overall network will be partitioned, the transferred data is stored on a device until new links are established. When a device scans for the presence of WiFi networks in range, it can detect the channel used, besides the signal strength, SSID or its MAC address. Then the device can either choose to become a client of an existing AP, which would imply using the same channel, or create an own AP using another channel. As adjacent networks use non-overlapping channels, theoretically, such an approach can indefinitely extend the overall network. Figure 1 in (Dubois et al. 2013) shows the existence of five opportunistically created WiFi infrastructure networks. The AP of each adjacent network operates on a different frequency, i.e. in total three different channels are used: channel 1, channel 6, and channel 11. When a device is associated with a network it can still discover other networks in range. Using a decentralized policy for self-organizing the network, the nodes perform the execution of connectivity operations based on a set of local rules that take into account frequencies and network traffic. For instance, a client might become an AP, if no APs are anymore available. Also, a client might become an AP in order to relieve an existing AP that is handling too many requests. Concluding, the approach of Dubois et al. (2013) seems to be worth considering for scaling opportunistic networking approaches as Wifi-Opp or the network paradigm presented in this thesis (see chapter 7 and 8).

---

[1] http://ml.ninux.org/pipermail/battlemesh/2011-October/000958.html

Kärkkäinen and Ott (2014) investigated an approach that enhances MANETs with stationary nodes (LIBEROUTERS), ergo it is a hybrid networking approach that combines the paradigms of opportunistic networking (Pelusi et al. 2006) and mesh-networks (Akyildiz & Wang 2005). The motivation behind this approach is that opportunistically created MANETs represent ever-changing networks, which implies that essential information can suddenly get lost due to the disappearance of nodes. Nodes may disappear due to getting out of range, lack of battery, or congested links. Consider the example of people residing in the same room and exchanging messages. As soon as the room is empty all information is gone, and somebody who enters the room one hour later is not going to be able to retrieve the relevant information. Therefore, Kärkkäinen and Ott (2014) argue the need to invest in stationary elements beyond smartphones, which in terms of information retrieval can function as pick-up stations. Their prototype comprises as stationary nodes, battery-powered Rasperry Pi[1] pieces, which are relatively cheap single-board computers. Those stationary nodes deploy wireless networks with the SSID "LIBEROUTER". When mobile users connect to the network a captive portal offers them to download a native Android application, which is required for communicating inside the local Liberouter network. This application remains running in the background, unless stopped by the user, and enables seamless communication with nearby Liberouter networks. For example, Node A (stationary) and Node B (mobile) might communicate at some point, but at a later point, a long time after B has already disappeared, Node C (mobile) will be able to retrieve from Node A the messages, which Node A has previously received from Node B. From the perspective of the network layer it makes no difference if messages contain text, images, audio, video, or byte code of an application intended for being deployed in local, neighbored networks. While LIBEROUTER is a promising low-cost approach, the success of its practical deployment remains to be seen. Besides, privacy issues related to the decentralized distribution of applications (see also section 7.3), in the Rescue stage (see section 2.1.1) the presence or absence of stationary nodes is unclear. One could think of technology-savvy users carrying single-board computers with them and being willing to deploy in them in the face of a disaster. Publicly provided stationary nodes can also be imagined, which can be accessed easily and be enabled in a straightforward manner, similar to a defibrillation apparatus being available at buildings that are open to the public, such as central stations, or airports. However, those publicly accessible elements might get damaged. Concluding, LIBEROUTER's practicality needs to be observed in the future.

6.4 Conclusion

This chapter detailed Bluetooth and WiFi based communication approaches applied by utilizing cell phones.

---

[1] Raspberry Pi, http://www.raspberrypi.org/

Bluetooth has primarily been designed for enabling secure communications that users perform on a daily or frequent basis, such as linking the phone with the car kit in order to easily answer calls while driving the car. Bluetooth-based approaches benefit from its widespread proliferation and its low energy footprint. Bluetooth allows for short-range interconnection of portable products requiring low power. As smartphones fall into the second power class of Bluetooth they only support ranges up to 10m, which can be disadvantageous given obstacles that decrease the maximal transmission range. Also, Bluetooth requires a relatively long time (up to 10s) for the discovery of devices. For the scope of this work, the strongest disadvantage is the cumbersome pairing of devices. This makes Bluetooth less suitable for serendipitous communication and not complying with QUAT-3. In an environment with significant mobility this is likely to lead to extremely slow name resolution, because many of the devices that the scanner attempts to contact will already have left the coverage area of the scanner.

In contrast to Bluetooth, WiFi in general allows for the quick construction of ad-hoc networks (QUAT-2 and QUAT-3). While, due to its nature, 802.11 in ad hoc mode suggests itself for the purpose of fostering the ad-hoc creation of network infrastructures, Dubois et al. (2013) point out that in practice it has several drawbacks. First, it is not available to most mobile users, as widespread mobile platforms do not support 802.11 in ad hoc mode. For instance, Android or iOS do not support the 802.11 ad hoc mode, unless the underlying operating system is reconfigured (see section 7.2.2.1). Further, such reconfiguration is rather a process to be performed by advanced mobile users, besides the risk to stop receiving critical updates. Therefore, systems built around the 802.11 ad hoc mode will not reach the critical mass of people in routine and disaster situations (QUAT-1), making this mode less suitable for the scope of this work. Second, the 802.11 ad hoc mode consumes significantly more power than the infrastructure mode (Perrucci et al. 2011). Third, all devices must use the same channel and thus do not scale (Wang & Ho 2011). Due to these limitations the 802.11 ad hoc mode has not yet yielded the success which the infrastructure mode has. Thus, the WiFi Alliance has investigated WiFi Direct as a software-based approach that is built upon the IEEE 802.11 in infrastructure mode.

WiFi Direct has been designed for quick, easy and secure peering of home devices via WiFi, such as connecting a camera with a printer. WiFi Direct encompasses new features over common WiFi, which basically are: power management for WLAN group owners (P2P GOs), service discovery prior to establishing a connection, and concurrent WLAN connections. While these features underline that WiFi Direct has a great potential for bringing device-to-device communication to the market, it is still an emerging standard that has some severe limitations. Regarding its energy footprint there are some pitfalls. As its discovery algorithm requires devices to keep awake, Kravets (2012) points out that WiFi Direct is not suitable to support the design of proximity-based applications. Additionally this WiFi Direct requires implementing

WPS, making it less suitable for supporting serendipitous communication between nearby devices (QUAT-4). WiFi Direct as a technology is still in its infancy. Implementations on current mobile platforms are still evolving or not available (see also section 7.2.2.1). Due to its limited distribution and the constraint that the owner of a P2P group must be a WiFi Direct certified device, it cannot properly address QUAT-1, and thus should be rather viewed as a supplement to the networking approach that was developed in the frame of this work.

For the scope of this thesis, common WiFi is the most appropriate technology in order to enable ad-hoc communication. Thus, this thesis investigates ways of opportunistically creating MANETs using commercially available smartphones that operate in the 802.11 infrastructure mode.

7 First System: Help Beacons

This chapter presents the iterative development of a lightweight, ad-hoc SOS system for smartphones called Help Beacons. Three prototypes have been developed in total. They exemplify how the quality attributes suggested in section 5.2 can be implemented for smartphones. This chapter begins with a general description of the system and then describes in detail the course of development for the three prototypes. The chapter ends with a conclusion of how the identified quality attributes have contributed to the resilience in the design of the system.

7.1 Concept

This section provides a general overview of the Help Beacons system, and discusses the reasoning for its development.

The Help Beacons system is a mobile SOS system that runs on commercially available smartphones and is independent from any existing network infrastructure. It enables people in distress to use their smartphones for communicating their situation via an ad-hoc emergency signal that can be received by professional first responders, helping them to locate casualties in disaster situations. For doing so, the Help Beacons approach exploits opportunities that already exist in established wireless network protocols and standards. This means, when creating ad-hoc communication links between neighboring smartphones, the Help Beacons approach exploits WiFi service set identifiers (SSIDs) for the discovery of devices and to convey short emergency messages inside the SSIDs. Additionally, it piggybacks on the WiFi connection process in order to exchange additional data beyond the information conveyed via SSIDs. One device (the "Beacon")[1] creates a WiFi network and advertises an emergency message inside the SSID, i.e. the human readable network name of the WiFi network. In turn, another device (the "Seeker") scans the environment for devices that advertise themselves as Beacons and instantiates brief connections to those in order to notify each Beacon that it has been discovered. In cases where connectivity is good enough, both devices (Beacon and Seeker) can use network sockets to exchange further information that would exceed the maximum length constraint of the SSID.

The concept of the Help Beacons system was inspired by how people make use of the names of their WiFi home networks to broadcast short messages. Such messages can be used for manifold purposes. In their longitudinal study, Wong et al. (2007) examine the use of WiFi network names to mark either public or private spaces.

---

[1] For the sake of readability the author will often write Beacon instead of Beacon device; analogous for Seeker.

Their empirical findings are based on two large Canadian cities, Montréal and Toronto. To mark a private network people often label it either by placing the focus on the location of a signal (e.g. *"53Tyrell"*), or use intimate nicknames or references that mean something to people within the house (e.g. *"sweetpea"*) in order to convey the privacy of their networks (Wong et al. 2007). Also, Wong et al. (2007) found out that people use names that can be interpreted for the intended users of the network, but also external users who only receive the signal (e.g. *"Todd's Net"*). Besides encrypting their WiFi network, some people assign names to their networks that clearly express the intended private use, such as *"backonyourbike"* or *"getyourwlan"* (Wong et al. 2007). To the contrary, public WiFi networks are unencrypted and often named after the property behind the network, such as a community, restaurant, university, or airport. Besides the signal, stickers being placed outside or inside of walls of buildings often support the visibility of public networks.

Furthermore, a survey by the Swedish broadband supplier Telia[1] showed that conflicts in neighborhoods are sometimes expressed via provocative names of WiFi networks. For example, the survey listed SSIDs, such as *"Turn the noise down"* or *"no trash in the stairwell"*, which in a way replace the angry notes inhabitants would usually put in laundry rooms, lifts, or the main entrance of multifamily houses. Simpson (2010) reports that further examples of such names conveying simple, anonymous messages can be *"remove the fluff from the filter"* or *"DontStealMyInternet"*.

---

[1] Telia, http://www.telia.se

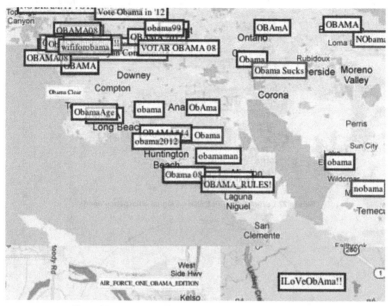

Figure 21 Exploiting WiFi SSIDs to convey political allegiances

Extracted from (Yau 2012)

As another example, Figure 21 illustrates how people creatively used SSID names to express political ideas in the context of the re-election of US president Barack Obama in 2012. Many people expressed their sympathy to Obama (or vice versa) by adapting the name of their WiFi home network, such as *"ILoVeObAma!!"* or *"Vote Obama in '12"*, or *"nobama"* (Yau 2012).

In summary, a WiFi network is visible in a certain range and the advertised SSID is usually the first thing people become aware of. Essentially, people can easily relate and understand SSID names. They represent a point of contact between people and the intangible element that wireless networks represent. This creates an interesting potential for emergency response which led to the creation of the concept of the Help Beacons system, displayed in Figure 22. It explores the idea of using WiFi SSIDs as beacons to ask for help, to offer resources, or to disclose locations.

Figure 22 Leveraging WiFi SSIDs to signal emergency needs

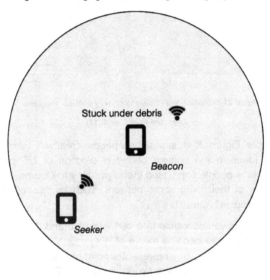

Figure 23 Tracking of a Beacon signal

Figure 23 highlights that the presence of a help beacon defines a sort of "I'm here" signal that can be tracked by other devices in the vicinity. Particularly, in this aspect the author saw a potential to support responders in finding missing persons and re-establishing communication in the face of disrupted network infrastructures.

7.2 First Prototype

This section describes the initial design and implementation of the first prototype of the Help Beacons system. It also explains how the feasibility of the system has been evaluated in an underground tunnel and the corresponding analysis. Parts of this section are based on research first published in (Al-Akkad, Ramirez, Boden, et al. 2014).

7.2.1 Design

The WiFi SSID sent out by a Beacon can carry useful information about the user. For instance, the information may contain her or his name, health status, or other important information. Technically, the idea is implemented by placing short messages inside the SSID in order to create an emergency beacon. A Seeker device uses its wireless interface to search for any Beacon devices in range, collecting the information they broadcasted. By piggybacking the handshaking process of WiFi networks, i.e. by associating with an unencrypted access point, the Seeker can notify the Beacon that it has received the broadcast signal. Afterwards, it can request further information or store additional information supporting the logistics of the rescuing process by connecting to a network socket provided by the Beacon.

Step	Description
1a	The device advertises a WiFi network using an SSID identifier
1b	The device advertises itself as a Beacon by means of a particular string contained in the SSID
1c	The device places a unique identifier at a defined position inside the SSID, e.g. a string pre-/suffix built on a MAC or IMEI of the device
2	The device runs a DHCP server assigning an IP address when a Seeker connects
3	The device runs a program that listens at a specific socket address, accepts incoming connections and interchanges details by the use of a protocol

Table 10 Setup of a Beacon

The Help Beacons approach towards opportunistic ad-hoc communication initially comprises two or more mobile devices. Table 10 depicts the setup process for a Beacon: at first, a device deploys a WiFi network that advertises itself as a Beacon by using a particular string of characters inside the SSID. The device runs a DHCP server for providing an IP address configuration for the Seeker, and listens to a specific socket address, i.e. the combination of an IP address and a port number, to exchange details when the Seeker device associates with it. According to Table 10, a Beacon could deploy a WiFi network with the SSID "*#%a5My leg is broken". The sequence of "*#%" would be the prefix, "a5" the unique id, and "My leg is broken" the help message.

Figure 24 illustrates the Seeker, which enables its WiFi interface, performs a scan for WiFi networks, and finds the Beacon by the particular string of characters placed inside its SSID.

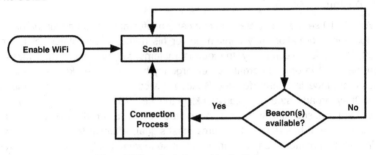

Figure 24 Flow chart of searching for Beacons

Figure 25 illustrates how the Seeker connects to the Beacon and writes its details to the specific socket address. Subsequently, it receives details from the Beacon and finally it disconnects.

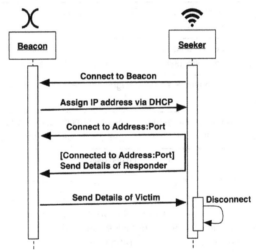

Figure 25 Sequence diagram of exchanging details between Beacon and Seeker

7.2.2 Implementation

The Help Beacons system consists of two applications. The first is a victim application that enables its users to create an emergency beacon by placing short messages inside the SSID of a WiFi hotspot (Beacon). The other application (Seeker) allows professional first responders to discover the requesting Beacons. The purpose of the Help Beacons system would be rather constrained if it would not be linked to other emergency response systems. In the BRIDGE project, the Seeker sends the collected data acquired from Beacons to a command center as shown in Figure 26. At the command center people can view the transferred data on a map illustrated in Figure 27 in order to support the response operation. The jagged arrow in Figure 26 hides the complexity the BRIDGE 'system of systems' is dealing with in order to transfer the collected data to a command center. In detail, a dedicated background process running on the Seeker device is responsible for sending the collected data. In the first instance, the data is sent to a mesh router, which then routes the data to a topic based proprietary publish-subscribe cloud service that pushes the data to the command center. Before, a daemon running at the premises of the command center initiated to subscribe to the Help Beacons topic.

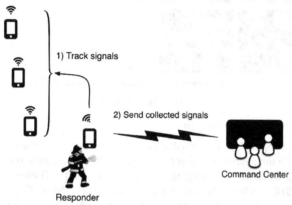

Figure 26 The big picture of deploying the Help Beacons system

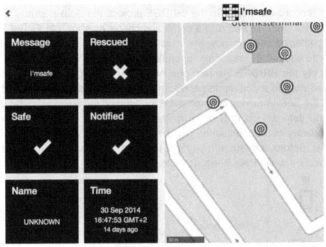

Figure 27 Beacons displayed on a map in the command center

Source: https://master-bridge.eu

7.2.2.1 Choice of Mobile Platform

When implementing mobile systems that enable the construction of ad-hoc networks, the choice of the mobile platform is very important. When the goal is to foster the prototyping of applications for challenging scenarios. According to Gartner (Rivera & van der Meulen 2014) Apple's iOS and Google's Android are the leading platforms for smartphones in the market. This makes them comply with QUAT-1. Both mobile platforms will be described in general and against the background of this work.

iOS is the mobile platform for the iPhone, a line of smartphones that was initially launched in 2007. Since then, iOS products, such as the iPod touch, iPhone, and iPad, have revolutionized the mobile market. One major enhancement is the way mobile users can interact with cell phones. The iPhone led the path to smartphones enabling people to touch and pinch the screen for navigation (Jindal 2012). The iPhone comes with a set of native apps, in particular utility apps such as a calculator or a mail program. Another important app is called App Store. The App Store enables access to an online distribution platform of the same name that facilitates users to purchase or download free apps. This shows a huge paradigm shift from how the apps were distributed before, when third-party app stores offered apps that were poorly integrated into the mobile platform. Instead of introducing something new, Apple reuses iTunes—originally a distribution platform for music, to distribute apps as well. Third-party apps were nothing new, though the App Store created a whole new user experience resulting in an increasing number of downloads (Jindal 2012). People cannot load apps aside from the App Store on their device, while Apple has strict requirements for legitimizing apps into the App Store. The iOS SDK offers developers a wide range of tool kits and Xcode is an IDE containing a suite of development tools. Users can develop and test applications by using a free copy of Xcode, but they cannot launch their apps on a physical device, nor publish them in the App Store, before first paying a developer fee of $99.00[1] per year. The primary programming language for building applications is Objective-C. While writing this work the relevant API versions were iOS v4 to iOS v7. The latest iOS version provides APIs for WiFi or Bluetooth, but not yet for NFC. Via the system settings, users can set up an access point for tethering Internet connection via 3G, 4G. The iOS platform neither supports the 802.11 ad hoc mode nor WiFi Direct; the 802.11 ad hoc mode can be used on jailbroken devices conflicting with QUAT-1. iOS offers no API to enable or disable a WiFi AP.

Android is a Linux based operating system. Developers can write apps with using a customized SDK of the Java programming language. The SDK is freely available for download in the Web. Many developers use Eclipse ADT as an IDE for the Android SDK. The Android equivalent for Apple's AppStore is the Google Play Store, which was formerly known as the Android Market. It is now the leading app store worldwide, seeing in the first quarter of 2014 45% more downloads than the AppStore (Perez 2014). To license apps in the Google Play Store developers have to pay a one-time fee of $25[2]. Aside from the Google Play Store, people can install third-party apps by granting permission in their system settings as displayed in Figure 28. Developers need to set so-called *permissions* to gain access to system services, such as input/output file handling, location or communication services. Android supports the coexistence of multiple processes, in which each app runs in its own process. Since Android SDK version 2.2 smartphones can be turned into a WiFi hotspot, which allows up to eight devices to connect to it. To programmatically enable or disable a WiFi infrastructure network, developers need to call hidden API methods via JAVA reflection. Of course, hidden methods hold the danger that they may disappear in future SDKs, but compared to iOS there is at least a possibility to make use of that feature. Operating the 802.11 ad hoc mode requires root access, which is forbidden in commercial phones. The implementation of WiFi Direct was still evolving at the time of writing this thesis. The author found out that the Android operating system does not support two basic operations without the need for user interaction: first, to enable WiFi Direct, and second, to accept incoming connections. This is also described in an issue tracker thread[3].

---

[1] iOS Developer Program, https://developer.apple.com/programs/ios/

[2] Android Developer Registration, https://support.google.com/googleplay/android-developer/answer/113468?hl=en

[3] Issue 30880: WiFi Direct API for connection acceptance, https://code.google.com/p/android/issues/detail?id=30880

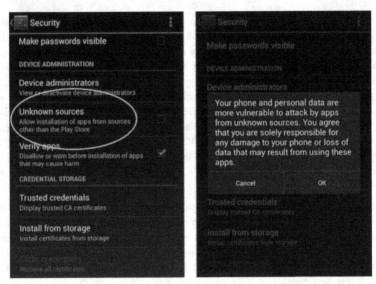

Figure 28 Settings allowing the installation of apps outside the Google Play store

In summary, both Android and iOS, represent promising mobile platforms for the pro-totyping of smartphone-based systems. However, in the scope of this work Android is the more open platform, as iOS fails to support setting up through programmatic code an AP in order to create a WiFi infrastructure network and does not allow for decentralized distribution of apps (see Table 11). Thus, for the scope of this work the Android platform is the more suitable mobile platform to continue with.

QUAT-...	Android	iOS
1	✓	✓
2	✓	✗
3	✓	✓
8	✓	✗

Table 11 Comparison of iOS and Android against the scope of this work

7.2.2.2 Victim Application (Beacon)

The victim application, and also the responder application, can be deployed on de-vices running Android (supported APIs range from 2.3.3 to 4.x). Besides Android be-ing the most widespread mobile operating system (Rivera & van der Meulen 2013), the Help Beacons system is supported even in older Android devices, with API ver-sions equal or newer than Android version 2.3.3. According to platform version statistics versions upwards of API 2.3.3 are installed on 99.3%[1] of all Android devices, which strongly supports a potential prevalence of such a system (QUAT-1). One goal was to design this application in a very minimalistic way, requiring no cumbersome configuration efforts of the user. To create a Beacon the user needs to push a red button, which is labeled with "Push S.O.S." (see right image in Figure 29).

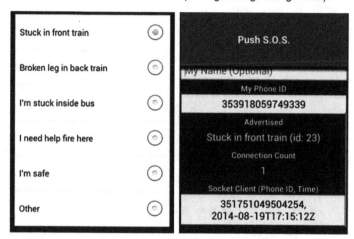

Figure 29 Initial UI of the victim app of the Help Beacons system

Users can select from predefined messages or manually type in a new one (see left image in Figure 29). The application will provide visual feedback to make the user aware that the device now broadcasts the selected/entered message. When the situation of the user changes, users can update their SSID broadcast accordingly. The user also gets notified when a Seeker device has connected to it and performed the exchange of details (see right image in Figure 29).

---

[1] Android platform versions, Google Inc., http://developer.android.com/about/dashboards/index.html, Accessed at 4th August 2014

```
private boolean processSetWifiApEnabled

    (boolean enable, WifiConfiguration wifiApConfig)
{

    boolean val = false;

    try {

        Method method = wifiManager.getClass().getMethod(

            WifiApService.SET_WIFI_AP_ENABLED,

            WifiConfiguration.class,

            boolean.class);

        val = (Boolean) method.invoke(

            wifiManager, wifiApConfig, enable);

        if (val)

            Log.i(TAG, "invocation successful.");

        return true;

    }

    catch (Exception e) {

        Log.e(TAG, e.getMessage());

    }

    return false;

}
```

Table 12 Code excerpt for deploying an AP in Android

As soon as the creation of a Beacon is triggered, a WiFi network is deployed. As Android provides this feature through a hidden API, the relevant methods for creating a WiFi network are invoked via JAVA reflection (see Table 12). Reflection is a technique that allows applications to examine and modify the structure and behavior of a program at run-time. In this particular case, reflection gives access to internal methods of the Android WifiManager[1] class loaded into the Java Virtual Machine. Accessing such methods directly, as programmers usually do for public methods, would result in errors at design-time.

To indicate that a WiFi network constitutes a Beacon the SSID is prefixed with an uncommon string (*#%). This allows a Seeker to distinguish a Beacon from other available networks. According to the 802.11 standard (2007) an SSID has a maximum length of 32 bytes (which can hold up to 32 ASCII characters). The design considers a Beacon to comprise four parts inside an SSID (see Figure 30): a prefix that indicates that this network represents a Beacon, a persistent id (two ASCII characters), and most importantly the emergency message. In the case the status of a person has become safe and s/he wants to inform others about her or his well-being, users can select a specific entry (i.e. "I'm safe") from the list. Then, the application will trigger to deploy a WiFi network that contains in its SSID, besides the prefix, a specific suffix that contains the reverted order of the prefix. In case a Beacon broadcasts a message containing this suffix the responder application ("Seeker") will recognize as a Beacon, though it will not connect to it, as it interprets the person behind the Beacon has become safe.

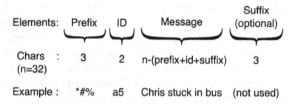

Figure 30 Example composition of a Help Beacons SSID

A "persistent" ID is used to be able to distinguish between equally labeled Beacons or to track devices that updated their SSID if the situation of the owner changed. Initially, the author considered tracking unique devices by using the BSSID that is automatically received when discovering a WiFi network. Usually, the BSSID is the MAC address of the WiFi interface and hence is fixed. However, with Android 4.x the second half of the BSSID is generated randomly. Therefore, the application needs to use another static ID, so it puts a shortened fingerprint of the IMEI consisting of two ASCII characters, inside the SSID. To hamper a reverse look-up of a fingerprint, i.e. to prevent that attackers can derive characters of the IMEI of a Beacon, the application combines a random seed with the IMEI (a unique device ID for mobile phones) to generate an MD5 hash. Finally, the application includes inside the SSID the first two characters of the hash and stores this shortened device ID for later use inside the phone's cache. In order to provide scalability for the ID, the composition of the SSID

---

[1] Android WifiManager class,
http://developer.android.com/reference/android/net/wifi/WifiManager.html

could be changed to allow for longer IDs (e.g. four characters), which implies to reduce one of the other elements (arbitrary message input, prefix).

After a WiFi network has been deployed, the Android operating system automatically performs two internal actions that are beneficial for the victim application: 1) it creates a DHCP server, and 2) it flushes its cache of the address resolution protocol (ARP). The DHCP server assigns an IP address to each connecting client, enabling clients to address the Beacon. The IP address of the AP is always 192.168.43.1. The system uses this static address for exchanging details, which cannot be placed inside the SSID due to the maximum size of 32 ASCII characters. This information includes elements such as the unique ID of a device (IMEI), or the time, a Beacon has been enabled. To facilitate the exchange of details, the Beacon device listens on a specific port (192.168.43.1:8888). After connecting to a Beacon, the responder application tries to establish a connection to this address, in order to exchange details. A proprietary protocol has been designed for this purpose. To trigger the exchange of details the Seeker device (i.e. responder application) tries to bind to a socket. The Help Beacons application supports the exchange of details via TCP sockets.

Flushing the ARP clears the history of registered physical addresses of clients that are or have been connected to the Beacon device. Therefore, the victim application deploys a dedicated thread that regularly checks the ARP cache for new entries in order to detect if a Seeker device has associated with the Beacon device. If a new entry appears, the application immediately informs its user that another device has associated with her or his device. Practically, this means that a responder device has found the signal, which the user's device is broadcasting. The notification is performed by means of a short pop-up message and an audio cue.

Section 4.2.3.1 suggests that people in disasters are willing to open their private WiFi networks. To avoid that other devices that are not part of the Help Beacons system connect to one of the Beacons during field tests, the Beacon application configures an encrypted WiFi network. Due to underlying phone settings sometimes conflicts arise that prevent enabling a Beacon. In such cases the application will automatically retry to enable Beacon and also inform the user via a pop-up message that the previous call failed but that the app will try again in one second.

The author used for development the following devices: Samsung Galaxy S1, S2, Tablet and a Nexus S. Based on tests with these Android devices the time to enable a Beacon can range from 0.5 to 2 seconds; this also depends on the firmware, CPU and further aspects. In the case that a responder cannot see or hear a victim, he or she can at least receive a signal conveying that a victim's phone is within this range. No severe issues were experienced in terms of energy consumption. Trifunovic et al. (2011) use the same APIs used by the Help Beacons system and show acceptable power usage values, i.e. a Beacon broadcast would last for 17 hours on an Android-based Nexus One device.

7.2.2.3 Responder Application (Seeker)

The second element of the Help Beacons system is a responder application that sniffs radio signals in order to seek Beacons. To trigger the discovery of Beacons the user needs to push the "Search" button illustrated in the left image in Figure 31. Then, the application sets up the Seeker device, i.e. it enables the WiFi interface of the device, and starts to search for Beacons (see right image in Figure 31). The Seeker device continuously searches the environment for Beacons and the received scan results are filtered based on the particular SSID prefix set by the Beacon device. When one or more Beacons have been discovered, the responder application initiates a connection to the discovered Beacon from which it receives a stronger signal.

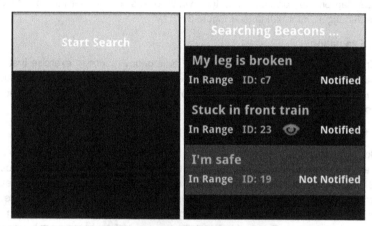

Figure 31 Initial UI of the responder application of the Help Beacons system

Figure 32 UI displaying details of a collected Beacon

According to tests with the development devices typical times to associate with a Beacon, including the attempt to exchange details, are 1.5 to 4s. As soon as the Seeker device is connected to the Beacon the application plays a short sound and vibrates in order to indicate the successful connection. Subsequently, a background process triggers the exchange of details via a network socket. Finally, the Seeker device disconnects in order to associate with other Beacons. The application highlights remaining beacons with the "Not Notified" label (see last entry in the right image in Figure 31); in this particular case the application has ignored the Beacon as it uses the suffix "%#*" in its SSID. In the case that details have been exchanged, the responder application plays another sound and visually highlights this to the user with an eye icon (see second entry in the right image in Figure 31). To see the details the user can tap on the corresponding item, which opens a new user interface that includes debugging information (see Figure 32).

7.2.3 Evaluation

The first prototype was tested as part of an emergency response exercise that was organized inside a tunnel. Several weeks before the exercise took place the author and his colleagues went to the premises to make feasibility tests of the developed technology.

7.2.3.1 Feasibility Study in Underground Tunnel

Thanks to the BRIDGE project the technical feasibility of the prototype could be tested in an underground test gallery (see both images Figure 33). The gallery is hosted by VSH[1], a partner of the BRIDGE project consortium. International response teams train tactical, strategic, and operational aspects in the underground facility. While doing so, these trainings are supported by large-scale tests in the areas including fire, smoke, and explosions. During this feasibility test a set of Android smartphones was distributed all around the facility (see left image and lower right image in Figure 34). As there were a lot of dust and debris in the tunnel the phones were placed inside plastic bags (see upper right image in Figure 34). While performing the experiments the phones were placed around curves, inside train wagons, a bus and cars, inside grooves on the walls or other places posing interesting challenges for the functioning of the Help Beacons system.

During the technical field tests, the author carried the Seeker device. When he was walking through the tunnel, he varied in the speed. The real-world tests led to the identification of two problems that the author was not able to identify beforehand while testing the system in a lab environment. Both problems hindered the overall process of the Seeker tracking and associating to available Beacons.

---

[1] Versuchsstollen Hagerbach (VSH), http://hagerbach.ch/en/

Figure 33 Arrangements of vehicles in an underground tunnel facility

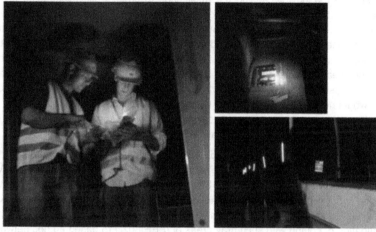

Figure 34 Exploring technology in an underground tunnel

The first problem was that the Seeker device was sometimes able to scan a Beacon, but was not able to associate with it, and then got stuck in a loop, hindering the overall process of searching for further Beacons. As long as other Beacons are in the range from which the Seeker receives a stronger signal and which the Seeker has not already notified of its presence, the Seeker will connect to those Beacons and merely add the tracked Beacon to its list (see Figure 31 above). Nevertheless, in the following three cases the Seeker will try to connect such a Beacon:

- when no other Beacons are available,

- when other Beacons are available but have already been notified, and

- when the signal received by this Beacon has been the strongest one among not yet notified Beacons.

Similar to the first problem the second one was, that during some test runs the Seeker device would connect to a Beacon, but then get stuck, instead of disconnecting from the Beacon and notifying the remaining Beacons previously discovered. This happened several times, although in the same test runs the Seeker previously was able to connect to other Beacons and exchange details with them. After having conducted several test runs, the author looked over the logs of the responder application (Seeker). Each time the Seeker scanned the environment for Beacons, the responder application logged the SSID of the Beacons and the received strength of the signal being broadcasted. The reason for the first problem, letting the overall search process to get stuck was, that when obtaining scan results the Seeker received right away weak signals, which fits into the problem of having problems to connect with a Beacon. The reason for causing the application to crash while exchanging details was that after the connection to a Beacon succeeded, the Seeker device tried to bind to a TCP/IP socket to exchange details (see section 7.2.2.3). For the creation of a socket connection, a certain bandwidth is required—otherwise the communication may stall—which was sometimes not available as the large amount of steel inside of the tunnel weakened the signals (see both images in Figure 33). Also, when obtaining a scan result of a Beacon, a strong signal was received resulting in a bandwidth, which would normally be sufficient for establishing a socket connection. However, as the author and his colleagues were moving, their position sometimes changed at the same time as the responder application tried to establish a connection.

In the abstract, these connection and communication problems can happen in the every day world. Often people using a smartphone, tablet or laptop can track a WiFi network, though connecting to it fails. Similarly, people manage to connect to a WiFi network, though communication in the network is not possible due to the lack of bandwidth. Such events represent certain gray areas in terms of connectivity. In their investigation of coping with such gray areas of IEEE 802.11b based ad hoc networks Lundgren et al. (2002) coin the term "communication gray zones". This means, there are several zones of connectivity between two devices, irrespective of using the IEEE 802.11 ad hoc or infrastructure mode. The author reasoned the existence of three different zones of connectivity. Figure 35 exemplifies these three zones by an 802.11-based infrastructure network, which consists of four devices (1AP, 3 STAs).

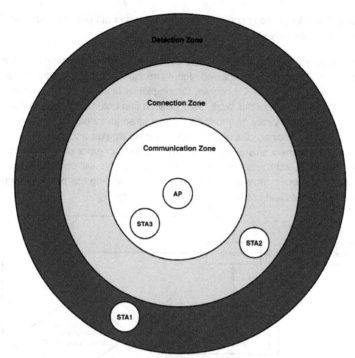

Figure 35 Three zones of connectivity

In the outer zone, which the author coined the *detection zone*, STA1 can only receive the signal of the AP, but STA1 is not able to establish a connection to the AP. Then, in the middle zone, the *connection zone*, STA2 is able to associate with a Beacon, though data transmissions, such as the exchange of details between a Seeker and Beacon, do not work due to low bandwidths. Ideally, devices stay in the *communication zone* as STA3. There, devices can send and receive properly data, as the bandwidth of the link between STA3 and AP is high enough.

It is arguable that both problems, i.e. not to be able to connect to Beacons or to exchange details with them, might have also occurred in lab tests. For instance, a lab test in which devices would be located more distant from each other. However, the author ran several tests in a lab environment, but did not face these problems. But, given the fact that inside the underground tunnel were several curves and a high amount of steel, eventually, showed the limitations in the current implementation.

7.2.3.2 Re-Design

In order to avoid communication gray zones Johnson and Hancke (2009) propose to change configurations to lock the broadcast rate to the rate that is used for unicast messages. A similar strategy could be applied to tackle both problems identified from conducting the feasibility study.

Search algorithm. To improve the way the Seeker searches for available Beacons, the Seeker could check if the received signal strength is strong enough before trying to associate with a Beacon. Of course, to completely disregard a Beacon would be impractical for the scope of this work, as a Beacon can potentially represent a sign of life. However, to simply rely on a minimal signal strength value would be a too rigid approach, as while moving, the signal could become weaker and thus in the second instance a fallback mechanism needs to terminate the sub process of connecting to a Beacon. Figure 36 highlights that the Seeker from now on, will connect to a Beacon by the use of a specific timeout value; besides, disregarding the previous step Beacons from which the Seeker has received a very low signal.

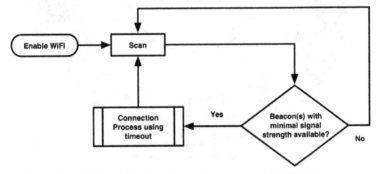

Figure 36 Flow chart of an enhanced algorithm to search for Beacons

The Android API constitutes a ScanResult object exposing all relevant information about a scanned WiFi network, i.e. its SSID, BSSID, signal strength and more. The Seeker respectively, will from now on only consider networks with minimal signal strength; for testing, the minimal signal strength value can be configured via the setting in the responder application. The ScanResult encapsulates the field `level` to indicate the signal strength in dBm or also dBm (decibel milli-Watts), which is a signal strength rating in decibels as a power rating compared to 1 milli-Watt. In order to simplify the use of such measurements, the Android API offers the use of the `WifiManager.calculateSignalLevel` method (see Table 13). This method takes the given level of the signal strength of the scanned network in dBm, and returns a value from 1 to the second parameter (20) as a rating of the signal strength of the network. The stronger a signal is received the higher the level will be.

```
for (ScanResult scanResult : scanResults){

    int level = WifiManager.calculateSignalLevel(

                                    scanResult.level, 20);

    if(level >= 5){

        //Connect to Beacon using a specific timeout value

    }

}
```

Table 13 Code excerpt for handling WiFi scan results in Android

Exchange of details. Similarly to the way of connecting to Beacons, the author thought of considering a minimal bandwidth value before letting the Seeker bind to a socket on which a Beacon listens. The Android API exposes the bandwidth of a connection by the field `LINK_SPEED_UNITS` of the `WifiInfo` class. In detail, the class WifiInfo `WifiInfoED` exposes the method `getLinkSpeed` that returns the current link speed units or bandwidth respectively in Mbps. Table 14 shows that the application would only try to exchange details via a TCP/IP socket in case the bandwidth is equal or higher than 54Mbps.

```
WifiInfo wifiInfo = wifiManager.getConnectionInfo();

//other code

int linkSpeed = wifiInfo.getLinkSpeed();

if(linkSpeed >= 54){

    //initiate to exchange details

}
```

Table 14 Potential Android code for exchanging details between Seeker and Beacon

One could argue that 54Mbps are a relatively high lower barrier, but the code depicted in Table 14 proved to be not applicable for phones running newer API versions of Android, i.e. 4.x versions. Testing the code on Android devices running API 4.0 and 4.1 resulted in no exchange of details at all, as the obtained link speed result was permanently a negative value despite a stable connection between the Seeker and Beacon. Uncommenting the code resulted in successful exchanges of details. Thus, in this regard similar to the process of searching for Beacons, from now on will be enhanced by the use a specific timeout value as displayed in Figure 37.

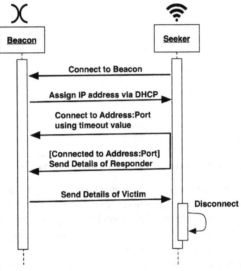

Figure 37 Sequence diagram of an enhanced way of exchanging details

As Android uses a static IP, i.e. `192.168.43`, to devices enabling an AP, the improved code piggybacks on this (see Table 15) by instantiating a socket connection to this address with the port `8888`. Several tests showed that the time out value of 3s is suitable. When the exchange of details has not been executed within the time window, the process of connecting to a socket is terminated. Subsequently, the Seeker disconnects from the Beacon and connects to the remaining not notified Beacons.

```
final String serverIpAdress = "192.168.43.1";

final int socketPort = 8888;

final int timeout = 3000;

SocketAddress socketAddress = new InetSocketAddress

                        (serverIpAddress, socketPort);

socket.connect(socketAddress, timeout);
```

Table 15 Improved code for exchanging details by the use of a timeout value

After the implementation had been revised, the author conducted several test runs without experiencing any problems. As these technical improvements resulted in a more robust prototype, the system was deployed in a real-world exercise.

7.2.3.3 Real-World Exercise in Underground Tunnel

The emergency response exercise took place in the same underground facility. The enhanced prototype was tested during the exercise based on the following scenario:

In the middle of a tunnel, several people get stuck in their vehicles due to an explosion in the back part of the tunnel. As some casualties lost network access in their phones, they launch an application that enables them to advertise emergency beacons. After a while a phone carried by a first responder discovers those beacons and connects with them in order to notify the victims of the responder's presence. As soon as the responder is able to connect to the outside world, a report generated from the data coming from the beacons is sent to the local command center.

Figure 38 depicts the three Beacon devices that were deployed during the exercise: one Beacon was placed inside a bus and the remaining Beacons inside two train wagons. After a conceptual introduction (see Figure 39), the author demonstrated the prototype to the front-line officer (FO) assigned for the exercise. The front-line officer is the firefighter who first enters the disaster scene and who provides a quick impression to the rest of the responder team. Initially, the FO expressed some reservations about the deployment of any digital technology due to bad experiences with a digital breathing device. Even so, he agreed to test the Help Beacons system, which basically meant that he would carry a Seeker phone during the exercise.

The Seeker phone was placed inside a plastic box attached to a cord (see left image in Figure 40), which the FO carried around his neck (see right image in Figure 40). This way the author hoped the FO would not be distracted by the device, but would have the possibility to look at the smartphone when he preferred to do so. During the exercise (see Figure 41) the FO was able to quickly receive the help calls that convey an idea of the status of the trapped people despite the harsh conditions. As the fixation of the phone in the box was rather amateurish, at some point the phone broke out of the box. So, the FO simply put the device in his pocket, a solution that — it turned out—for the FO worked better than the protective box.

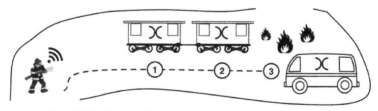

Figure 38 Distribution of Beacons during an underground tunnel exercise

99

Figure 39 Hands-on experience of the Help Beacons system with the front-line officer

Figure 40 Boxed Seeker phone and wearable box to hang around the neck

Figure 41 Front-line officer using the Help Beacons system in a real-world exercise

After the evaluation, several interviews were conducted with the participants to gather feedback from end-users. The interview with the FO who used the responder application was particularly informative. From the first impression, the FO felt that using the responder application could be distracting from the actual work, especially when the first responders first enter an emergency site.

FO: For the officer in charge at the front it is difficult, as the officer does not know what is expecting her or him. For me personally, it was rather distracting. (...) You know when you stand there, in the tunnel it is really difficult to focus on the application.

Apart from the possible distractions, the FO also mentioned that the initial focus of first responders would not be to find all trapped persons. At the same time, he indicated that the application could also conflict with existing protocols of rescue operations with regard to the order in which victims are salvaged.

FO: For example, if I see there is fire, I will command that the fire hoses will be rolled out, regardless of finding persons there or not. Further, if your application detects a beacon, and tells me a person is stuck inside on one of the train wagons, but I see another person over there near to the fire, I will first rescue the person next to the fire.

The FO found the concept useful, however, for later stages of the response operation, or where the data collected in the field might be routed to the personnel working at the remote command center. The command center could then analyze the data in order to support responders in the field to find people who may have been overlooked.

FO: But, I see the benefit of the application in its implicit use. I mean when it is linked to a rear command center. If I tell the command center, we checked everything and rescued all persons. But, they received a beacon call that does not match with one of the rescued persons. They can say "Stop, go back there and check if somebody is there".

The FO also added that the system would be useful in larger scale emergencies, which are not as constrained as the tunnel scenario, and where the focus would be more on finding missing persons.

FO: Inside the tunnel you usually find all people easily. I think it is rather helpful in other disasters, such as a flooding or an earthquake. You could set up a beacon conveying a GPS or a message saying, "I live in the Main Street No. 15 and I'm stuck inside the debris". This could be a big advantage. You could direct upon this information a helicopter to get people from the roof. Of course, you could try to make an emergency call, but usually the dispatch center is too busy or the network is congested or damaged.

Not least, in further discussion with the FO and other fire fighters who participated in the exercise, the professionals wondered how victims would install the required app in the first place. So far, the author made the assumption that the application was already installed on the smartphones. Thus, it could be seen as an integral part of the underlying mobile operating system, similar to the emergency call feature in cell phones.

7.2.4 Analysis

Analyzing the evaluation of the system in the scope of the larger exercise points to several limitations:

- Finite way of localization,

- Distractions of users from the physical world,

- Narrowness of tunnel scenario,

- No evaluation with victims, and

- Assumption of preinstalled victim app.

Localization. Currently, the responder can only rely on a description of the SSID in order to get an idea where a victim is trapped. As no GPS service would have been accessible in a tunnel, its usage was omitted on purpose. However, for the use in the scope of outdoor operations, localizing victims via GPS represents a promising approach besides a potential description inside the SSID.

Distractions of users from the physical world. Besides the task of finding victims, the front-line officer had to focus on many other tasks in the exercise: to check the path, to delegate other responders, to observe the fire, to report to the command center. Thus, in the beginning the use of the Help Beacons system was distracting for the FO, as he had to focus on many other tasks. Sounds and vibrations of the Seeker phone that notified about the tracking, connecting, or exchanging details with a given Beacon were not helpful in this sense. The FO pointed out that there are a lot of impressions when responders enter the impact zone of a disaster. So, due to the evolving nature of emergency response, the FO considered that the Help Beacons system is rather useful for later phases to check if a responder or a team of responders has overlooked some persons.

Narrowness of tunnel scenario. Exploring the technology in the described exercise was very helpful to prove its technical feasibility and to understand its implications of the domain. However, the FO explained that inside the tunnel usually trapped people are found after some while. Thus, to examine further benefits and also limitations of the system, the FO recommended evaluating the system in a scenario where victims and their phones would be more dispersed across a larger area. For instance, in an earthquake or flooding scenario people are scattered in impact zones where preexisting network infrastructures often become disrupted (see also section 4.2.1.3).

No evaluation with victims. A further limitation is that no "victims" have been evaluated. This was not possible due to safety regulations within the impact zone of the exercise, i.e. people were not allowed to stay inside the vehicles. Also, it is arguable that it is difficult to define what expertise or authority qualifies a "victim". Even so, the plan is to conduct evaluations in which people play the role of civilians in distress (see section 7.4). By doing so, the author hopes to gain further feedback on the constraints of the system.

Assumption of preinstalled victim app. One question that often arose when explaining the victim application to responders before and after the exercise was: "How do I get this app on my phone?" Right now, it is not realistic to assume that such an app, when available in the usual App stores (e.g. Google Play, AppStore), would be pre-installed on a majority of devices—especially since the assumed disruptions of infrastructure would prevent users from accessing the app stores during the emergency. Thus, the design of the second prototype will tackle the challenge of deploying the application without the need of having Internet access.

7.3 Second Prototype

This section describes the second prototype of the Help Beacons system. One concern raised by the professionals in the previous evaluation was the problem of assuming that the victim application is preinstalled on the victims' phones. This section concerns the investigation of approaches enabling the decentralized distribution of mobile applications without Internet access. The benefits and constraints of the different approaches are contrasted with each other. One approach is implemented, forming the second prototype of the Help Beacons system. Finally, the enhanced Help Beacons system is discussed with professional responders during a workshop.

7.3.1 Design

Unless stated otherwise, this section is based on research that has originally been published in (Al-Akkad & Raffelsberger 2014; Al-Akkad & Vinkovits 2014).

The way of distributing mobile applications in a decentralized manner was discussed with several professionals and as well with some technicians inside the BRIDGE project. It was agreed on that at least the smartphone would be required, besides other additional devices, to distribute an application in a decentralized manner. As a result of these discussions, five different approaches have been developed. In the following, the approaches will be presented and examined based on the proposed quality attributes (see section 5.2):

Distribution via ad-hoc networked devices running captive portals. The first approach is based on the presence of an ad-hoc deployed wireless network, such as WiFi routers or cell towers. In previous disasters such as the 2009 L'Aquila earthquake in Italy, some mobile operators extended their coverage with additional mobile stations in order to cover homeless camps (see section 4.2.3.1). This observation shows that people or organizations may respond by the deployment of network devices filling gaps of communication. Similarly, an open, i.e. unencrypted, WiFi network could be deployed and configured to distribute a mobile application. The left image in Figure 42 shows how users carrying a smartphone could access this network and as soon as they try to access the Internet, they would be automatically redirected to a special web page that could include information on how to acquire an application. For instance, the acquisition could be managed by providing a download link. The web page would be hosted locally on the deployed device and hence be available despite the lack of Internet access. The deployment of this approach is based on the *captive portals* technique that people normally experience after connecting to public WiFi hotspots deployed at universities or hotels. In terms of ad-hoc communication (QUAT-2) the main disadvantage of this approach is that it relies on the practical deployment of wireless devices running a captive portal. In other words, a fire fighter or other professional responders need to be able to deploy or carry wireless devices. Another limitation is that this approach lacks in terms of establishing quick connectivity (QUAT-3), as users would first need to enter a specific URL and then find out that their request is being redirected to a static page. Newer API versions of mobile platforms support this action by directing users immediately to the login window.

Figure 42 Captive portal and captive portal with QR code

a. 1) Connect 2) Redirect 3) Download

b. 1) Connect 2) Scan QR code triggering the download

Download via ad-hoc networks with QR code. The process of invoking the download page could be improved by exploiting quick response (QR) codes. Several recent studies, such as (Gebrekristos et al. 2008; Seeburger 2012), have shown enhanced interactions by combining QR codes with cell phones. Similarly, when deploying an ad-hoc device in the aftermath of a disaster, leaflets or posters could be distributed, which include a QR code that advertises an emergency application. The right image in Figure 42 illustrates such an example. Assuming that a device is already connected to a local WiFi network, scanning a QR code with the phone's camera would result in being directed to a static page offering the download link for the dedicated application. Besides the above-mentioned disadvantages of deploying an ad-hoc device, this approach also requires placing QR codes on walls or other places in the affected disaster zone. Therefore, this approach addresses QUAT-2 even less.

Cell broadcast. Cellular networks provide communication services that allow one-to-many communication links. For instance, the GSM standard defines Cell Broadcast[1] (CB), as a mobile service to send short text messages with a length of up to 93 characters to all users in one or more network cells. Similarly, UMTS offers Multimedia Broadcast Multicast Services (MBMS) that allows cell towers to transmit multimedia data (e.g. mobile TV and radio broadcasting) and files. If a cell tower survives the adverse effects of a disaster, this approach is a probably the fastest way for distributing applications (QUAT-3), as the application is directly being pushed to mobile users. This approach is similar to the previous two approaches, as it requires additional elements of network structure. However, this approach assumes that some pre-existing infrastructural elements, namely cell towers as depicted in Figure 43, are still operational. Therefore, this approach also strongly lacks in terms of ad-hoc communication (QUAT-2). Also, people are rather unfamiliar with the cell broadcast service, as it emerged just recently and it is not widely deployed by mobile providers, making this approach not comply with QUAT-1. Thus, the main downfall of this approach is that it requires the support of mobile providers, which need to trigger the

---

[1] Cell Broadcast, http://www.cellbroadcastforum.org/whatisCB/

deployment of the dedicated emergency application. Additionally, mobile devices may not support or have disabled the reception of cell broadcasts.

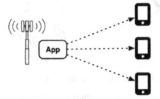

Figure 43 Cell broadcast

Viral deployment. Compared to all other approaches the approach illustrated in the left image in Figure 44 requires no presence of preexisting infrastructure at all, and therefore completely complies with QUAT-2. As a result of this, it allows to distribute the application from phone to phone complying with QUAT-8. This approach reuses the paradigm of the Help Beacons approach to exploit the SSID to convey an emergency need. In this particular case an SSID would be broadcasted that conveys the sharing of an app, such as `"Get Emergency App"` and point to a web page that provides a download link for the application. In order to acquire the application, mobile users would need to connect to an open (i.e. unencrypted) WiFi network and then open the web browser. Any request would be redirected to the download page distributing the application that is hosted on the device that provides the WiFi network. In contrast to all previous approaches this would support the re-distribution of application between mobile users. For instance, once an application has been installed, it could open another WiFi network advertising the download link and hence be distributed from phone to phone. While this approach is the only "infrastructure-less" one, it is at the same time the least user-friendly one. Not least, compared to all previous approaches, this one would allow to some extent for serendipity (QUAT-4). This means, mobile users who would be interested in acquiring a dedicated application would be notified of the presence of a WiFi network with a name that conveys the provision of a certain application. The process of connecting to a WiFi network and downloading the app certainly requires more time than in all previous approaches, and therefore this approach does not properly address QUAT-3.

Figure 44 Distribution of an app from phone to phone

a. Viral deployment of an app via the SSID, b. viral deployment of an app via a generic app

Viral deployment via a generic application. To ease the process of acquiring the application via the last approach, the use of a generic application could handle the exchange of other applications (see right image in Figure 44). Such a "generic distribution application" could offer a catalogue of apps that can be exchanged between smartphones without requiring Internet access. Besides disaster situations, any other contexts could be addressed, in which spontaneous deployment of applications would be desired. For example, recently some airlines started to offer passengers to consume multimedia services via 'on board' available WiFi hotspots. However, in order to join the network passengers have to pre-install a dedicated app from the airline. This presents a weakness or constraint in situations where consumers are not aware of such an application. This approach would be easier to use than the previous one, as the user has to interact with one application only. Preferably, the exchange of applications would be handled over a standardized and open protocol. However, given the fact that mobile users would need to have the generic application preinstalled, which is currently not the case, this approach does not comply with QUAT-1.

Summarizing, the author identified five approaches that enable the distribution of applications to 'air-gapped' phones. Table 16 contrasts the different approaches against five of the suggested quality attributes defined in section 5.2. The "viral" approach is the one that matches best with the suggested quality attributes. Therefore, this work will investigate the possibilities of implementing such an approach.

Quality Attribute	Captive Portal	QR Code	Cell Broadcasts	Viral	Viral Via App
Prevalence (QUAT-1)	3	3	1	4	0
Ad-hoc communication (QUAT-2)	2	1	0	4	3
Quick connectivity (QUAT-3)	2	3	4	1	3
Serendipity (QUAT-4)	1	2	N/A	2	3
Decentralized distribution (QUAT-8)	1	2	N/A	4	4
Total	9	11	5	15	13

Table 16 Comparison of the different deployment approaches

(Bad=0, rather bad=1, alright=2, rather good=3, good=4)

7.3.2 Implementation

The second prototype has been built around the following scenario:

In the aftermath of an earthquake the mobile network is down for a longer period of time. A special victim app has been launched which enables ad-hoc communication between neighboring devices. The victim app can be shared from phone to phone.

People, who have installed the application, are able to communicate their needs via a mesh of networked devices.

Originally, the idea was to use URL redirecting in order to intercept URL requests of connected client phones. This would redirect calls of users to a static web page. But, as Android does not provide an API to forward URL requests, the approach would be to explicitly indicate the URL of the static web page inside the SSID. For instance, an example SSID would be a message indicating to go to a particular socket address, such as "GOTOURL192.168.43.1:9999". In order to obtain the victim application a mobile user would first need to connect to a Beacon and then manually enter the URL "192.168.43.1:9999", which brings users to a dedicated web page as illustrated Figure 45.

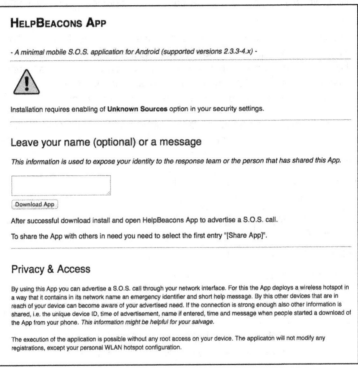

HELPBEACONS APP

- A minimal mobile S.O.S. application for Android (supported versions 2.3.3-4.x) -

Installation requires enabling of **Unknown Sources** option in your security settings.

Leave your name (optional) or a message

This information is used to expose your identity to the response team or the person that has shared this App.

Download App

After successful download install and open HelpBeacons App to advertise a S.O.S. call.

To share the App with others in need you need to select the first entry "[Share App]".

Privacy & Access

By using this App you can advertise a S.O.S. call through your network interface. For this the App deploys a wireless hotspot in a way that it contains in its network name an emergency identifier and short help message. By this other devices that are in reach of your device can become aware of your advertised need. If the connection is strong enough also other information is shared, i.e. the unique device ID, time of advertisement, name if entered, time and message when people started a download of the App from your phone. *This information might be helpful for your salvage.*

The execution of the application is possible without any root access on your device. The applicaton will not modify any registrations, except your personal WLAN hotspot configuration.

Figure 45 Download page to obtain the victim app in a decentralized manner

The dedicated web page on top explains the purpose of the application and immediately afterwards indicates that users need to configure the settings on their phone, i.e. enable the "Unknown Sources" option, in order to install applications aside the app store (see section 7.2.2.1). Before downloading the application users can leave their name as sort of a trace. When a Seeker will exchange details with a Beacon, this information will be retrieved. In this way, a response team can see who has acquired the app dynamically. Then it is explained that users can select an additional entry inside the prepared list of messages called "[Share App]" in order to offer the download of the app in a decentralized manner (see left image in Figure 46). The right image in Figure 46 shows that this will set up a Beacon that advertises a message containing the request to visit a specific socket address. The bottom of the page provides in detail how the application affects the privacy and access of data. In order to handle the viral distribution of the victim application, the victim application itself runs a simple HTTP web server.

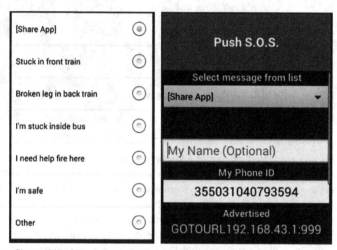

Figure 46 UI of the victim application enabling users to distribute virally the app

7.3.3 Evaluation

The second prototype was evaluated during a BRIDGE end-user workshop (see Figure 47). The system was presented and discussed with three professionals in the emergency response domain.

Section 7.3.2 has shown a way to implement the viral deployment via SSID approach for the Android system. Android does allow deploying an HTTP Server, however, it does not provide an API[1] to redirect URL requests, which people would enter into their web browsers. As a fallback solution, the socket address of the download page was wrapped inside the broadcasted SSID. Though, this approach is way too difficult to be evaluated with common users. Technology-savvy people might understand the intention behind a WiFi network whose name conveys the request to go to a specific socket address. Alternatively, it would be possible to set up a dedicated AP that

---

[1] Android version 2.3.3 – 4.x

hosts the application, i.e. to choose the approach of deploying an ad-hoc network running a captive portal. Then, the AP could redirect all HTTP requests to a download page, which eases the procedure, as users do not have to manually enter the download URL into their browser. However, this would require additional hardware and will not be feasible in every scenario.

Figure 47 Demonstrating second prototype during a user workshop

The system was evaluated as part of a larger workshop to prepare for an upcoming large-scale exercise (see section 7.4.3). Several professional responders participated in the workshop. The Help Beacons system was presented to three professionals: a fire fighter (FF), a police officer (PO), and a head of division from the German technical relief (TR). After giving a short presentation and hands-on demonstration of the prototype, the author and his colleagues discussed the concept with the professionals. Although, the author explained that the smartphone was only used temporarily for the Seeker device, the FF was reluctant to use the system and feared it would require too much interaction, distracting him from his main tasks.

The PO who was at the same the head of the exercise explained:

PO: I think, during the upcoming exercise, it would make sense to probe your system with the search and rescue team that rechecks for victims and the presence of terrorists on the ship. You could equip some students on the board of the ship with some mobile phones.

The participants provided also some feedback around the interaction of the system. The PO mentioned, for example, that both the responder application and victim application should not make any sounds, but rather vibrate in order to avoid distraction and avoid drawing unwanted attention to the user in dangerous situations such as acts of terrorism.

In fact, TR raised the issue if it is realistic that people would have the victim app preinstalled or download it in daily life. Thus, the author explained to him that he investigated several approaches that would enable the distributing of mobile applications requiring no Internet access. However, at the same time the author pointed out that current mobile operating systems do not offer convenient ways to distribute applications in a decentralized manner. It turned out that the TR himself was involved in a national project where the goal is to calm down mass of people visiting a large event, such as a concert or soccer game.

TR: *In the frame of this project routers were deployed in a soccer stadium, offering the download of a dedicated app, which in an emergency would give instructions to visitors. We found out that people mostly would not download such an application, as they mistrusted the application to gather too much personal data.*

Related to the explained mistrust to share virally applications, TR pointed to the danger of fake Beacons.

TR: *What would happen when people set up a fake beacon? This might jeopardize the loop of searching for available beacons?*

Not least, one technical issue arose while testing the system with newer phones from a project partner. The exchange of details between the Seeker and Beacon would not work properly.

7.3.4 Analysis

In general, all interviewed professionals saw a purpose in deploying the Help Beacons system, albeit the FF at first showed a strong reluctance. The TR hinted to the problem of trust when trying to distribute such an application in a decentralized manner. In summary, the finding is that currently available mobile operating systems do not really foresee to download applications from neighboring devices, including ad-hoc deployed WiFi hotspots or pass them from phone to phone. However, such distribution mechanisms may be crucial to distribute emergency applications in the aftermath of a disaster. But, at the same such decentralized approaches could be misused in daily life. For freely available applications, except for counting the number of downloads, no real damage might be caused due to a decentralized distribution. However, for commercially available applications, decentralized approaches, may induce vulnerabilities to the intellectual property of app vendors. In the following, these vulnerabilities are described:

Currently, when mobile users download applications from a distribution store, they authenticate themselves through a username/password scheme requiring users to register before with an online account. Similarly, for decentralized distribution approaches the use of trusted certificates could be used to enable secure connections between a phone to another phone or an ad-hoc router or other devices. However, in this case, the question arises how people could work around a delayed purchase of commercial apps. In the centralized app distribution store model, commercial applications usually require payment before usage.

Assumed there would be the possibility of relaying invoices over decentralized networks for the purchase of commercial apps, the author could think of two scenarios for misusing such an approach:

First, people might on purpose not go 'online' after having obtained a commercial application. Of course, this could be counteracted by the use of several strategies, such as watermarks, blocking the application after a certain amount of time, or launches, or clicks. However, in case of commercial applications that are only used for a short while, such as casual games, a blockade may not affect the user at all. Or people might be able to uninstall and re-install and use the app, unless no restriction is put inside the registry. Further, before users need to go 'online', they could under-take a system reset to an earlier point of time, or a complete reset, which would dissolve any hints for obligations of open invoices. Of course, the source of distribution might later go online and transmit data revealing the IDs of people with whom s/he shared the app, but at some point such linkage of traces might become confusing.

Second, in terms of technology-savvy people, a decentralized distribution approach might be harmed by the use of disassemblers. A disassembler is a reverse engineering tool, i.e. a computer program that supports to convert the binary coded machine language of an executable program into the human readable assembly language. Currently, disassembler tools are available, such as these two tools[12], which offer to dissemble binary code. As in theory disassemblers allow users to receive nearly original code, people may copy the code, develop and distribute their own app, and even earn money through this.

In summary, due to security restrictions on mobile platforms the quality attribute decentralized distribution (QUAT-8) is difficult to implement for smartphones. To resort to an external device, as a router, seems to be the only feasible solution. Otherwise, the use of "rooted" or "jailbroken" smartphones would be required, which does not comply with QUAT-1. To install mobile applications aside the centralized authority of an app store, of course, holds certain risks, for users and vendors as well. To investigate these security issues goes beyond the scope of this work.

7.4 Third Prototype

This section describes the development of the third prototype. The prototype was evaluated as part of large-scale "terrorist attack" scenario. Compared to the previous real-world exercise evaluation described in section 7.2.3 'victims' have been involved. Before exploring the system in the exercise, a feasibility study was conducted. Moreover, the overall system was discussed with a group of practitioners as part of a workshop. The overall goal was to examine the applicability of the system from a higher-level perspective.

---

[1] android-apktool, https://code.google.com/p/android-apktool/

[2] A Guide to Debugging Android Binaries, http://bit.ly/1g8flgS

7.4.1 Design

Fake Beacons. In the last evaluation the head of division for civil protection pointed out a weakness in the process of searching for Beacons. So far the improved process (see Figure 36) considers a Seeker to connect to a Beacon by using a timeout of 30s. As long as Beacons are configured with the same password and security protocol, no problems would arise. But in the case a 'fake' Beacon is set up, the process could run into an endless loop. A 'fake' Beacon is a device, which advertises itself as a Beacon, but does not offer other devices to connect to it. To rigorously dispel 'fake' Beacons could be misleading, as it might be possible that the Seeker tracks a 'fake' Beacon, but later tracks another Beacon that is broadcasting the same message the 'fake' Beacon previously had broadcasted. Therefore, the approach is to put 'fake' Beacons temporarily on a blacklist. After some while, the Seeker will again consider to connect to such a Beacon message. Doing so would not hinder the process of connecting to other available Beacons.

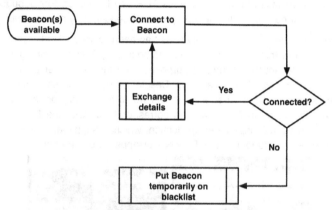

Figure 48 Flow chart of an enhanced connection process

Positioning. As proposed by the front-line officer who tested the Help Beacons prototype in the first evaluation (see section 7.2.3.3), another enhancement is the use of GPS positioning in order to better support the logistics of the salvaging victims. When the Beacon and Seeker exchange details the GPS coordinates and a corresponding timestamp would be included. In the case the victim cannot acquire a GPS fix, the Seeker device will use its GPS position at the time it tracked the Beacon. This is another example of how the prototype implements the graceful degradation quality attribute. As a tracked Beacon means that it is in a range of circa 100m, the GPS position of the Seeker at that time still provides a rough indication of the position, in case the Beacon fails to provide a GPS position. The same approach of graceful degradation (QUAT-6) is used in case the Seeker cannot connect to the Beacon.

7.4.2 Implementation

Blacklisting. Beacons that are considered to be 'fake' beacons are blacklisted. When the corresponding timestamp expires after one minute, the Seeker will try to connect to the Beacon if it is still in range.

Positioning. When the user launches the victim application in the background it is checked if the GPS feature in the phone is enabled. In case GPS is not activated, the application asks the user if s/he likes to enable GPS. Retrieving an initial GPS fix requires 30s to 2 minutes, depending on the device and free sight to the satellites.

UDP protocol. As an alternative to TCP/IP socket the system will also consider the use of UDP. For each (UDP, TCP/IP) sort of socket connection a dedicated thread will be initiated. The Seeker will terminate both threads as soon one of the threads has managed to obtain details from the Beacon. The Seeker can use both concurrently or exclusively. The author experienced that UDP is faster in most cases, though sometimes fails and in these cases TCP can take over. For debugging purposes the Seeker can set up to use both protocols concurrently or exclusively.

User interface. The UI of both applications has been revised. The left image in Figure 49 depicts how the victim application has been simplified by omitting information that was only relevant for debugging purposes. And the responder application from now on indicates a new state for a victim. Besides being in distress or 'safe', a victim can get the status 'rescued' when a responder would checks him or her out (see right element in right image in Figure 49). In correspondence with the BRIDGE project partner developing the map-based application, which is supposed to be used in the command center, 'rescued' or 'safe' Beacons disappear from the map.

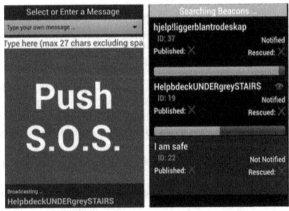

Figure 49 Enhanced UI of the victim app and responder app

7.4.3 Evaluation

The BRIDGE project had the possibility to participate in a large-scale exercise that took place in the port area of a Norwegian city, which has a high concentration of industries for petrol and natural gas. The overall goal of the exercise was to assess organizational practices and cross-collaboration between the three main response units (police, fire brigade, and ambulance). As some research on local risks hinted to man-made disasters in the industrial area being located at the port, the exercise simulated a "terrorist attack" on the basis of the following scenario:

Four terrorists reach the mainland by a boat. They quickly affix explosive bodies to pots of a chemical plant. Shortly, the chemical factory is blown up. Due to the explosion a lot of people got wounded. Besides the chemical plant, the terrorists also enter a ferry and a terminal where the ferry has docked at this terminal. The terrorists shoot any person who could possibly thwart them. The extent of brutality is devastating.

During the exercise a special police unit entered the ferry to search for the terrorists and victims. The ferry itself was the home for students who received navy lesson, besides normal high school lesson. Several of those students acted as 'victims' during the exercise. Before the exercise, all students received several instructions from their supervisors to play their role of a 'victim' as realistically as possible. The exercise committee made three students available that could use the victim application during the exercise in order to call for help. The three students' were 1 male (V1) and 2 females (V2 and V3) and between 15-16 years old.

7.4.3.1 Feasibility Study on Ferry

To explore the feasibility of the system, a pre-study was conducted on the ferry a few days before the large-scale exercise took place. Based on the previous evaluation, the ferry was considered to be the main evaluation site for the Help Beacons system.

First, the author presented the core idea of the system to the three students. Then, they showed the author and his colleagues the facility. Finally, the test runs were conducted with the students through "hide and seek" test runs (see Figure 50): the author carried the Seeker device in order to locate Beacons that had been set up by the three students.

Figure 50 Conducting 'hide and seek' experiments with 'victims' on the ferry

In the beginning, the students kept on the sound feature of the victim application, making it quite easy to locate them. Then, the students switched the sound off, as it would obviously alarm terrorists with regard to the large-scale exercise. As the ferry was a quite familiar place for the students, they knew to hide quite well and the author and his colleagues had difficulties to locate them receiving no more sounds. GPS would not work anyway inside the ferry. Thus, acting from necessity the author looked into the Android WiFi settings, which indicate the signal strength of an available WiFi network, and which helped to locate the victims.

7.4.3.2 Re-Design

When preparing for the exercise the assumption was made that the technology would be deployed outdoors having free sight to receive easily a GPS connection. As the opposite became the case, the 'hide and seek' tests hinted to the need to provide a means for indoor positioning. To simply use the sound was not sufficient in the current scenario. Therefore, the responder application was enhanced to include a signal strength bar (see first two entries in right image in Figure 49). This signal strength bar shows the received signal more precisely than the Android WiFi settings, which only highlights or shades the four semicircles of the WiFi logo. The responder application maps the received signal to a scale from 1 to 20, whereby 20 is the highest value. When no signal at all is received for a Beacon, the bar disappears from the UI. Having enhanced the system for indoor positioning, the third prototype was deployed in the large-scale exercise to locate three 'victims'.

116

7.4.3.3 Large-Scale Exercise in a Terrorist Scenario

In the following the course of the response operation is described from the perspective of deploying the Help Beacons system.

Figure 51 Special police unit before entering the ferry

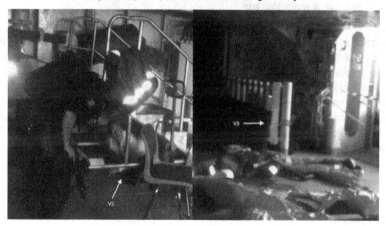

Figure 52 Victims on ferry hiding from the terrorists

During the exercise the focal point of the responders would be to follow their tactics and procedures. Therefore, it would upfront not be clear which responder would be part of the team that would enter the ferry in order to chase for the terrorists and in the second instance to help victims. Thus, the head of the exercise committee suggested that the author should follow this dynamically created team while carrying a

Seeker device. Indeed, during the exercise a special unit of the police was formed dynamically and then entered the ferry (see Figure 51). At some point this team entered the ferry accompanied by the author carrying a Seeker device. In order to indicate their presence researchers and also people from the press were asked to wear yellow vests that indicated their affiliation.

The right image in Figure 49 depicts which distress signals the victims broadcasted during the exercise via their phones and how the Seeker phone discovered these signals. During the special police unit discovered one of the three persons broadcasting a Beacon, namely the one hiding on the deck in the back of the cabins. However, the remaining two students (see both images in Figure 52) were later discovered by the support of the responder application sniffing for the presence of Beacons. One victim device was possible to retrieve a GPS fix. The two other Beacons were complemented by the GPS position the responder device had acquired when discovering these two Beacons. The collected beacons were finally forwarded to an operational control room where the Beacons were visualized on the map by means of their (precise or approximated) GPS positions.

The remainder of this section summarized the feedback that was collected from the victims and the police officer the author mainly had followed when searching for the hidden victims behind the Beacons.

7.4.3.4 Feedback from Victims

One day after the exercise the author met the students and conducted semi-structured interviews. The 'victims' raised several concerns regarding the applicability of the system. V2 pointed out that the victim application could be misused to play a joke on the emergency personnel. Aligned to this V3 explained that initially—after playing 'hide and seek'—she liked the idea of using WiFi SSIDs to convey emergency needs. However, she explained that in hindsight, given the terrorist scenario the current setup of the system is not a good idea, as besides responders also the terrorists would be able to see messages and then harm people. However, for other scenarios this setup would be useful.

V3: If I had run wild in the woods the app would be great, but it is not good in case of a terroristic attack.

A general concern mentioned by all three students is the dissemination of data to untrusted people. Their desire would be that only the police or any further response unit would be able to pick up their emergency messages.

When V1 and V2 were asked about the limited size of a message, they explained that the current number of characters is enough, though it would require some creativity; of course, this also depends on the name of the ship and further contextual aspects. Another proposal made by V2, would be to take pictures and add keywords and then send this data out when exchanging details between the Beacon and the Seeker device.

Also, V3 pointed out that she would like the Seeker device to connect to her phone, when she set up her status to 'safe' in order to know that the personnel in the field and in the control room have become aware of her new state.

Both V1 and V2 agreed to download the application from a dedicated device, in case Internet connection is disrupted. Though, they would prefer to have the application preinstalled.

V1: I propose to have it shipped in every phone, already when you buy it.

Not least, V2 expressed the difficulty to design for each context.

V2: The area was dark; when I was using the app, it would lighten up the area. So if the terrorists were near they would see the light.

7.4.3.5 Feedback from Police Officer

Two weeks after the exercise the author organized via the telephone a semi-structured interview with one police officer of the special unit who interacted with the Help Beacons system while being assisted from the author.

The police officer (PO) explained that their main mission was to chase the terrorists, and at the same time take care of the health personnel to enter safe areas in order to do their job. PO explained that during the operation his team and he faced a lot of problems with the radio resulting often into broken pieces of communication. For instance, when the police found out that at least one of the terrorists had entered the ferry. Initially, the special police unit did not go on the ferry as some smoke was coming out. Though, after several unsuccessful attempts of contacting the fire brigade the special police unit decided to go onto the ferry despite the absence of any 'green light' confirmed by the fire brigade.

PO: After a while we tried to get hold to somebody of the fire department, because we wanted to be told what kind of smoke is coming from the boat before we went in. So, we have the correct equipment immediately to go in. We waited like 5-10 minutes, which felt in this situation like years. Finally, we couldn't wait anymore, and as we understood there are problems with the radio, we went into the boat. It was our own decision, as we saw the smoke, decreasing, we saw our chance to get inside the ferry.

PO explained that as the radio was not working, i.e. their leader standing outside near the ferry could not instruct them, as he would have liked to. In response to this, for instance, the special police unit tried to go for sounds and also talking to victims or other witnesses who had seen some of the terrorists.

At the same time the PO made clear that locating victims was not the highest priority in the beginning of their mission, but later in the progress of the operation it became more important.

PO: First of all we had to locate the terrorist to avoid any further harm. That was a big challenge, as while we were searching for the terrorists, we encountered a lot of injured and shocked people.

Further, the PO made clear that during the beginning of a mission he and his colleagues normally have their hands full and cannot use additional devices such as the Seeker device.

PO: I had my private phone with me, but I didn't use it. Our mission does not allow us to use phones [...] but if things calm down, we might have one hand for free.

Author: But in the first instance you might have one 'ear' free. For example, if your leader has received a signal of a beacon, he could give you a hint via radio.

PO: Yes. The leader should not use both hands for weapons. So he has one hand free, which he could work with more than one device and provide information to us and to the other members outside.

Author: What would be if the radio were not working? You could activate your smartphone?

PO: Good backup plan if the radio is not working, so we could listen whatever is going on from our commanders [...] that could go through our personal phone.

Reflecting on the feedback about the current setup, which was collected from the victims, the author asked the PO to estimate the benefits of an inverted setup. This means, victims would carry a Seeker device, and accordingly a responder would carry a Beacon device. At first, the PO did not see a big danger in the current setup.

PO: I mostly agree that terrorist would get this information as well [...] people send information to police that they need help and where they are [...] it might be possible to check out who is sending the message [...] depending on how many people are there.

Thereupon, the author re-discussed the current setup with the PO making the PO rethink his previous statement.

PO: Maybe it is better that we send out the signal in order to help the people around us and tell them where they can meet us. If in worst case the terrorists can see us, we are somehow ready to cope with them as well. Maybe we have a description of them. Instead of the terrorist can sort of see where the victims are hiding [...] I think it would be very interesting to try out the other way around, I guess this could be helpful.

7.4.3.6 Workshop with professionals

In addition, to evaluating the system as part of a large-scale exercise, one day after the exercise took place a workshop with professionals was organized. Six professionals attended the workshop (see also Figure 6):

- A head of the fire brigade (FB),

- A head of the ambulance service (AS),

- An officer of a European federal police (FP),

- An inspector at a police college (PC),

- A head of division for civil protection (CP), and

- An industrial manufacturer (IM).

The overall goal of this workshop was to receive multiple high-level perspectives from different crisis stakeholders on the applicability and possible implications of using the Help Beacons system inside the emergency response domain.

At first the professionals confirmed the trend towards equipping field personnel with wireless devices, such as smartphones or tablet computers. Then, the CP made the request to investigate speech in order to confirm people that their signal has been tracked. He critically pointed out that receiving a confirmation without talking to personnel might be interpreted as numbers when being in the queue of hotlines.

The author also confronted the professionals regarding an inverted setup. In this context, the PC floated in the idea of a terrorist carrying a responder device and stressed that this would present a risk. FB supported this by giving an example of a sniper in Norway who called the police asking for help and as a result two police officers were fatally injured. In contrary, the CP seized a suggestion being based on the idea of an inverted setup of the Help Beacons system.

CP: Responders who carry devices that broadcast a sort of "we are in here and we are trying to get through to you". I guess that makes more sense. It is similar to current practices of fire fighters [...] when responders enter a house they talk to the persons inside the house in order to get relevant information from the people.

CP further pointed out that his organization follows a system of grids and sectors, which they do sweep automatically. He elaborated how the system could become useful in this context.

CP: If you would have used something like this in Haiti [...] they would put up the beacons on the roof of the buildings [...] that these buildings were already examined by an engineer so that they cross out the building [...] in a search and rescue mission you could think of having just one signal saying "this sector is searched or not"[...] if you then would have a huge map of a city, and this sector would go green, so to say [...] that could help to direct forces in the response operation.

The AS asked for civilian-to-civilian communication. Although, it is conflicting with the risk that a person who is behind a 'victim' may actually be a terrorist, he justified his opinion by explaining that for other scenarios on the other hand a civilian-to-civilian communication would be helpful. For instance, in the aftermath of a flooding or an earthquake, volunteers or local residents could use the system supporting them while trying to help affected people.

The IM proposed to link the responder application via the GPS feature with a map-based application that also would work in off-line modus by caching GPS positions. Having this in place, the IM explained the use case of a responder independently looking for victims in the vicinity without having received instructions to go 'here' or 'there'.

Finally, the FB underlined the limitation of relying on changes being only visible through the WiFi SSID.

FB: What happens if a victim moves elsewhere? I mean assume a person would significantly change its position. Then the location that you have obtained earlier when connecting to a victim's phone would become obsolete.

Figure 53 Workshop with professionals

7.4.4 Analysis

The last evaluation allowed gaining insights into the applicability of the Help Beacons system in the practice of emergency response under the specific circumstances of a terror attack. Both user groups (victims and responders) voiced concerns about potentially disclosing their location to the terrorists / assaulters. This has specific implications both in terms of technical specifications and for the use of the prototype.

122

Hence, in the following the focus is on the aspect of negotiating (in) visibility and security.

Both victims and professionals raised concerns over the broadcasting of a distress signal hinting at or describing the victims' location. In a 'terrorist attack', terrorists using phones with WiFi capability could retrieve such information on the presence, and potentially descriptions of the locations of victims, as the default settings of their phone would notify them of any discovered WiFi network in range. It is therefore a challenge in a terrorist attack for victims to manage their visibility.

The professionals also pointed out the inverted situation where terrorists might pretend to be a responder by using a stolen Seeker device. While the benefit of the Help Beacons system unfolds through the ubiquity of WiFi SSIDs, at the same time the system can be misused to setup wrong messages. Given the 'terrorist attack' scenario one of the terrorist could have set up a wrong message and by this harm responders trusting such distress signal.

Both evaluations have revealed several implications for an enhanced, fourth prototype of the system. As highlighted through the discussions visibility and security can be managed either through technical implementation or by good instructions (which might translate into interface design) of the user. In the following, the author proposes several design suggestions in order to addresses the identified issues.

Enhancing the validity of data. To complicate the process of setting up a message would decrease the simplicity of the Help Beacons system making its usage less attractive. The Seeker already puts 'fake' messages temporarily on a blacklist. In order to indicate to a Seeker that the state of a Beacon has changed, the composition of the SSID could be revised to consider one byte of the SSID that displays each time a randomly generated ASCII-character. Then, the Seeker would notify a change in the SSID and try to connect again to the updated Beacon. Of course, this approach would reduce the space reserved for the help me by one further character. To recognize that the state of a Beacon has changed could also be dealt with at the site of the Seeker:

- When tracking again the same Beacon, the Seeker could compare the location of the Beacon with the location the Seeker had when it tracked Beacon for the first time, or

- To refresh Beacons after a certain time interval, then the Seeker would track and connect with the Beacons, as if the Seeker has never encountered the Beacons beforehand.

To prevent the misuse of a responder device by a 'terrorist' fingerprints or other biometric-related authentication schemes could be used. The exchange of details could be secured by an extensible authentication protocol. However, securing the data of Beacons would maybe limit mobile users. It would definitely make it harder for other people in the area to pick up Beacons by chance. Including voluntary helpers into emergency response is an important strategy, especially in "larger" disasters and early stages of emergencies, so it is important to keep such systems as open as possible, but without putting volunteers at risk. From the perspective of the police, validity also referred to the question if messages retrieved by the system were still relevant or had become obsolete. When victims change their location but not their emergency message, i.e. the information placed in the SSID, their location will not be updated in the system, if they are tracked again, since the responder device does not register this as an updated position. This will only happen if they also change their emergency message. This was pointed out as a weakness of the system by the head of fire department. For the future, it would be desirable if the Seeker notices a change of location of the same entity and thereupon would connect again to the corresponding Beacon. As a solution, a future prototype might automatically update the position if either of the two indicators – emergency message or GPS coordinates – have changed, or there might be an alert pop up, indicating to the user that for location change to be registered they also have to change the message. The same goes for security related visibility issues.

Managing (in-) visibility of Beacons. The strategy of exposing the presence of a 'victim' through a Beacon is useful for disaster scenarios in which exposing the presence of a victim does not provoke to be harmed, such as an earthquake or flooding, or extensive fires. In the large-scale 'terrorist attack' scenario, however, it turned out to be inadequate as the distress signal could alert the terrorists to locate victims and harm them. Thus, the design of an inverted setup of the Help Beacons system was proposed. This means, a responder would carry a device that broadcasts an *"I'm a responder that is here to help you"* message of sorts, which in turn victims carrying devices (that are set up in the WiFi scan mode) would be able to discover and connect to in order to notify the responder device (i.e. in this case the Beacon) of their presence. Such an inverted setup would be more suitable in situations in which the victim(s) behind a Beacon would rather like to be invisible in terms of WiFi radio. The inverted setup would also have advantages with regard to the number of messages that could be picked up by the Seeker at the same time, as such a setup would allow for several concurrent connections at the same time. Furthermore, it would be more power efficient for the victim devices to operate in a scanning mode rather than advertising beacons actively. And last but not least, it would also be easier to port such implementations to other mobile platforms as iOS. However, the police also expressed concerns about giving away their position in a terrorist attack scenario. A possible solution for this would be to attach the Seeker device to an unmanned aerial vehicle (UAV), if the area of operation allows it. This approach would be useful, in particular for situations in which it is dangerous for professional responders to approach an impact zone, or to cover a wide area.

Supporting negotiation and awareness. It would also be important to add support for the negotiation of the visibility of help calls and the validity of exchanged messages. At the same time, it is important not to make the use of such tools too complicated, especially for the victims who need to operate the application in distress. Hence, it would be very promising to experiment with approaches that provide awareness about the functioning of the applications. The functioning in terms of what the tool is actually doing and what possible consequences could occur. Moreover, to allow users to decide if they want to send their messages and give away their positions over unencrypted channels, or if they would prefer to stick to encrypted channels. A more advanced concept for user interaction would also allow for mixed setups of the application. In the sense of a hybrid approach that is able to switch between different modes of operation, depending on the context of the situation and the preferences of the users. This would allow for a fine-grained negotiation in terms of the above-mentioned visibility and validity. The security of the user might be negotiated by access control or by an extra screen in the process of setting up a Beacon that asks the user about the specific context of the emergency.

7.5 Conclusion

This chapter presented the iterative development of a lightweight mobile ad-hoc SOS system. Its usage is intended for situations of disrupted network infrastructures. For this, the Help Beacons system exploits the WiFi SSID and enables the ad-hoc construction of short-lived connections between neighboring WiFi devices. In iterative cycles, three prototypes have been designed and evaluated, which helped to continuously inform the design of the system.

Quality	Goal	Concrete Implementation
Prevalence	Reach of wide population of people	WiFi, SSID
Ad-hoc communication	Independent from preexisting networks	WiFi infrastructure (AP/Client)
Quick connectivity	Smooth creation of networks	Setup of Beacon/Seeker
Serendipity	Coincidental communication	Uncommon Prefix in SSID
Graceful degradation	Targeted use of still functioning services	Connection process, Exchange of details, Retrieval of position
Short-lived interactions	Efficient use of scarce Resources	Seeker search algorithm
Self-management	Adapt to unanticipated events	Temporarily blacklisting of Beacons to which connection is not possible
Decentralized Distribution	Loose dependency to centralized entity	Viral deployment via SSID

Table 17 Quality attributes contributing to Help Beacons system

The system implements all eight, empirically grounded quality attributes that were proposed in chapter 5. How each of these quality attributes has contributed to the design of the system is enlisted in Table 17. In summary, the implementation of all qualities proved to be promising in order to design a resilient ad-hoc communication system. The only exception was the decentralized distribution (QUAT-8), which revealed itself as difficult given current conditions provided by mobile operating systems. To reuse established protocols and networking standards proved to be helpful in order to design the core infrastructure features for a simple but robust mobile SOS system. Overall, the author received positive feedback on the potentials of the technology for supporting the practices of emergency response and how the system can be extended for future works. Due to the evolving nature of emergency response work, the introduction of the Help Beacons system was perceived to be more useful at later stages in the process, as it needed time for the network to emerge and stabilize.

8 Second System: Local Cloud

This chapter presents the iterative development of the second system developed in the frame of this work. The Local Cloud system is a messenger application that reuses the same network paradigm as the Help Beacons system in order to opportunistically enable local P2P networks between smartphones. Two prototypes have been developed which provide an additional reference how to implement the quality attributes defined in section 5.2. First, the chapter describes the core idea and concept of the system, and then describes in detail the course of development for the two prototypes. This chapter concludes by explaining how the considered qualities have contributed to the resilience in the design of the presented mobile ad-hoc system.

8.1 Concept

The Local Cloud concept envisions the idea of sharing information in a P2P fashion by opportunistically creating MANETs and interconnecting them by means of devices moving from one MANET to another until eventually data can be shared with the online world. This idea behind one or more local cloud[1] is inspired by patterns observed in disasters with large geographic extension, such as the earthquake in Chile in 2010 (see section 4.2.2.4), which created "islands" of connectivity whose users stranded within the affected territory. As people traveled, they moved across these islands. This observation shows an interesting opportunity: people moving across separated "islands" of connectivity could propagate messages from one cloud to other clouds. Eventually, a device carried or deployed by a person may be able to gain Internet access and relay the collected data, acting as a mediator between isolated areas and the online world. This relaying mechanism can facilitate the construction of temporary bridges to move data across poorly connected areas, and moreover support the distribution of important information for the population and the search for missing people. Figure 54 illustrates how messages could be shared inside a MANET (*dotted lines*) and transported from a MANET to another one (*dashed lines*) until messages would finally flow into the online world.

---

[1] For the sake of readability the author will often solely write "cloud" instead of "local cloud".

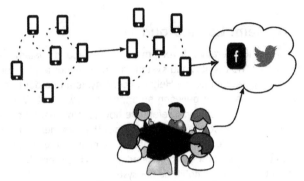

Figure 54 Local Cloud concept

The concept of the Local Cloud system is similar to store-and-forward mechanisms. These mechanisms have been used successfully in other networks with restricted availability such as FidoNet[1], which in the mid 90's used residential phone calls to move millions of message posts and emails across bulletin board systems.

8.2 First Prototype

This section describes the first prototype of the Local Cloud system. The prototype is tested in a simulated sniper scenario. Parts of this section were originally published in (Al-Akkad, Raffelsberger, et al. 2014), but have been partially rewritten and extended to fit the format and structure of the thesis.

8.2.1 Design

Technically, the Local Cloud concept can be constructed by leveraging the WiFi capabilities in smartphones, namely the 802.11 infrastructure mode. Table 18 explains the setup of deploying a local cloud (HUB).

Figure 55 depicts the flow chart of enabling the HUB mode. In particular, in case no device has associated with the HUB device, the device disables the advertised wireless network after a certain time interval and switches into client mode to look for other potentially available HUBs. The flow chart in Figure 56 depicts how a second device, called the client, enables its WiFi interface. The client scans its vicinity for some time interval for the availability of WiFi networks. The client finds the HUB device and identifies it as a HUB by means of recognizing the marking string of characters contained in the SSID.

---

[1] FidoNet, http://www.fidonet.org

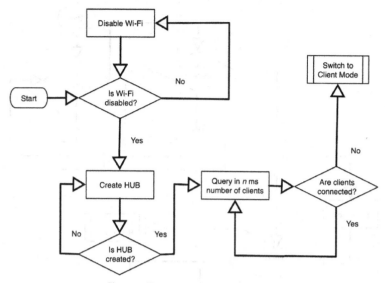

Figure 55 Flow chart of enabling HUB mode

Step	Description
1a	The device establishes a WiFi network that it advertises using an SSID identifier.
1b	The device advertises itself as a HUB by means of a particular string contained in the SSID.
1c	The device places a unique identifier at a defined position inside the SSID, e.g. a string pre-/suffix built on the MAC or IMEI of the device.
2	The device runs a DHCP server.
3	The device runs a program that listens at a specific socket address, accepts incoming connections and exchanges details by the use of a protocol.

Table 18 Setup of a HUB

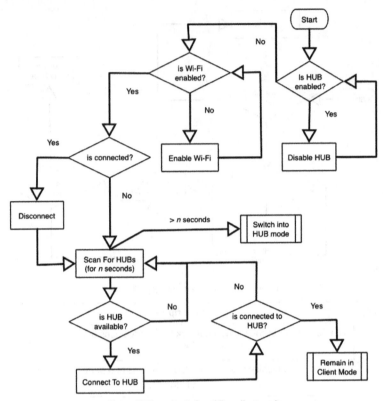

Figure 56 Flow chart of enabling client mode

8.2.2 Implementation

This section describes the functionalities of the first prototype.

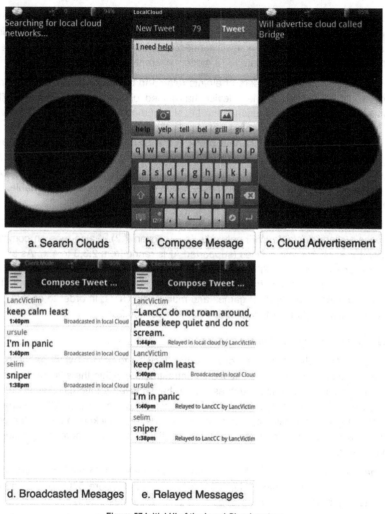

Figure 57 Initial UI of the Local Cloud system

8.2.2.1 Core

Connectivity. Complying with QUAT-3 when designing the Local Cloud prototype the goal was to hide the complexity of the following two tasks from the users:

- Creating a WiFi network and deploying a P2P communication on top of it.

- Searching for a local cloud and joining its P2P communication.

Recovery. When a client loses connection to a HUB, the client device will try to recover by searching for other clouds. In case it finds another cloud or the original cloud reappears, the client device will connect to it, otherwise the application will setup the client device to switch into HUB mode, i.e. create an own cloud.

UI. The application notifies users of events related to the connectivity. For example, users would be notified, if their device has joined or created a local cloud. This means, as soon as a user launches the Local Cloud application, the phone uses its WiFi radio to search for available local clouds. To advertise the presence of a local cloud the prototype places a certain prefix in the SSID, i.e. '#&*'. When the user launches the application, it automatically searches for clouds (see Figure 57a). If a local cloud is found, the device connects to its corresponding WiFi network and joins the P2P communication overlay. In case that there is no local cloud available, the application creates automatically a new local cloud (see Figure 57c).

As the Local Cloud system reuses the same technical implementation as the Help Beacons system to create WiFi networks (see section 7.2), it also runs on commercial, off the shelf Android devices (supported APIs range from 2.3.3 to 4.x). As a middleware for establishing P2P communication, the AllJoyn[1] framework was utilized. AllJoyn is an open-source framework that has been used for the development of several commercial multiplayer games and multimedia chats. In order to enable P2P communication the first prototype used AllJoyn's version 2.2.

8.2.2.2 Integration with Twitter service

Complying with QUAT-1, the author made the decision to utilize Twitter as the basic everyday service to run over a 'recovered' infrastructure within the system. In recent years, microblogging services such as Twitter have played an increasingly important role in citizen involvement in emergency response (Starbird & Palen 2011; Perng et al. 2013). Providing access to everyday services that are well known among the population, such as microblogging, has the potential to afford a more integrated response effort.

In order to compose and send a message, users can type in messages via a UI, which is similar to available Twitter clients (illustrated in Figure 57b). Users can opt for attaching images to their messages. As soon as a message is broadcasted in a local cloud, it appears on top of the list of messages. As soon as a wireless device detects that a connection to a Twitter server is possible, for example via its cellular or WiFi interface, locally collected data can be transported to the online world. Tweets are posted to a dedicated Twitter account simulating a local command center. In order to post or query tweets the prototype leverages the Twitter4J[2] library.

---

[1] AllJoyn, https://www.alljoyn.org
[2] Twitter4J, http://twitter4j.org

Immediately after tweets have been posted successfully, the Local Cloud application queries latest tweets related to the Twitter username of the command center. In case, the local cloud to which the relaying device was previously connected is still in range, the user will be asked if s/he likes to reconnect to inform former peers. Having confirmed this, the device will synchronize the status of tweets that have been relayed and tweets that have been received from the account of the command center. Further, it will send a request to former peers to send tweets that have been shared in the local cloud while the 'relaying' device was disconnected. This enables a two-way communication between peers in the local cloud and the command center.

As peers can join different MANETS and also connect to the online world, the mobile system distinguishes between five types of messages that are:

1. Broadcasted inside a local cloud,

2. Relayed by a device into another local cloud,

3. Broadcasted inside a local cloud and sent to Twitter, i.e. messages that were composed by the author who carries the relaying device,

4. Relayed from a local cloud to Twitter, but the author of the message has not yet been informed, and

5. Relayed from a local cloud to Twitter, and the author of the message have been informed.

Due to the relay of data the fourth or fifth type of messages have implications on the originality of the content of the tweets. Thus, to indicate that the content of a tweet has not been composed by the Twitter user who posted it, the Local Cloud system uses the ~ sign before posting a tweet.

To indicate the type of messages the author constrained the length of a message to 90 characters, since the total length of a Tweet is limited to 140 characters. A tweet is augmented to contain following constructs besides the actual message (see also Figure 57d and Figure 57e):

```
~<usernameOfOriginalAuthor>:_<message>_(<timestamp>_<day_and_month>)_<@user
nameOfLocalPolice>
```

8.2.3 Evaluation

This section describes the setup and the course of evaluating the first prototype.

8.2.3.1 Setup

The prototype was evaluated in the frame of a simulated shooting at an English university. The goal of this evaluation was to explore to which extent the Local Cloud system could support the flow of tweets between students—being disrupted from existing infrastructure—and the local police. Four students (S1-S4) acted as 'victims' during the evaluation. The group of students comprised two females and two males ranging from 25 to 35 years (see Figure 58). After giving a short introduction, the author gave each student a smartphone on which the prototype was pre-installed. Two professionals acted in the role of personnel at the local police (see Figure 59): a police officer (PO) that in her unit is responsible for analyzing social media generated data and (MR) a leader of an organization that rescues people in remote environments like mountains.

During the evaluation tweets that were relayed from the students to the local police were monitored and accordingly reacted to. For the test the agreement with the students was that one of the students (S3) would relay data, which has been previously shared in a local cloud, to the police as soon as s/he gains connectivity to Twitter. The author created a fake Twitter account for the same person and another one for the police. For the evaluation it was assumed that the students know about the account of the local police, but not vice versa. The prototype used in the evaluation supported to broadcast messages inside a local cloud which then could be relayed to Twitter, but it did not support that messages could hop from one cloud to another.

Figure 58 Preparative demonstration to students acting as 'casualties'

Figure 59 Evaluation with professionals acting as the local police

Tweets containing images have a high payload and require significantly more time to be sent than tweets that only contain text. Thus, the author applied a simple heuristic to select the order to send tweets: first, 50% of the available text-only tweets are sent, followed by 50% of the image tweets. Other heuristics that better balance the bandwidth share of text-only and image tweets go beyond the scope of this work.

8.2.3.2 Insights gained from Sniper Scenario at University

Generally, the students liked the Local Cloud concept, as it provides important uses for an emergency situation, building on their familiarity with Twitter. Users liked the possibility to communicate despite a lack of mobile reception, even if it would not work perfectly, it would be "better than nothing" (S2). However, there were concerns about the degree of user interaction. During the evaluation, the messages shared in a local cloud were relayed to Twitter via a wireless network corresponding to the university. In that regard, S4 suggested the application should switch to the right network automatically, because in an emergency situation the situation of a person might deteriorate. Further, some students found it difficult to distinguish right away the different types of messages despite their different colors and syntax.

S1: "Messages that have been tweeted by someone else's device or mine could be categorized into different groups. Listing the latest messages on top makes you neglect the state of previous messages."

The professionals, on the other hand, agreed on the need to consider that networks may break down as they had experienced this. In that regard, users saw a potential in the prototype, because it could provide a way to get in touch when other systems would fail. Based on his experiences, MR elaborated on the benefit of using text-based technology instead of voice communication.

MR: "If we are on a rescue and can't talk to people, we automatically send text messages with all our information to contact us when they get a signal. We actually ran a whole rescue on text."

However, both professionals raised also concerns of deploying the system. The PO was afraid of the awareness of the messages send on Twitter, which can be received by everyone.

PO: "So in our case, maybe the parents of the children would get a bit nervous, or it would attract bystanders, if they see our responses."

Further, the PO pointed out ways to work around the limited size of tweets in order to communicate emergency needs, for example by using a website with information and point to the URL with the Local Cloud system.

Thereupon, the author discussed the style of addressing police and people. In that regard, the PO explained that it would be okay for her to receive direct messages from specific users over Twitter. She also explained that she would send direct messages to users herself in cases where she wanted to talk to people in an emergency situation directly.

PO: "[...] because then it is controlled what is for them and what is for general knowledge."

However, the MR raised concerns about using the Local Cloud system in remote environments due to obstacles and long distances between people. Another aspect he stressed was the short battery lifetimes of cell phones he continuously has to deal with. So one of the first questions he usually asks victims in an emergency situation is *"how much battery you've got left?"*. He would then regularly tell them to save their batteries, and not call anyone else until the situation has been resolved.

MR: "We have to be forceful, because if you don't, often they waffle [...]."

Reflecting on the university campus the MR expressed the need of transporting data from one cloud to another before it enters the online world. In particular, he said it would not be sufficient to transmit information just in local "pockets of people", but to span the whole area.

MR: "You don't want to have a small cluster of information."

The PO and the MR also raised concerns regarding the trustworthiness of tweets in general. As the police officer explained, it would be important to know if a message is authentic, and not coming from a "fake profile". The MR supported that view, and stressed the need to know if the situation or a person would be dangerous in order to ensure the safety of the personnel.

To scrutinize the potential of leveraging technology that supports the transport of data—despite disrupted infrastructure—into social media streams, the author also asked both professionals how their organization uses social media in general. The police officer explained that the police see a certain need to use social media because they don't want to be "left behind". So they would do, as much as possible, and while there would be a set of policies regarding the use of social media, they don't restrict the use too much.

PO: "[...] because then that wouldn't be social media."

The MR further explained that they would use social media to inform people about what they are doing in order to get public support in terms of the necessary charity.

8.2.4 Analysis

The evaluation revealed interesting insights into the implications of the design for the practice of emergency response. The first insight is the advantage of the Local Cloud concept in exploiting an everyday service such as Twitter as a ubiquitous stream of social media to push data into the online world. In this sense, the students addressed the Twitter account of the simulated local police, whose name was similar to the real local police. At some point the Twitter account of the actual local police was following the fake account the author had created, as PO indicated.

PO: "We had a couple of followers, among them the local police. I blocked them [...] Then I protected the messages and wrote 'test' in the description of my profile"

MR: "Which tells you the power of what you are doing. We're just having a test, and possibly creating panic throughout Cumbria and Lancaster."

Both professionals were able to see the benefit of the system to enable communication between the public and authorities or non-governmental organizations. According to the evaluation, it is helpful to indicate the route which messages took before they were posted on Twitter.

MR: "Tracking of messages to see where they are going, I think this would calm people down."

In this context, the use of the micro-syntax proved to be promising, as long as the application generates it automatically.

PO: "To put a ~ sign at the beginning of a message and the rest is clever [...] I think as long as the system does this automatically it may help".

In that regard, it is important to take into account the communication protocols of emergency responder organizations, which can be quite different even within the same countries (Denef et al. 2013).

Also, the evaluation showed that the authenticity of information (e.g. fake profiles etc.) is an important issue for the professionals, which needs to be addressed in future work. Further, an important, albeit Twitter-specific technical problem, is that a tweet is limited to 140 characters, and that the Local Cloud system brings that down to only 90 characters for the actual message. Future work could look into micro-syntaxes that would allow for more space, but provide the same information. Of course, this would reduce the human readability of a tweet, but using tools that automatically extract the required information could resolve this issue. In this sense, the Local Cloud system fits on the edge of discussions of micro-syntax systems to support the coordinated analyzes of social media generated data (Starbird & Stamberger 2010; Imran et al. 2013).

On the other hand, the evaluation also pointed to a set of limitations:

Integrity of relayed messages. The way of messages are interchanged between a local cloud and the online world also leaves room for improvement from a practical perspective. PO explained that sending direct messages would have the advantage to avoid peripheral worriedness of beloved ones or attracting bystanders. The evaluation shows that the authenticity of information is a topic for future work. Given the fact that the Local Cloud system currently communicates over open communication channels, the perpetrator might also get access to the exchanged information, which could even increase the threat.

Multi-hop messages. The current implementation supported only one hop communication between a local cloud and the online world. As stressed by MR, there is a need to enhance the implementation to work over more than one hop. This implies a more complex synchronization between several MANETs. While this goes beyond the scope of this work, the author refers at this point to previous research of store-and-forward mechanisms (Delosieres & Nadjm-Tehrani 2012; Raffelsberger & Hellwagner 2013), which could be considered in order to enhance the design of the Local Cloud system for the use of a protocol to route and synchronize messages between clouds.

Battery life. The HUB uses more energy than the client but there is no role change implemented in the current prototype. Hence the HUB device's battery depletes faster, which can be problematic as the evaluation showed.

8.3 Second Prototype

This section presents the enhanced design and implementation of the second prototype, which implements complex mechanisms that originally have been published in (Al-Akkad, Ramirez & Zimmermann 2014). This section then illustrates how these mechanisms were evaluated in a lab environment.

8.3.1 Design

The last evaluation hinted to the problem, that the device that originally created a local cloud (HUB) remains in this state despite draining battery or other conflicting states. If the HUB device disappears, due to a depleted battery or getting out of range, client devices need to restart the application. To deal with this complexity, the author enhanced the process of creating local clouds between neighboring smartphones. Essentially, the process is augmented with the exchange of contextual connectivity parameters between the HUB and client device in order to maintain opportunistic communications.

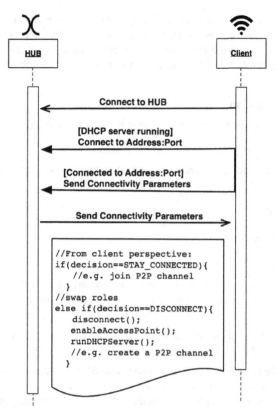

```
//From client perspective:
if(decision==STAY_CONNECTED){
    //e.g. join P2P channel
}
//swap roles
else if(decision==DISCONNECT){
    disconnect();
    enableAccessPoint();
    runDHCPServer();
    //e.g. create a P2P channel
}
```

Figure 60 Sequence diagram and pseudo code of the enhanced connection process

The contextual data that can be considered for connectivity parameters can be mani-fold. For instance, useful information includes parameters such as the current battery level, the battery charging state, the list of WiFi access points that are in the vicinity of the device or the number of connected clients if the device hosts a WiFi access point. Additionally, the context parameters may include information that is provided by applications that run on the device. Especially, this includes information that is col-lected by the Local Cloud application itself. For instance, the recognized local clouds, i.e. WiFi networks that comply with the naming scheme inside the WiFi SSID. All this information can be useful to decide whether to participate in an existing or to create a new local cloud.

Figure 60 illustrates the enhanced connection process between the client and HUB. The client connects to the HUB and obtains an IP address from the HUB via DHCP. Afterwards, the client connects to a predefined default IP address and port. Using the IP connection and a proprietary protocol, the client sends its contextual connectivity parameters to the HUB. The client also sends its IMEI for identification purposes. The HUB compares the received connectivity parameters from the client to its own parameters and replies to the client through the established socket connection. The reply indicates either that the HUB remains in its role or it passes the role to the client, i.e. both devices swap roles.

8.3.2 Implementation

This section describes the implementation of the second prototype.

8.3.2.1 Creation and maintenance of local clouds

The second prototype considers three contextual connectivity parameters in order to negotiate the role of devices:

- Battery level,

- Visible HUBs, and

- Connected clients

Battery level. The battery level reflects the last broadcasted state of the battery. In order to receive this value in Android, applications need to register for events broadcasted by the `android.os.BatteryManager`.

Visible HUBs. The number of visible HUBs can be acquired by receiving WiFi scan results, which are broadcasted nearly every second by the Android system.

Connected clients. To acquire this value in Android, applications have to register for events broadcasted by the `android.net.wifi.WifiManager`. There exists no API to directly acquire the number of connected clients. One possibility would be to access the routing table of the HUB device. However, accessing the corresponding files would require root access. This means, special privileges that are not available by default on commercial Android phones. Although it is possible to allow users to get such privileged control of the device (i.e. so called "rooting" of the device), this approach would conflict with QUAT-1. Therefore, the number of connected clients is acquired by reading the entries of the ARP cache, which is accessible in the Android system and contains the MAC to IP address mappings. The IP addresses are subsequently pinged. In detail, an ICMP echo request is sent to the IP address of a particular client in order to determine if the device is still available. This said, the number of connected clients is the number of local IP addresses that responded to the echo requests.

Negotiation of roles. The prototype uses a proprietary format in order to exchange connectivity parameters between the HUB and a client. Table 19 exemplifies how a request and a corresponding reply could look like resulting in swapping of roles, and Table 20 illustrates the results when both devices would remain in their current roles.

The pseudo code in Table 21 exemplifies on which basis the HUB makes the decision to swap roles (`return 1`) or to remain in current roles (`return 0`). The messages to negotiate the roles of the devices are exchanged via a TCP/IP socket. For this the HUB device creates a server socket, right after having deployed an AP. As soon as a client device connects to the hotspot, it binds to the socket.

Persistence of decisions. In the case two devices are connected, but due to various reasons (range, battery etc.) get disconnected, and reconnect later, it would be cumbersome to renegotiate the role, as this was recently performed. Therefore, the client device caches the ID of the HUB in case the decision was to remain in the current roles. The HUB device exposes its ID via the WiFi SSID. The ID is composed of two ASCII characters, which are the first two characters of the MD5 hash value of the phone's IMEI. The IDs inside the cache expire after five minutes.

	Source	Message	Parameters
Request	Client	87.2#[1]1	Battery level, visible HUBs
Reply	HUB	0#61.2#0	Decision, battery level, clients
Result	N/A	N/A	Both devices swap roles

Table 19 Example format for a request/reply pair resulting in swapping of roles

	Source	Message	Parameters
Request	Client	87.2#1	Battery level, visible HUBs
Reply	HUB	0#81.2#3	Decision, battery level, clients
Result	N/A	N/A	Both devices remain in their role

Table 20 Example format for a request/reply pair resulting in remaining in roles

```
if(hubBatteryLevel > 60.0f && connectedClients >= visibleHubs)

        return 0;

if(visibleHubs > connectedClients)

        return 1;

if(hubBatteryLevel<=40.0f && clientBatterLevel>60.0f)

        return 1;
```

Table 21 Pseudo code of an exemplified decision making for negotiating roles

---

[1] # is used as a separator

8.3.2.2 Further enhancements

Due to rather unsatisfying experiences in terms of reliability with AllJoyn's 2.2 Android implementation, the author replaced it with an own lightweight UDP multicast implementation in order to enable P2P communication. Furthermore, the design of the UI was enhanced (see Figure 61) and users are notified of any Local Cloud connectivity relevant aspects.

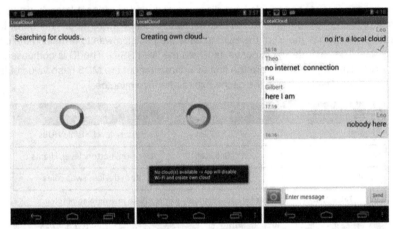

Figure 61 Enhanced UI of the Local Cloud system

8.3.3 Evaluation

This section describes performance measurements of the core mechanisms of the Local Cloud system. In particular, the time for switching roles between the client and HUB are measured, which is an important performance metric since it determines how long the communication between both devices is disrupted which will heavily influence the user experience. Table 22 shows the list of test devices, which are classified on the basis of pre-tests for creating and connecting to a HUB. Each test comprised exactly two devices. Although, the LG Nexus indicates better hardware properties, the Galaxy Nexus performed better in these pre-tests. For the evaluation, the author selected three groups of devices listed in Table 23.

Device	Abbreviation	CPU	RAM	Android Version	Classification
Galaxy S1	S1	1 GHz	512 MB	2.3.3	Weakest
Galaxy S2	S2	1.2 GHz	1 GB	2.3.3	Weak
LG Nexus	LG	1.5 GHz	2 GB	4.2.2	Strong
Galaxy Nexus	GN	1.2 GHz	1 GB	4.2.2	Strongest

Table 22 Test devices

Group	Device 1	Device 2
Weak	Galaxy S1	Galaxy S2
Medium	Galaxy S2	Galaxy Nexus
Strong	Galaxy Nexus	LG Nexus

Table 23 Test groups

As a test base the mechanism of swapping roles has been applied. These mechanisms covers all relevant four actions:

- t_ClientToHub[1] denotes the time in milliseconds a device requires to switch from Client into HUB mode. The performance measurement t_ClientToHub starts when the device in Client mode receives a reply from the Hub_{old} and ends when the $Client_{new}$ connects to Hub_{new}.

- t_HubToClient denotes the opposite process, i.e. the time in milliseconds a device in HUB mode requires to switch into Client mode. The performance measurement t_HubToClient starts when the device in HUB mode receives a request from $Client_{old}$ and stops when it is connected to Hub_{new}.

- t_CreateHub measures the time in milliseconds to create a HUB. This is the time that starts when a device in Client mode ($Client_{old}$) receives a reply from Hub_{old} and ends when being Hub_{new}.

- t_ConnectToHub measures the time in milliseconds from when a device in Client mode ($Client_{new}$) receives a scan result of available Hubs until it is connected to a Hub_{new}.

Time measurements for all four actions are conducted in a swapping roles experiment (see previous section) comprising two smartphones deployed in a lab setting. This means, while for one device t_ClientToHub is measured, at the same for the other device t_HubToClient is measured.

Both t_CreateHub and t_ConnectToHub are measurements of actions that are included in the process of switching roles. Figure 62 shows that t_CreateHub is included in t_ClientToHub, and Figure 63 shows that t_ConnectToHub is included in t_HubToClient.

---

[1] For the sake of readability only the first character of HUB is written in capital letters when referring to it in a performance measurement (e.g. t_ClientToHub) or when indicating if the device was previously a HUB (Hub_{old}) or has recently switched into this role (Hub_{new}).

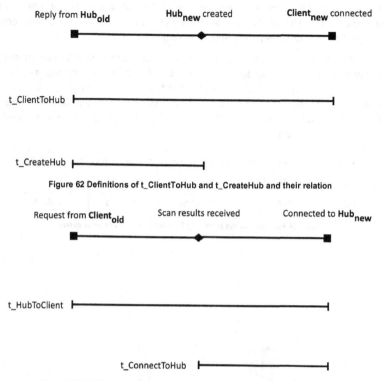

Figure 62 Definitions of t_ClientToHub and t_CreateHub and their relation

Figure 63 Definitions of t_HubToClient and t_ConnectToHub and their relation

The author tested these four actions on the three specified groups. All measurements were repeated 50 times to increase the statistical significance. The average results of the performance measurements for the devices of the weaker group are shown in Table 24. Accordingly, Table 25 contains the average results for the medium group and Table 26 the average results of the devices from the strong group. Each value in the table denotes the average of 50 samples. Figure 64, Figure 65 and Figure 66 provide the corresponding graphical representation of each table. The error bars in the diagrams indicate the 95% confidence interval.

Table 24 and Table 25 highlight that the stronger device results into lower results for t_ClientToHub while at the same time the weaker device shows lower results for t_HubToClient. For example, Figure 64 demonstrates that in the weak group (S1, S2) the S2 device—which is the stronger device—requires less time than the S1 device to switch from Client into HUB mode, but needs more time the other way around. However, in Table 26 the results show the opposite, i.e. the stronger device (LG) has higher results for t_ClientToHub, while the weaker device shows lower results for `t_HubToClient`. However, this might be due to the software issues or firmware not well suited for LG. The GN is the older device and thus more matured in this regard. Anyways, both devices are nearly equally strong.

In order to compare `t_CreateHub`, the author computed the maximum and minimum time the test devices require to create a HUB. Table 27 shows the results of maximum and minimum required times in milliseconds of 50 measurements. Max and Min values for S2 are taken from S1-S2 experiment since S2-GN also has the same result, and Max and Min values for GN are taken from the GN-S2 experiment because GN-LG also has the same result.

Devices	t_ClientToHub	t_HubToClient	t_CreateHub	t_ConnectToHub
S1	11763,7	5427,9	5676,14	1213,14
S2	5764,85	11743,56	3816,96	1657,36

Table 24 Average results of testing four actions with the weak group

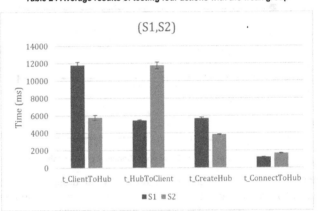

Figure 64 Performance results of the four mechanisms with the weak group

Devices	t_ClientToHub	t_HubToClient	t_CreateHub	t_ConnectToHub
S2	13863,62	7001,92	3879,44	1189,64
GN	7108,56	13616,48	1317,86	6998,44

Table 25 Average results of testing four actions with the medium group

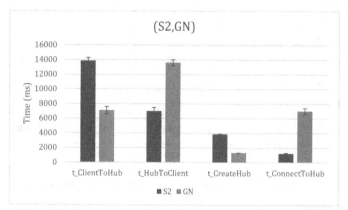

Figure 65 Performance results of the four mechanisms with the medium group

Devices	t_ClientToHub	t_HubToClient	t_CreateHub	t_ConnectToHub
GN	7884,86	10849,98	1302,06	4297,46
LG	10790,28	7887,2	1685,86	1680

Table 26 Average results of testing four actions with the strong group

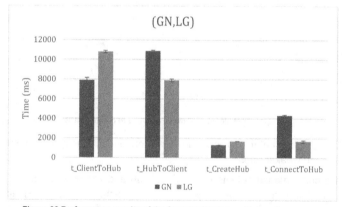

Figure 66 Performance results of the four mechanisms with the strong group

147

Devices / Creation of HUB	S1	S2	LG	GN
Min	5329	3509	1519	1233
Max	8458	4353	1994	1427

Table 27 Minimum and maximum required time to create a HUB

8.3.4 Analysis

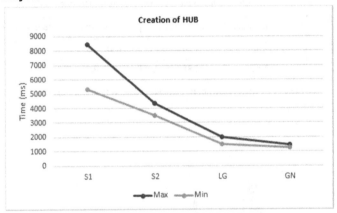

Figure 67 Minimum and maximum time to create a HUB

Figure 67 highlights that the stronger devices require significantly less time to create a HUB than the weaker ones.

Both overarching measurements (t_ClientToHub and t_HubToClient) are entangled. In the following, this dependency between both actions is explained with t_HubToClient. The measurement t_HubToClient is performed on the device that switches from HUB to Client mode (Hub_old, Client_new). This action is triggered by the request that Client_old has sent to Hub_old, and finishes until Client_new connects to Hub_new.

In principle the t_ClientToHub of the weaker device is congruent with the t_HubToClient of the stronger device. This little deviation results from using a pull mechanism to check for newly connected clients (see section 3.7 for details). In particular, all results are additionally delayed by the interval of this check, which in worst case can cause a 1s delay.

The sub actions measured in `t_CreateHub` and `t_ConnectToHub` indicate considerably less time than the corresponding overarching actions. In this context, the question arises: what causes such high values for the remaining time? For instance, Table 10 shows that the LG device yields an average time of roughly 2s to create a HUB and the counterpart (GN) takes about 4s to connect to this HUB. However, the total average time for switching from the Client to HUB role is nearly 11s, and not 6s as someone may expect. The difference of several seconds is a result of the specific events that have been chosen to perform these measurements. In particular, the Android notification that a new wireless network has been created is used to determine `t_CreateHub`. However, this event does not practically imply that the wireless network is discoverable from another Client device right away. Additionally, the connection process requires some time. First, the device that tries to connect to the wireless network (i.e. the new Client) receives WiFi scan results only in a certain interval, which is about 1s for most devices. Afterwards, the Client device tries to establish a connection to the HUB that involves the assignment of IPs and more, which again takes some time.

8.4 Delineations

8.4.1 Help Beacons System

This section distinguishes the Local Cloud system from the Help Beacons system that has been described in the previous chapter.

While the Local Cloud and the Help Beacons system share the same networking paradigm and the same technical implementation to create these networks, they differ in an important point, since the Local Cloud application relies on context information in order to manage opportunistic networks.

In the Help Beacons system the role of the user defines also its role in the creation of the opportunistic network. In particular, victims that use the Help Beacons application in order to send a distress signal create opportunistic networks, i.e. they act as a so-called HUB. First responders then can join these networks, i.e. they act as so-called clients. Although, a reversed setup where first responders create opportunistic networks, i.e. take the role of a HUB and victims join these networks is possible, the roles are still fixed and pre-determined by the application designer.

The Local Cloud application is different in the sense that each user may either create an opportunistic network or join an existing network. Hence, the roles within the opportunistic network are dynamic which requires that the nodes within a network negotiate the roles in the network. Considering the current context of the devices and the network is important in order to optimize this process. Thus, each device has to collect and manage context parameters that are used in this process. The second prototype of the Local Cloud system supports collecting context information that is relevant for the creation and management of opportunistic networks and could be reused by applications that use this type of networks.

8.4.2 WiFi Direct

This section explains the group formation process of WiFi Direct and then contrasts it to the way the Local Cloud system creates local MANETs.

The fastest procedure for the group formation is when a P2P Device *autonomously* forms a P2P group, i.e. the GO pre-configured. Also, two P2P Devices, which previously have met and stored network credentials and the corresponding client and owner roles, can quickly rejoin into a P2P Group by using a flag present in Beacon frames and further constructs. Here, the specification refers to *persistent* groups. When two WiFi Direct devices meet for the first time, which the specification refers to as the *standard* group formation, they need to go through a negotiation procedure determining the role of the P2P GO and P2P Client. Figure 2 in (Camps-Mur et al. 2013) illustrates the different orders of phases for all three P2P group formations.

In the case WiFi Direct starts with performing a common 802.11 scan, i.e. the scanning process defined in IEEE Std 802.11-2007 (IEEE 2007). Though, after this scan the *discovery* algorithm is enhanced with a *Find Phase* ensuring that two simultaneously P2P devices arrive on a common channel. For this a P2P device cycles between a state where it waits on a fixed channel for Probe Request frames (the *Listen State*) or a state where it transmits Probe Request frames on a fixed list of channels (the *Search State*). Figure 4 in (Wi-Fi Alliance 2010) illustrates the convergence of two WiFi Direct P2P devices by randomizing the time lasting in both states and on the same channel. The time to converge is reduced by using a small set of so-called Social Channels (Channels 1,6 and 11 in the 2.4 GHz band).

Having completed successfully the Find Phase, the GO Negotiation Phase continues in which both devices agree on which device will be the owner and the operating channel (either 2.4 GHz or 5 GHz bands). For agreeing on the role of a device both devices exchange numerical values, so called GO Intents, within a three-way handshake. The device transmitting the higher GO Intent value becomes the P2P group owner. To prevent conflicts when both devices sent the same GO Intent value, a tie-breaker bit is set randomly each time a GO Negotiation request is sent. Subsequently, the communication is secured in the *Provisioning* Phase, and not least the P2P GO acts as a DHCP server to provide IP addresses to the connected P2P Client.

The second prototype of the Local Cloud system uses three similar procedures to create and maintain networks. Of course, as the Local Cloud system uses WiFi in infrastructure mode, both devices need to be already interconnected to execute the procedure of role negotiation. WiFi Direct overcomes this hurdle by cycling between the states of 'listen' and 'search'. Further, Local Cloud does not offer autonomous negotiation, i.e. to pre-configure statically which device functions as a HUB or client. On the contrary, WiFi Direct autonomous group formation allows for pre-configure the roles of P2P devices.

8.5 Conclusion

This chapter presented the iterative development of the Local Cloud system. Two prototypes have been developed. The second prototype implements six of the eight quality attributes suggested in section 5.2. Table 28 lists how each quality contributed to the system. Two of the eight proposed quality attributes are not applicable to the Local Cloud system. In the scope of the Help Beacons system short-lived interactions (QUAT-5), proved to be a quite useful strategy for disseminating data. However, this quality attribute does not match with the concept behind the Local Cloud system, as the its main function is to form local MANETs, in which people for some while are supposed to communicate with each other in a P2P fashion. Also, the decentralized distribution (QUAT-8) of the system is not really applicable. Due to the ubiquity of mobile applications, enabling Twitter functionality or any other chat messengers, it is rather appropriate to provide an application upfront that considers a normal mode and a disaster mode that would be used in situations of disrupted infrastructure, similar to the Twimight application described above in 6.3.2.

Quality	Goal	Concrete Implementation
Prevalence	Reach of wide population of people	WiFi, SSID, Twitter
Ad-hoc communication	Independent from preexisting networks	WiFi infrastructure (AP/Client)
Quick connectivity	Smooth creation of networks	Setup of HUB/Client
Serendipity	Coincidental communication	Uncommon Prefix in SSID
Graceful degradation	Targeted use of still functioning services	Recovery Process Heuristic to send messages
Short-lived interactions	Efficient use of scarce Resources	N/A
Self-management	Adapt to unanticipated events	Maintenance of local MANETs
Decentralized Distribution	Loose dependency to centralized entity	N/A

Table 28 Quality attributes contributing to Local Cloud system

Altogether, the concept behind the Local Cloud system was well received by the professionals. However, one main concern stated, is that in remote areas the strength and reach of WiFi signals can be significantly reduced. Designing resilient systems that do not rely on the preexisting network infrastructure, but which can still be available and useful for remote environments remains an open and challenging issue. The role swapping mechanism implemented by the Local Cloud system is already a step towards overcoming such "islands" of connectivity. Combining such a mechanism with strategies of delay-tolerant networks could be an appropriate approach.

9 Conclusions

This chapter summarizes the contributions of the thesis and possible aspects for future work.

9.1 Contributions

This thesis has contributed to the field of crisis informatics by addressing the three research questions that have been introduced at the outset of this work.

RQ1 How do people creatively use remnants of technology in disaster situations?

RQ2 Which quality attributes for ubiquitous systems can support resilience in such situations?

RQ3 How can such quality attributes be implemented for smartphones?

The author addressed RQ1 by collecting empirical data from primary and secondary sources and filtering this data into three categories of how people creatively use remnants of technology to communicate their needs in disaster situations (see also chapter 4). RQ2 was addressed by developing a conceptual framework that comprises eight quality attributes (see also chapter 5), whose formulation is empirically grounded based on the findings gained from addressing RQ1. RQ3 was addressed through the iterative design and evaluation of two concrete systems (see chapter 7 and chapter 8) in order to provide an account for the quality attributes that resulted from answering RQ2.

RQ1 has been addressed in chapter 4 by investigating how people creatively use remnants of technology in disaster and crisis situations in which the access to network infrastructure is disrupted. The three categories, which were identified on the basis of the constant comparative method, show that in a disaster or crisis situation literally formulated *"not all is gone"*. Remnants of technology are often still functional, and people become creative in using these remnants to propagate information and work around communication hurdles due to the disruption of the underlying network infrastructure. The author of this thesis argues that observing how people solve communication breakdowns in the light of disruptions can provide a key source for inspiration of defining qualities for the design of a resilient technology. So far, within the research field of crisis informatics, a lot of research has examined how people use ICT services when the underlying network infrastructure is still functioning. However, only little research has looked into the use of ICT during disaster situations in which network infrastructure was not (or was only partially) functioning, such as the use of technology in war zones. By answering RQ1 this thesis contributed to this stream of research.

RQ2 has been tackled in chapter 5 by developing a conceptual framework consisting of eight empirically grounded quality attributes. Implementing those quality attributes can potentially support the resilience in the design of mobile ad-hoc systems. It is important to note here, although these quality attributes are empirically grounded, they are not strictly contingent on their empirical source. This means that developing systems that implement those quality attributes might not have necessarily helped in all of the disaster and crisis situations that have inspired their formulation, because this thesis has focused on certain aspects of the analyzed disasters. Hence, the collection of quality attributes should be understood as a conceptual framework for designing systems that foster resilience by supporting the ad-hoc construction of new network infrastructure. Moreover, while answering RQ3 it became clear that the suggested quality attributes are neither finite nor generalizable for all scenarios (see section 7.4.4), but in some cases can even conflict. For instance, to implement the quality attribute of decentralized distribution (QUAT-8) for current smartphones in a "user-friendly" way would require patching the phone. However, patching the phone would hinder our ability to reach the critical mass of people, and thus conflict with the goal to benefit from the ubiquity of a technology or system respectively being consolidated in the quality attribute of prevalence (QUAT-1).

To address RQ3 two mobile ad-hoc systems have been developed which implement the quality attributes that resulted from answering RQ2. Both systems were designed and evaluated in iterative cycles with end-users in simulated disaster scenarios in order to explore the technical feasibility of both systems and its specific implications for certain disaster scenarios as well as to the domain of emergency response in general. After analyzing the feedback from both user groups, insights were gained which were continuously considered to improve the design of both systems.

First, chapter 7 presented the development of the Help Beacons system—a lightweight, ad-hoc SOS system to support the salvage of victims. In particular, its lightweight approach for enabling serendipitous communication between smartphones proved to be a good design choice. Its deployment in two real-world exercises (see sections 7.2.3 and 7.4.3) was successful, although the terrorist scenario revealed unforeseen contingencies that illustrated the importance of taking contextual factors as well as sense-making processes on behalf of the users into account (see section 7.4.4). The decentralized distribution remains an open issue. In fact, the viral deployment strategy (see section 7.3) works on commercial Android phones, though it is scarcely user-friendly. The positive feedback hinted to a lot of extensions that future work could tackle (such as the development of an inverted setup of the application), and therefore underline the viability of the concept.

Second, chapter 8 demonstrated the development of the Local Cloud system—an offline P2P messenger that leverages Twitter as an everyday communication channel to spread information. The local mobile ad-hoc network instantiated by the system can be reused by any other application. Evaluating the concept in a sniper scenario showed the potential of the system to create an information flow between formal and informal response. The performance results of the comprehensive mechanisms of the Local Cloud system (see section 8.3), showed promise for use in the face of disrupted network infrastructure.

In conclusion, both systems implement concepts that can have a strong impact on the use of technology in disaster situations, although the lightweight implementation of the Help Beacons system seems to be more adequate given the capabilities of currently available smartphones; though, with newer devices, the performance results of the Local Cloud system were significantly better (see section 8.3.4). The technical backbone of the Local Cloud system builds on core features of the Help Beacons systems, and extended the functionality with some more comprehensive mechanisms to construct and maintain local mobile ad-hoc networks. The conducted evaluations and gained insights therefore revealed, in general, positive user feedback on resilient mobile ad-hoc systems, which are per se ubicomp systems, and therefore are an answer to RQ3—completing this thesis' response to the three original research questions set out in the introductory chapter.

As with every thesis, this work also has limitations in a broader context of research. In terms of HCI for emergency response, providing solutions that are applicable in practice is a major challenge. Turoff (2002) points out that a system not used on a daily basis will not be used in an emergency or disaster situation. Designing both systems in a minimalist way is, of course, one helpful aspect that reduces the learning curve when introducing a new tool inside an organization. The evaluation of the Help Beacons prototype in the large-scale exercise (see chapter 7) has hinted towards the complex implications and needs for negotiations of technologies that such use contexts can entail. But it would take a much deeper evaluation of the technology being used over a long time in practice (Kuutti & Bannon 2014), and possibly also additional context studies in the sense of design case studies (Wulf et al. 2011), in order to better understand the complexities that can arise when technology is introduced into fields as unpredictable and unstable as emergency response. Due to the novelty of the designed systems as well as to limitations of the project in which this work has been conducted, this thesis has rather focused on the usefulness of the developed solutions, leaving a deeper appropriation study in the sense of Stevens et al. (2010) for future work.

9.2 Future Work

The following paragraphs summarize seven potential aspects to be explored in future work. Some aspects were not considered upfront. Other aspects came to surface when conducting the evaluations.

To enhance the networking approach. Several aspects related to the presented networking approach could be enhanced, for instance, energy efficiency, security, and scalability. One way to preserve *energy efficiency* was already exemplified by the Local Cloud system, which allows configuring WiFi networks considering connectivity parameters including the battery level of phones. However, the way of advertising the network as a point of interest (i.e. a Beacon/Local Cloud) to other peers could be enhanced in order to preserve the battery life of phones more properly. Trifunovic et al. (2013) have already looked into power saving strategies. To provide better means for *security*, the approach could be enhanced with an extensible authentication protocol (EAP[1]). Furthermore, the usage of a standardized protocol to exchange messages remains an open issue. Also, the integrity and validity of messages transmitted via TCP/IP sockets, as well as SSIDs could be enhanced. In this context, besides the SSID, other parts of the WiFi beacon as defined in the IEEE 802.11 standard (2012) could be exploited if they become available. Könings et al. (2013) use vendor-specific elements in order to convey privacy related information between devices. However, their implementation would require patching commercially available phones to allow for exchanging information in WiFi beacons. From the last evaluation of the Help Beacons system (see section 7.4), it became clear that for some scenarios, users should be able to make their own semantic interpretation to setup the visibility and validity of distress calls, perhaps in the sense of the Speakeasy approach (Edwards et al. 2009) for discovering devices. The scalability of the networking approach has only been tested in smaller settings.

To combine the networking approach with other approaches. The presented networking approach has the potential to support spontaneous interactions, as well as location-based and pattern-based approaches. *Location-based approaches*, such as Foursquare[2] or Google Latitude[3], automatically detect the location of mobile users via a cellular/WiFi fingerprint, or GPS, or a combination of all three. Users are offered to check in to a centralized application server in order to expose their location and receive information about nearby friends. Typically, the location of people is pushed to a cloud service requiring Internet access. While location-based approaches are already commonly used, their usage is constrained to situations in which network infrastructure is still functioning. *Pattern-based approaches*, on the other hand, are based on the idea of social mobility patterns, presuming, for instance, that people in specific localities (e.g. concerts) share similar interests (Karamshuk et al. 2011), or that people usually take the same route to work or to leisure activities (Urry 2002; González et al. 2008), or that a certain availability of WiFi hotspots in urban areas is given (Balasubramanian et al. 2010; Whitbeck et al. 2012). In terms of scalability, pattern-based approaches hold a great potential. However, disaster situations have the tendency to be unpredictable and break common patterns, so that the approach presented in this thesis could be seen as a complement. Future work could look into sophisticatedly combining all three approaches with each other.

---

[1] EAP, http://tools.ietf.org/html/rfc3748

[2] Foursquare, https://foursquare.com/

[3] Google Latitude, https://latitude.google.com/latitude

To observe events in the hacking community. Hacking reflects a process of solving a task in an unorthodox way (Levy 2010). Nowadays, the original field of hacking has expanded into many new facets: sites of innovation emerged that have started to turn Do-It-Yourself (DIY) ubicomp things into products (Lindtner et al. 2014) and spread across the globe into so-called 'hackerspaces' (Savage 2013). Conti (2006) suggests that hackers are people that do not follow conventions, and thus represent a community that becomes creative in finding both the vulnerabilities and possibilities inherent in technology. While usually such endeavors might be considered as harmful, in disaster situations such skills may become quite useful. Further, Conti underlines that ideas expressed in the hacking community should be considered by academia when surveying related work. In the context of this work, one good example is the Emergency S.O.S Beacon[1] system. It emits help messages through Morse codes over AM radio, which is receivable in a one-mile range using simple radio transceivers. Such a system is quite similar to the presented Help Beacons system. Also, considerable ad-hoc networking projects[2][3] exist, which presented in hacking forums. If this community finds possibilities to distribute mobile applications in a decentralized but also user-friendly manner, there may well be other lessons to learn.

To enhance the developed systems. In the scope of the Help Beacons system one idea is to invert the setup, i.e. the roles of the Beacon (victim phone) and Seeker (responder device) would swap. The advantage of such an approach would be in terms of the invisibility of victims' phones. Besides, having a solution that allows simultaneous connections between responder and victim devices (see also section 7.4). Another idea is to combine the system with a UAV system. Tracking WiFi phones via an UAV has already been investigated by some research (Yanmaz 2012; Wang et al. 2013). Transforming an UAV as an enhanced Seeker device could strongly help to increase the scalability of the system.

To enhance the way of interaction. With respect to the current implementation of the Help Beacons concept, a responder would certainly not use a normal smartphone. Studying which device and form of interaction (e.g. vibration or speech) is adequate could increase the usability of the system. Moreover, to examine to which extent both systems could be enhanced to use seams (Chalmers & Galani 2004) in their design also represent an open design space.

To extract system features into a generic framework. Promising core features and utility features (in terms of networking) were identified during the iterative development. These features could be extracted into a *generic framework* in order to increase the reusability of the code. Application developers could use such a framework as the backbone for any application that needs to support serendipitous interac-

---

[1] Emergency S.O.S Beacon, http://badwolf.hackhut.com/2011/02/20/555-contest-entries-badwolf/

[2] Auto-Bahn project, http://blog.spiderlabs.com/2011/08/auto-bahn.html

[3] beddernet, http://code.google.com/p/beddernet/

tions. Any scenarios where mobile users still face communication hurdles could be addressed. For example, one application could be a multi-player game that enables mobile users (travelling alone) to (re-) connect on the fly during their train rides through remote areas. Actually, a whole community[1] emerged from the discussion pertaining to providing technology that also works offline.

To maintain the collection of quality attributes. As a matter of fact, the collection of quality attributes in section 5.2 is neither finite nor generalizable for all scenarios. New empirical data could lead to further findings, which in turn can inspire us to think of new qualities or refine existing qualities. Other works might suggest alternative ways of thinking about the problem space, being either narrower or wider in scope. Sakurai et al. (2014) orient themselves to only four principles (universality/ubiquity/uniqueness/unison), which partly match with some of the quality attributes defined in this thesis, but their focus has been particularly for deploying a system in the early stages of disaster relief.

9.3 Closing Remarks

This thesis investigated the ad-hoc construction of smartphone-based communication for disaster situations in which preexisting network infrastructure has collapsed. As people in their daily life have got used to continuously sending and receiving up-to-date information via ICT services, there is a similar need to do this when in disaster situations. Providing solutions that on the one hand run independently from preexisting network infrastructure and on the other hand can reach the critical mass of people, is a gap in the field of HCI and ubicomp.

To the best of the author's knowledge, no research has tackled the challenge that has been identified in this thesis in a user-oriented way, i.e. by empirically investigating into the problem space, working out a conceptual framework, and implementing this by several practice-centered prototypes. By doing so, this thesis has successfully shown how to develop resilient, ad-hoc communication systems based on off-the-shelf smartphones, and therefore provided a basis for tackling a long-standing gap inside the HCI and ubicomp community.

---

[1] Offline First community, http://offlinefirst.org/

References

Abolhasan, M., Hagelstein, B. & Wang, J.C.-P., 2009. Real-world performance of current proactive multi-hop mesh protocols. In *Proceedings of the 15th Asia-Pacific Conference on Communications. APCC '09*. pp. 44–47. doi:10.1109/APCC.2009.5375690.

Ahson, S.A. & Ilyas, M., 2011. *Near Field Communications Handbook, First Edition*, Boca Raton: Auerbach Publications.

Al-Akkad, A. & Raffelsberger, C., 2014. How Do I Get This App? A Discourse on Distributing Mobile Applications Despite Disrupted Infrastructure. In *Proceedings of the 11th International Conference on Information Systems for Crisis Response and Management. ISCRAM'14*. Penn State University, Pennsylvenia, USA: ISCRAM.

Al-Akkad, A., Raffelsberger, C., Boden, A., Ramirez, L. & Zimmermann, A., 2014. Tweeting "When Online is Off"? Opportunistically Creating Mobile Ad-hoc Networks in Response to Disrupted Infrastructure. In *Proceedings of the 11th International Conference on Information Systems for Crisis Response and Management. ISCRAM'14*. Penn State University, Pennsylvenia, USA: ISCRAM.

Al-Akkad, A., Ramirez, L., Boden, A., Randall, D. & Zimmermann, A., 2014. Help Beacons: Design and Evaluation of an Ad-hoc Lightweight S.O.S. System for Smartphones. In *Proceedings of the 32nd SIGCHI Conference on Human Factors in Computing Systems. CHI '14*. New York, NY, USA: ACM, pp. 1485–1494. doi:10.1145/2556288.2557002.

Al-Akkad, A., Ramirez, L., Denef, S., Boden, A., Wood, L., Büscher, M. & Zimmermann, A., 2013. "Reconstructing Normality": The Use of Infrastructure Leftovers in Crisis Situations As Inspiration for the Design of Resilient Technology. In *Proceedings of the 25th Australian Computer-Human Interaction Conference: Augmentation, Application, Innovation, Collaboration. OzCHI '13*. New York, NY, USA: ACM, pp. 457–466. doi:10.1145/2541016.2541051.

Al-Akkad, A., Ramirez, L. & Zimmermann, A., 2014. Method for organizing a wireless network. *European Patent Office*, Application No. 13171881.9, Publication No. 2814299A1. Retrieved from https://depatisnet.dpma.de/DepatisNet/depatisnet?docid=EP000002814299A1 [Accessed on December 20, 2014].

Al-Akkad, A. & Vinkovits, M., 2014. Increasing Users' Autonomy in Obtaining Mobile Applications. In *Autonomy in Technology Design. Workshop at the SIGCHI Conference on Human Factors in Computing Systems*. CHI'14. New York, NY, USA: ACM.

Al-Akkad, A. & Zimmermann, A., 2012. Survey: ICT-supported Public Participation in Disasters. In *Proceedings of the 9th International Conference on Information Systems for Crisis Response and Management*. ISCRAM'12. Vancouver, BC, Canada: ISCRAM.

Al-Akkad, A. & Zimmermann, A., 2011. User Study: Involving civilians by smart phones during emergency situations. In *Proceedings of the 8th International Conference on Information Systems for Crisis Response and Management*. ISCRAM'11. Lisbon, Portugal: ISCRAM.

Akyildiz, I.F. & Wang, X., 2005. A survey on wireless mesh networks. *IEEE Communications Magazine*, 43(9), p.23–30. doi:10.1109/MCOM.2005.1509968.

Allen, E., 2012. First an electricity blackout and now CELL PHONE coverage is down as users in Manhattan battle signal failures. *Daily Mail*. Retrieved from http://www.dailymail.co.uk/news/article-2225217/Superstorm-Sandy-New-York-CELL-PHONE-coverage-users-battle-signal-failures.html [Accessed on March 1, 2014].

Al-Ani, B., Mark, G., Chung, J. & Jones, J., 2012. The Egyptian Blogosphere: A Counter-narrative of the Revolution. In *Proceedings of the 15th Conference on Computer Supported Cooperative Work*. CSCW '12. New York, NY, USA: ACM, pp. 17–26. doi:10.1145/2145204.2145213.

audiotranskription.de, 2014. *f4 & f5*, Retrieved from http://www.audiotranskription.de/english/f4.htm [Accessed on March 1, 2014].

Balasubramanian, A., Mahajan, R. & Venkataramani, A., 2010. Augmenting Mobile 3G Using WiFi. In *Proceedings of the 8th International Conference on Mobile Systems, Applications, and Services*. MobiSys '10. New York, NY, USA: ACM, pp. 209–222. doi:10.1145/1814433.1814456.

Baldoni, R., Contenti, M. & Virgillito, A., 2003. The evolution of publish/subscribe communication systems. In *Future Directions in Distributed Computing*. Berlin, Heidelberg: Springer-Verlag, pp. 137–141.

Bassoli, A., Brewer, J., Martin, K., Dourish, P. & Mainwaring, S., 2007. Underground Aesthetics: Rethinking Urban Computing. *IEEE Pervasive Computing*, 6(3), p.39–45. doi:10.1109/MPRV.2007.68.

BBC News, 2011. Egypt protest deaths "over 800." Retrieved from http://www.bbc.co.uk/news/world-middle-east-13134956 [Accessed on December 16, 2014].

Bell, M., Hall, M., Chalmers, M., Gray, P. & Brown, B., 2006. Domino: Exploring Mobile Collaborative Software Adaptation. In *Proceedings of the 4th International Conference on Pervasive Computing*. PERVASIVE'06. Berlin, Heidelberg: Springer-Verlag, pp. 153–168. doi:10.1007/11748625_10.

Benight, C.C., Freyaldenhoven, R.W., Hughes, J., Ruiz, J.M., Zoschke, T.A. & Lovallo, W.R., 2000. Coping Self-Efficacy and Psychological Distress Following the Oklahoma City Bombing1. *Journal of Applied Social Psychology*, 30(7), p.1331–1344. doi:10.1111/j.1559-1816.2000.tb02523.x.

Betz, M. & Wulf, V., 2014. EmergencyMessenger: A Text Based Communication Concept for Indoor Firefighting. In *Proceedings of the 32nd SIGCHI Conference on Human Factors in Computing Systems*. CHI '14. New York, NY, USA: ACM, pp. 1515–1524. doi:10.1145/2556288.2557188.

Beven, J.L. & Kimberlain, T.B., 2009. *Tropical Cyclone Report: Hurricane Gustav, (AL072008) 25 August – 4 September 2008*, National Hurricane Center.

Bhat, V., Parashar, M., Liu, H., Khandekar, M., Kandasamy, N. & Abdelwahed, S., 2006. Enabling Self-Managing Applications using Model-based Online Control Strategies. In *Proceedings of the International Conference on Autonomic Computing*. ICAC '06. IEEE, pp. 15–24. doi:10.1109/ICAC.2006.1662377.

Blake, E.S., Kimberlain, T.B., Berg, R.J., Cangialosi, J.P. & Beven, J.L., 2013. *Tropical Cyclone Report: Hurricane Sandy (AL182012) 22–29 October 2012*, National Hurricane Center.

Bluetooth SIG Inc., 2004. *Bluetooth core specification v2.0*, Retrieved from http://www.bluetooth.com [Accessed on July 8, 2014].

Bluetooth SIG Inc., 2010. *Specification of the Bluetooth System v4.0*, Retrieved from http://www.bluetooth.com [Accessed on July 21, 2014].

Bødker, S. & Grønbaek, K., 1991. Cooperative Prototyping: Users and Designers in Mutual Activity. *International Journal of Man-Machine Studies*, 34(3), p.453–478. doi:10.1016/0020-7373(91)90030-B.

Borcea, C., Gupta, A., Kalra, A., Jones, Q. & Iftode, L., 2007. The MobiSoC Middleware for Mobile Social Computing: Challenges, Design, and Early Experiences. In *Proceedings of the 1st International Conference on MOBILe Wireless MiddleWARE, Operating Systems, and Applications*. MOBILWARE '08. ICST,

Brussels, Belgium, Belgium: ICST (Institute for Computer Sciences, Social-Informatics and Telecommunications Engineering), pp. 27:1–27:8.

Bruno, R., Conti, M. & Passarella, A., 2008. Opportunistic networking overlays for ICT services in crisis management. In *Proceedings of the 5th International Conference on Information Systems for Crisis Response and Management*. ISCRAM'08. ISCRAM Press.

Camps-Mur, D., Garcia-Saavedra, A. & Serrano, P., 2013. Device-to-device communications with Wi-Fi Direct: overview and experimentation. *IEEE Wireless Communications*, 20(3), p.96–104. doi:10.1109/MWC.2013.6549288.

Camps-Mur, D. & Loureiro, P., 2014. (E^2 D) Wi-Fi: A Mechanism to Achieve Energy Efficient Discovery in Wi-Fi. *IEEE Transactions on Mobile Computing*, 13(6), p.1186–1199. doi:10.1109/TMC.2013.149.

Chalmers, M. & Galani, A., 2004. Seamful Interweaving: Heterogeneity in the Theory and Design of Interactive Systems. In *Proceedings of the 5th Conference on Designing Interactive Systems: Processes, Practices, Methods, and Techniques*. DIS '04. New York, NY, USA: ACM, pp. 243–252. doi:10.1145/1013115.1013149.

Charmaz, K., 2006. *Constructing Grounded Theory: A Practical Guide Through Qualitative Analysis*, SAGE.

Charron, G. & Arnaud, E., 2012. *A full-scale displacement and humanitarian crisis with no solutions in sight*, IDMC (Internal Displacement Monitoring Centre). Retrieved from http://www.internal-displacement.org/middle-east-and-north-africa/syria/2012/a-full-scale-displacement-and-humanitarian-crisis-with-no-solutions-in-sight [Accessed on December 16, 2014].

Choney, S., 2012. Chile asks those who have Net, phones to share. *NBC News*. Retrieved from http://nbcnews.to/11g5zeM [Accessed on March 1, 2014].

CNN News & Lionheart Books Ltd., 2005. *CNN Reports: Hurricane Katrina: State of Emergency*, Andrews McMeel Publishing.

CNN Wire Staff, 2011. Report: Suspect in Norway attacks bought chemicals, tools on eBay. *CNN International*. Retrieved from http://www.cnn.com/2011/WORLD/europe/07/31/norway.attacks.ebay/index.html [Accessed on December 16, 2014].

Comfort, L.K., 1999. *Shared Risk: Complex Systems in Seismic Response*, Amsterdam; New York: Emerald Group Publishing Limited.

Conti, G., 2006. Introduction. *Communications of the ACM*, 49(6), p.32–36. doi:10.1145/1132469.1132497.

Conti, M. & Giordano, S., 2007a. Multihop Ad Hoc Networking: The Reality. *IEEE Communications Magazine*, 45(4), p.88–95. doi:10.1109/MCOM.2007.343617.

Conti, M. & Giordano, S., 2007b. Multihop Ad Hoc Networking: The Theory. *IEEE Communications Magazine*, 45(4), p.78–86. doi:10.1109/MCOM.2007.343616.

Conti, M. & Kumar, M., 2010. Opportunities in Opportunistic Computing. *Computer*, 43(1), p.42–50. doi:10.1109/MC.2010.19.

Corbin, J. & Strauss, A., 2008. *Basics of Qualitative Research: Techniques and Procedures for Developing Grounded Theory* Auflage: Third., Los Angeles, California: Sage Publications Inc.

Coyle, D. & Meier, P., 2009. *New Technologies in Emergencies and Conflicts: The Role of Information and Social Networks*, United Nations Foundation & Vodafone Foundation.

Cucurull, J., Asplund, M. & Nadjm-Tehrani, S., 2010. Anomaly Detection and Mitigation for Disaster Area Networks. In *Proceedings of the 13th International Conference on Recent Advances in Intrusion Detection*. RAID'10. Berlin, Heidelberg: Springer-Verlag, pp. 339–359.

Darrow, B., 2012. Data centers batten down as Hurricane Sandy blows in. *GIGAOM*. Retrieved from https://gigaom.com/2012/10/29/data-centers-batten-down-as-hurricane-sandy-blows-in/ [Accessed on March 1, 2014].

Davies, N., Friday, A., Newman, P., Rutlidge, S. & Storz, O., 2009. Using Bluetooth Device Names to Support Interaction in Smart Environments. In *Proceedings of the 7th International Conference on Mobile Systems, Applications, and Services*. MobiSys '09. New York, NY, USA: ACM, pp. 151–164. doi:10.1145/1555816.1555832.

Delosieres, L. & Nadjm-Tehrani, S., 2012. BATMAN Store-and-Forward: the Best of the Two Worlds. In PerCom Workshops '12. IEEE Computer Society, pp. 727–733.

Denef, S., Bayerl, P.S. & Kaptein, N.A., 2013. Social Media and the Police: Tweeting Practices of British Police Forces During the August 2011 Riots. In *Proceedings of the 31st SIGCHI Conference on Human Factors in Computing Systems*. CHI '13. New York, NY, USA: ACM, pp. 3471–3480. doi:10.1145/2470654.2466477.

Dewey, J., 1983. The Pattern of Inquiry. In *Logic: Theory of Inquiry*. Henry Holt and Company.

Dilmaghani, R.B. & Rao, R.R., 2008. An Ad Hoc Network Infrastructure: Communication and Information Sharing for Emergency Response. In *Networking and Communications, 2008. WIMOB '08. IEEE International Conference on Wireless and Mobile Computing*. pp. 442–447. doi:10.1109/WiMob.2008.103.

Dourish, P. & Bell, G., 2011. *Divining a Digital Future: Mess and Mythology in Ubiquitous Computing*, The MIT Press.

Dubois, D.J., Bando, Y., Watanabe, K. & Holtzman, H., 2013. Lightweight Self-organizing Reconfiguration of Opportunistic Infrastructure-mode WiFi Networks. In *Proceedings of the 7th International Conference on Self-Adaptive and Self-Organizing Systems*. SASO '13. IEEE, pp. 247–256. doi:10.1109/SASO.2013.41.

Dynes, R.R., 1970. *Organized Behavior in Disaster*, Heath LexingtonBooks.

Edwards, W.K., Bellotti, V., Dey, A.K. & Newman, M.W., 2003. The Challenges of User-centered Design and Evaluation for Infrastructure. In *Proceedings of the 21st SIGCHI Conference on Human Factors in Computing Systems*. CHI '03. New York, NY, USA: ACM, pp. 297–304. doi:10.1145/642611.642664.

Edwards, W.K., Newman, M.W., Sedivy, J.Z. & Smith, T.F., 2009. Experiences with Recombinant Computing: Exploring Ad Hoc Interoperability in Evolving Digital Networks. *ACM Transactions on Computer-Human Interactions*, 16(1), p.3:1–3:44. doi:10.1145/1502800.1502803.

Estrin, D., 2010. Participatory sensing: applications and architecture [Internet Predictions]. *IEEE Internet Computing*, 14(1), p.12–42. doi:10.1109/MIC.2010.12.

Fall, K., 2003. A Delay-tolerant Network Architecture for Challenged Internets. In *Proceedings of the 2003 Conference on Applications, Technologies, Architectures, and Protocols for Computer Communications*. SIGCOMM '03. New York, NY, USA: ACM, pp. 27–34. doi:10.1145/863955.863960.

Farnham, S., Kirkpatrick, R. & Pedersen, E., 2006. Observation of Katrina/Rita deployment: Addressing social and communication challenges of ephemeral groups. In ISCRAM Press.

Feeney, L.M. & Nilsson, M., 2001. Investigating the energy consumption of a wireless network interface in an ad hoc networking environment. In *Proceedings of the 20th Annual Joint Conference of the IEEE Computer and Communications*

Societies. INFOCOM '01. IEEE, pp. 1548–1557 vol.3. doi:10.1109/INFCOM.2001.916651.

Ferro, E. & Potortí, F., 2005. Bluetooth and wi-fi wireless protocols: a survey and a comparison. *IEEE Wireless Communications*, 12(1), p.12–26. doi:10.1109/MWC.2005.1404569.

Fontana, A. & Frey, J.H., 1994. Interviewing: The Art of Science. In *Handbook of Qualitative Research*. SAGE, pp. 361–376.

Galea, S., Ahern, J., Resnick, H., Kilpatrick, D., Bucuvalas, M., Gold, J. & Vlahov, D., 2002. Psychological Sequelae of the September 11 Terrorist Attacks in New York City. *New England Journal of Medicine*, 346(13), p.982–987. doi:10.1056/NEJMsa013404.

Gardner-Stephen, P. & Palaniswamy, S., 2011. Serval Mesh software-WiFi Multi Model Management. In *Proceedings of the 1st International Conference on Wireless Technologies for Humanitarian Relief*. ACWR '11. New York, NY, USA: ACM, pp. 71–77. doi:10.1145/2185216.2185245.

Gebrekristos, M., Aljadaan, A. & Bihani, K., 2008. QR-Codes for the Chronically Homeless. In *Proceedings of the Extended Abstracts on Human Factors in Computing Systems*. CHI EA '08. New York, NY, USA: ACM, pp. 3879–3884. doi:10.1145/1358628.1358947.

Gilbert, C., 1998. Studying Disaster: Changes in the Main Conceptual Tools. In *What is a Disaster? Perspectives on the Question*. London and New York: Routledge.

Glaser, B.G. & Strauss, A., 1967. *The Discovery of Grounded Theory: Strategies for Qualitative Research*, Aldine Transaction.

Glaser, B.G. & Strauss, A.L., 1966. *Awareness Of Dying*, Transaction Publishers.

Glinz, M., 2007. On Non-Functional Requirements. In *Proceedings of the 15th International Requirements Engineering Conference*. IEEE, pp. 21–26.

Goldman, P., 2014. Israeli "SOS" Apps Launched in Wake of Recent Kidnappings. *NBC News*. Retrieved from http://www.nbcnews.com/news/investigations/feud-erupts-over-ags-claim-sandusky-abused-boys-investigation-dragged-n141126 [Accessed on January 7, 2014].

González, M.C., Hidalgo, C.A. & Barabási, A.-L., 2008. Understanding individual human mobility patterns. *Nature*, 453(7196), p.779–782. doi:10.1038/nature06958.

Gubbi, J., Buyya, R., Marusic, S. & Palaniswami, M., 2013. Internet of Things (IoT): A vision, architectural elements, and future directions. *Future Generation Computer Systems*, 29(7), p.1645–1660. doi:10.1016/j.future.2013.01.010.

Hagar, C. & Haythornthwaite, C., 2005. Crisis, Farming & Community. *The Journal of Community Informatics*, 1(3).

Auf der Heide, E., 2004. Common Misconceptions about Disasters: Panic, the "Disaster Syndrome," and Looting. In *The First 72 Hours: A Community Approach to Disaster Preparedness*. iUniverse Inc., pp. 340–380.

Helbing, D. & Mukerji, P., 2012. Crowd Disasters as Systemic Failures: Analysis of the Love Parade Disaster. *EPJ Data Science*, 1(7).

Hersman, E., 2012. The 4636 SMS Shortcode for Reporting in Haiti. *Ushahidi*. Retrieved from http://www.ushahidi.com/2010/01/17/the-4636-sms-shortcode-for-reporting-in-haiti/ [Accessed on March 1, 2014].

Hoffman, R.R., Crandall, B. & Shadbolt, N., 1998. Use of the Critical Decision Method to Elicit Expert Knowledge: A Case Study in the Methodology of Cognitive Task Analysis. *Human Factors: The Journal of the Human Factors and Ergonomics Society*, 40(2), p.254–276. doi:10.1518/001872098779480442.

Hofmann, P., Kuladinithi, K., Timm-Giel, A., Goerg, C., Bettstetter, C., Capman, F. & Toulsaly, C., 2006. Are IEEE 802 Wireless Technologies Suited for Fire Fighters? In *Proceedings of the 12th European Wireless Conference - Enabling Technologies for Wireless Multimedia Communications*. EW '06. pp. 1–5.

Holling, C.S., 1973. Resilience and Stability of Ecological Systems. *Annual Review of Ecology and Systematics*, 4(1), p.1–23. doi:10.1146/annurev.es.04.110173.000245.

Hollnagel, E., Paries, J., Woods, D.D. & Wreathall, J., 2011. *Resilience Engineering in Practice*, Ashgate Publishing, Ltd.

Hossmann, T., Legendre, F., Carta, P., Gunningberg, P. & Rohner, C., 2011. Twitter in Disaster Mode: Opportunistic Communication and Distribution of Sensor Data in Emergencies. In *Proceedings of the 3rd Extreme Conference on Communication: The Amazon Expedition*. ExtremeCom '11. New York, NY, USA: ACM, pp. 1:1–1:6. doi:10.1145/2414393.2414394.

IAGS, 2004. The Cost of September 11. *Institute for the Analysis of Global Security.* Retrieved from http://www.iags.org/costof911.html [Accessed on December 16, 2014].

IEEE, 2012. IEEE Standard for Information technology–Telecommunications and information exchange between systems Local and metropolitan area networks–Specific requirements Part 11: Wireless LAN Medium Access Control (MAC) and Physical Layer (PHY) Specifications. *IEEE Std 802.11-2012 (Revision of IEEE Std 802.11-2007)*, p.1–2793. doi:10.1109/IEEESTD.2012.6178212.

IEEE, 2007. IEEE Standard for Information Technology - Telecommunications and Information Exchange Between Systems - Local and Metropolitan Area Networks - Specific Requirements - Part 11: Wireless LAN Medium Access Control (MAC) and Physical Layer (PHY) Specifications. *IEEE Std 802.11-2007 (Revision of IEEE Std 802.11-1999)*, p.1–1076. doi:10.1109/IEEESTD.2007.373646.

Imran, M., Elbassuoni, S., Castillo, C. & Meier, P., 2013. Extracting Information Nuggets from Disaster-Related Messages in Social Media. In *Proceedings of the 10th International Conference on Information Systems for Crisis Response and Management.* ISCRAM'13. ISCRAM Press.

Iosifidis, G., Gao, L., Huang, J. & Tassiulas, L., 2014. Enabling crowd-sourced mobile Internet access. In *Proceedings of the 33rd Annual International Conference on Computer Communications.* INFOCOM '14. IEEE, pp. 451–459. doi:10.1109/INFOCOM.2014.6847968.

ISO/IEC, 2011. *ISO/IEC 14443-3:2011 Identification cards -- Contactless integrated circuit cards -- Proximity cards -- Part 3: Initialization and anticollision,* Retrieved from http://www.iso.org/iso/catalogue_detail.htm?csnumber=50942 [Accessed on July 21, 2014].

ISO/IEC, 2014. *ISO/IEC 25000:2014 Systems and software engineering -- Systems and software Quality Requirements and Evaluation (SQuaRE) -- Guide to SQuaRE,* Retrieved from http://www.iso.org/iso/home/store/catalogue_tc/catalogue_detail.htm?csnumber=64764 [Accessed on June 19, 2014].

Jennex, M.E., 2012. Social Media – Truly Viable For Crisis Response? In *Proceedings of the 9th International Conference on Information Systems for Crisis Response and Management.* ISCRAM 2012. Vancouver, BC, Canada: ISCRAM.

Jindal, G., 2012. A Comparative Study of Mobile Phone's Operating Systems. *International Journal of Computer Applications & Information Technology*, 1(3), p.10–15.

Johnson, D. & Hancke, G., 2009. Comparison of Two Routing Metrics in OLSR on a Grid Based Mesh Network. *Journal of Ad Hoc Networks*, 7(2), p.374–387. doi:10.1016/j.adhoc.2008.04.006.

Jones, A., Danzico, M., Barford, V. & Cullinane, S., 2011. As it happened: Norway attacks. *BBC News*. Retrieved from http://www.bbc.co.uk/news/world-europe-14254705 [Accessed on January 3, 2014].

Kahn, R.L. & Cannell, C.F., 1957. *The dynamics of interviewing: theory, technique, and cases*, Wiley.

Karamshuk, D., Boldrini, C., Conti, M. & Passarella, A., 2011. Human mobility models for opportunistic networks. *IEEE Communications Magazine*, 49(12), p.157–165. doi:10.1109/MCOM.2011.6094021.

Kärkkäinen, T. & Ott, J., 2014. Liberouter: Towards Autonomous Neighborhood Networking. In *Proceedings of the 11th IEEE/IFIP Annual Conference on Wireless On-deman Network Systems and Services*. WONS'14. IEEE, pp. 162–169.

Kavanaugh, A., Hassan, R., Elmongui, H., Magdy, M., Sheetz, S., Yang, S., Fox, E. & Shoemaker, D., 2012. Between a Rock and a Cell Phone. In *Proceedings of the 9th International Conference on Information Systems for Crisis Response and Management*. ISCRAM'12. Vancouver, BC, Canada: ISCRAM.

Kelman, B., 2014. Va. Tech shooting survivor recounts ordeal. *USA Today*. Retrieved from http://www.usatoday.com/story/news/nation/2014/07/14/virginia-tech-shooting-survivor-school-officers-conference/12653945/ [Accessed on December 16, 2014].

Kendra, J.M. & Wachtendorf, T., 2003. Elements of Resilience After the World Trade Center Disaster: Reconstituting New York City's Emergency Operations Centre. *Disasters*, 27(1), p.37–53. doi:10.1111/1467-7717.00218.

Kennedy, D., 2009. Powerful Italian quake kills many. *BBC News*. Retrieved from http://news.bbc.co.uk/2/hi/europe/7984867.stm [Accessed on December 16, 2014].

Knabb, R., Rhome, J. & Brow, D., 2005. *Tropical Cyclone Report: Hurricane Katrina*, National Hurricane Center.

Könings, B., Schaub, F. & Weber, M., 2013. Prifi Beacons: Piggybacking Privacy Implications on Wifi Beacons. In *Proceedings of the Conference on Pervasive and Ubiquitous Computing Adjunct Publication*. UbiComp '13 Adjunct. New York, NY, USA: ACM, pp. 83–86. doi:10.1145/2494091.2494115.

Kotz, D., 2013. Number injured in marathon bombing revised downward to 264. *The Boston Globe*. Retrieved from https://www.bostonglobe.com/lifestyle/health-wellness/2013/04/23/number-injured-marathon-bombing-revised-downward/NRpaz5mmvGquP7KMA6XsIK/story.html [Accessed on December 16, 2014].

Kravets, R.H., 2012. Enabling Social Interactions off the Grid. *IEEE Pervasive Computing*, 11, p.8–11. doi:10.1109/mprv.2012.29.

Kreps, G.A., 1984. Sociological Inquiry and Disaster Research. *Annual Review of Sociology*, 10, p.309–330.

Kreps, G.A. & Bosworth, S.L., 1994. *Organizing, Role Enactment, and Disaster: A Structural Theory*, University of Delaware Press.

Krishnamoorthy, S. & Agrawala, A., 2012. Context-aware, Technology Enabled Social Contribution for Public Safety Using M-Urgency. In *Proceedings of the 14th International Conference on Human-computer Interaction with Mobile Devices and Services*. MobileHCI '12. New York, NY, USA: ACM, pp. 123–132. doi:10.1145/2371574.2371594.

Kuutti, K. & Bannon, L.J., 2014. The Turn to Practice in HCI: Towards a Research Agenda. In *Proceedings of the 32nd SIGCHI Conference on Human Factors in Computing Systems*. CHI '14. New York, NY, USA: ACM, pp. 3543–3552. doi:10.1145/2556288.2557111.

Kwok, R., 2009. Personal technology: Phoning in data. *Nature News*, 458(7241), p.959–961. doi:10.1038/458959a.

Lamont, C.K. & Boujneh, H., 2012. Transitional Justice in Tunisia: Negotiating Justice during Transition. *Politička misao*, 49(5), p.32–49.

Landgren, J. & Nulden, U., 2007. A Study of Emergency Response Work: Patterns of Mobile Phone Interaction. In *Proceedings of the 25th SIGCHI Conference on Human Factors in Computing Systems*. CHI '07. New York, NY, USA: ACM, pp. 1323–1332. doi:10.1145/1240624.1240824.

Legendre, F., 2011. 30 Years of Ad Hoc Networking Research: What About Humanitarian and Disaster Relief Solutions? What Are We Still Missing? In *Proceedings of the 1st International Conference on Wireless Technologies for Humani-*

tarian Relief. ACWR '11. New York, NY, USA: ACM, pp. 217–217. doi:10.1145/2185216.2185279.

Levy, S., 2010. *Hackers: Heroes of the Computer Revolution - 25th Anniversary Edition*, Sebastopol, CA: O'Reilly Media.

Ley, B., Ludwig, T., Pipek, V., Randall, D., Reuter, C. & Wiedenhoefer, T., 2014. Information and Expertise Sharing in Inter-Organizational Crisis Management. *The Journal of Collaborative Computing and Work Practices*, 23(4-6), p.347–387. doi:10.1007/s10606-014-9205-2.

Ley, B., Pipek, V., Reuter, C. & Wiedenhoefer, T., 2012. Supporting Improvisation Work in Inter-organizational Crisis Management. In *Proceedings of the 30th SIGCHI Conference on Human Factors in Computing Systems*. CHI '12. New York, NY, USA: ACM, pp. 1529–1538. doi:10.1145/2207676.2208617.

Lien, Y.-N., Chi, L.-C. & Huang, C.-C., 2010. A Multi-hop Walkie-Talkie-Like Emergency Communication System for Catastrophic Natural Disasters. In *Proceedings of the 39th International Conference on Parallel Processing Workshops*. ICPPW '10. pp. 527–532. doi:10.1109/ICPPW.2010.77.

Lindtner, S., Hertz, G.D. & Dourish, P., 2014. Emerging Sites of HCI Innovation: Hackerspaces, Hardware Startups & Incubators. In *Proceedings of the 32nd SIGCHI Conference on Human Factors in Computing Systems*. CHI '14. New York, NY, USA: ACM, pp. 439–448. doi:10.1145/2556288.2557132.

Lotan, G., Graeff, E., Ananny, M., Gaffney, D., Pearce, I. & Boyd, D., 2011. The Revolutions Were Tweeted: Information Flows during the 2011 Tunisian and Egyptian Revolutions. *International Journal of Communication*, 5, p.1375–1405.

Ludwig, T., Reuter, C. & Pipek, V., 2013. What You See is What I Need: Mobile Reporting Practices in Emergencies. In *Proceedings of the 13th European Conference on Computer Supported Cooperative Work*. ECSCW'13. Paphos, Cyprus: Springer London, pp. 181–206.

Lukowicz, P., Baker, M.G. & Paradiso, J., 2010. Guest Editors' Introduction: Hostile Environments. *IEEE Pervasive Computing*, 9(4), p.13–15. doi:10.1109/MPRV.2010.80.

Lundgren, H., Nordström, E. & Tschudin, C., 2002. Coping with Communication Gray Zones in IEEE 802.11B Based Ad Hoc Networks. In *Proceedings of the 5th International Workshop on Wireless Mobile Multimedia*. WOWMOM '02. New York, NY, USA: ACM, pp. 49–55. doi:10.1145/570790.570799.

Luqman, F., Sun, F.-T., Cheng, H.-T., Buthpitiya, S. & Griss, M., 2011. Prioritizing Data in Emergency Response Based on Context, Message Content and Role. In *Proceedings of the 1st International Conference on Wireless Technologies for Humanitarian Relief.* ACWR '11. New York, NY, USA: ACM, pp. 63–69. doi:10.1145/2185216.2185244.

Lu, S., Shere, S., Liu, Y. & Liu, Y., 2011. Device discovery and connection establishment approach using Ad-Hoc Wi-Fi for opportunistic networks. In *Proceedings of the International Conference on Pervasive Computing and Communications Workshops (PERCOM Workshops).* IEEE, pp. 461–466. doi:10.1109/PERCOMW.2011.5766934.

Manoj, B.S. & Baker, A.H., 2007. Communication Challenges in Emergency Response. *Communications of the ACM,* 50(3), p.51–53. doi:10.1145/1226736.1226765.

Manyena, S.B., 2006. The concept of resilience revisited. *Disasters,* 30(4), p.434–450. doi:10.1111/j.0361-3666.2006.00331.x.

Marable, M. & Clarke, K., 2007. *Seeking Higher Ground: The Hurricane Katrina Crisis, Race, and Public Policy Reader, First Edition,* New York: Palgrave Macmillan.

Mark, G.J., Al-Ani, B. & Semaan, B., 2009. Resilience Through Technology Adoption: Merging the Old and the New in Iraq. In *Proceedings of the 27th SIGCHI Conference on Human Factors in Computing Systems.* CHI '09. New York, NY, USA: ACM, pp. 689–698. doi:10.1145/1518701.1518808.

Mark, G. & Semaan, B., 2008. Resilience in Collaboration: Technology As a Resource for New Patterns of Action. In *Proceedings of the 12th Conference on Computer Supported Cooperative Work.* CSCW '08. New York, NY, USA: ACM, pp. 137–146. doi:10.1145/1460563.1460585.

Martín-Campillo, A., Crowcroft, J., Yoneki, E. & Martí, R., 2013. Evaluating Opportunistic Networks in Disaster Scenarios. *Journal of Network and Computer Applications,* 36(2), p.870–880. doi:10.1016/j.jnca.2012.11.001.

Martín-Campillo, A., Crowcroft, J., Yoneki, E., Martí, R. & Martínez-García, C., 2010. Using Haggle to Create an Electronic Triage Tag. In *Proceedings of the 2nd International Workshop on Mobile Opportunistic Networking.* MobiOpp '10. New York, NY, USA: ACM, pp. 167–170. doi:10.1145/1755743.1755775.

Martín-Campillo, A., Martí, R., Yoneki, E. & Crowcroft, J., 2011. Electronic Triage Tag and Opportunistic Networks in Disasters. In *Proceedings of the Special Work-*

shop on Internet and Disasters. SWID '11. New York, NY, USA: ACM, pp. 6:1–6:10. doi:10.1145/2079360.2079366.

Mattise, N., 2013. Boston cellular networks flooded, but service was not cut off: Heavy usage after marathon bombings—not an intentional shutdown—degraded service. *Ars Technica*. Retrieved from http://arstechnica.com/information-technology/2013/04/boston-cellular-networks-flooded-but-service-was-not-cut-off/ [Accessed on March 1, 2014].

McSaveney, E., 2014. The 2011 Christchurch earthquake and other recent earth-quakes. *Te Ara - the Encyclopedia of New Zealand*. Retrieved from http://www.teara.govt.nz/en/historic-earthquakes/page-13 [Accessed on De-cember 16, 2014].

Mehendale, H., Paranjpe, A. & Vempala, S., 2011. LifeNet: A Flexible Ad Hoc Net-working Solution for Transient Environments. In *Proceedings of the Confer-ence of the ACM Special Interest Group on Data Communication*. SIGCOMM '11. New York, NY, USA: ACM, pp. 446–447. doi:10.1145/2018436.2018513.

Mileti, D.S., Drabek, T.E. & Haas, J.E., 1975. *Human Systems in Extreme Environ-ments: A Sociological Perspective*, Institute of Behavioral Science, University of Colorado.

Millar, L., 2010. Tens of thousands isolated at quake epicentre. *ABC News*. Re-trieved from http://www.abc.net.au/news/2010-01-17/tens-of-thousands-isolated-at-quake-epicentre/1211748 [Accessed on December 16, 2014].

Minichiello, V., Aroni, R., Timewell, E. & Alexander, L., 1992. *In-depth Interviewing: Researching People*, South Melbourne: Routledge.

Mogensen, P., 1992. Towards a provotyping approach in systems developement. *Scandinavian Journal of Information Systems*, 4(1).

Mokryn, O., Karmi, D., Elkayam, A. & Teller, T., 2012. Help Me: Opportunistic smart rescue application and system. In *Proceedings of the the 11th Annual Mediter-ranean Ad Hoc Networking Workshop (Med-Hoc-Net)*. IEEE, pp. 98–105. doi:10.1109/MedHocNet.2012.6257129.

Neal, D.M., 1997. Reconsidering the phases of disaster. *International Journal of Mass Emergencies and Disasters*, 15(2), p.239–264.

NFC Forum, 2014a. Our Mission & Goals. Retrieved from http://nfc-forum.org/about-us/the-nfc-forum/ [Accessed on July 21, 2014].

NFC Forum, 2014b. *Technical Specifications*, Retrieved from http://members.nfc-forum.org/specs/spec_list/ [Accessed on July 21, 2014].

Nordström, E., Gunningberg, P. & Rohner, C., 2009. Haggle: A Data-centric Network Architecture for Mobile Devices. In *Proceedings of the MobiHoc S3 Workshop of the ACM International Symposium on Mobile Ad Hoc Networking and Computing*. MobiHoc S3. New York, NY, USA: ACM, pp. 37–40. doi:10.1145/1540358.1540370.

NZPA, 2011. Christchurch earthquake: Phone lines still damaged. *The New Zealand Herald*. Retrieved from http://www.nzherald.co.nz/nz/news/article.cfm?c_id=1&objectid=10708456 [Accessed on March 1, 2014].

O'Keefe, E., 2009. FEMA Chief Fugate Wants Public Involved in Preparation Efforts. *The Washington Post*. Retrieved from http://www.washingtonpost.com/wp-dyn/content/article/2009/06/03/AR2009060303404.html [Accessed on July 23, 2014].

Olaore, O., 2011. Politexting: Using Mobile Technology to Connect the Unconnected and Expanding the Scope of Political Communication. In *Proceedings of the 28th Information Systems Educators Conference*. ISECON '11. Wilmington North Carolina, USA: EDSIG.

O'Neill, E., Kostakos, V., Kindberg, T., Schiek, A.F. gen., Penn, A., Fraser, D.S. & Jones, T., 2006. Instrumenting the City: Developing Methods for Observing and Understanding the Digital Cityscape. In *Proceedings of the 8th International Conference on Ubiquitous Computing*. UbiComp'06. Berlin, Heidelberg: Springer-Verlag, pp. 315–332. doi:10.1007/11853565_19.

Online Geography Resources, 2009. *MEDC Earthquake Case Study - L'Aquila, Italy*, Retrieved from http://ibgeography-lancaster.wikispaces.com/file/view/lquila-text-sources.pdf [Accessed on March 1, 2014].

Palen, L., Anderson, K.M., Mark, G., Martin, J., Sicker, D., Palmer, M. & Grunwald, D., 2010. A Vision for Technology-mediated Support for Public Participation & Assistance in Mass Emergencies & Disasters. In *Proceedings of the 2010 ACM-BCS Visions of Computer Science Conference*. ACM-BCS '10. Swinton, UK, UK: British Computer Society, pp. 8:1–8:12.

Palen, L. & Liu, S.B., 2007. Citizen Communications in Crisis: Anticipating a Future of ICT-supported Public Participation. In *Proceedings of the 25th SIGCHI Conference on Human Factors in Computing Systems*. CHI '07. New York, NY, USA: ACM, pp. 727–736. doi:10.1145/1240624.1240736.

Palen, L. & Vieweg, S., 2008. The Emergence of Online Widescale Interaction in Un-expected Events: Assistance, Alliance & Retreat. In *Proceedings of the 12th Conference on Computer Supported Cooperative Work*. CSCW '08. New York, NY, USA: ACM, pp. 117–126. doi:10.1145/1460563.1460583.

Palen, L., Vieweg, S. & Anderson, K.M., 2011. Supporting "Everyday Analysts" in Safety-and Time-Critical Situations. *The Information Society*, 27(1), p.52–62. doi:10.1080/01972243.2011.534370.

Palen, L., Vieweg, S., Liu, S.B. & Hughes, A.L., 2009. Crisis in a Networked World Features of Computer-Mediated Communication in the April 16, 2007, Virginia Tech Event. *Social Science Computer Review*, 27(4), p.467–480. doi:10.1177/0894439309332302.

Pallardy, R., 2014. Chile earthquake of 2010. *Encyclopedia Britannica*. Retrieved from http://www.britannica.com/EBchecked/topic/1669019/Chile-earthquake-of-2010 [Accessed on December 16, 2014].

Papandrea, M., Vanini, S. & Giordano, S., 2009. A lightweight localization architec-ture and application for opportunistic networks. In *Proceedings of the Interna-tional Symposium on a World of Wireless, Mobile and Multimedia Networks Workshops, 2009. WoWMoM 2009*. IEEE, pp. 1–3. doi:10.1109/WOWMOM.2009.5282438.

Pelusi, L., Passarella, A. & Conti, M., 2006. Opportunistic networking: data forward-ing in disconnected mobile ad hoc networks. *IEEE Communications Maga-zine*, 44(11), p.134–141. doi:10.1109/MCOM.2006.248176.

Perez, S., 2014. Google Play Still Tops iOS App Store Downloads, And Now Narrow-ing Revenue Gap, Too. *TechCrunch*. Retrieved from http://techcrunch.com/2014/04/15/google-play-still-tops-ios-app-store-downloads-and-now-narrowing-revenue-gap-too/ [Accessed on July 24, 2014].

Perng, S.-Y., Büscher, M., Wood, L., Halvorsrud, R., Stiso, M., Ramirez, L. & Al-Akkad, A., 2013. Peripheral response: microblogging during the 22/7/2011 Norway attacks. *International Journal of Information Systems for Crisis Re-sponse and Management*, 5(1), p.41–57.

Perrucci, G.P., Fitzek, F.H.P. & Widmer, J., 2011. Survey on Energy Consumption Entities on the Smartphone Platform. In *Proceedings of the 73rd Vehicular Technology Conference*. VTC '11 Spring. Budapest, Hungary: IEEE, pp. 1–6. doi:10.1109/VETECS.2011.5956528.

Perry, R., 1998. Definitions and the development of a theoretical superstructure of disaster research. In *What is a Disaster? Perspectives on the Question.* London and New York: Routledge.

Pietiläinen, A.-K., Oliver, E., LeBrun, J., Varghese, G. & Diot, C., 2009. MobiClique: middleware for mobile social networking. In *Proceedings of the 2nd workshop on Online social networks.* ACM, pp. 49–54. doi:10.1145/1592665.1592678.

Pipek, V. & Wulf, V., 2009. Infrastructuring: Towards an Integrated Perspetive on the Design and Use of Information Technology. *Journal of the Association for Information Systems,* 10(5), p.306–332.

Powell, J., 1954. *An Introduction to the Natural History of Disaster,* College Park: University of Maryland Disaster Research Project.

Pullar-Strecker, T., 2011. Phone network hit by Christchurch quake. *Fairfax Media.* Retrieved from http://www.stuff.co.nz/business/industries/4688732/Phone-network-hit-by-Christchurch-quake [Accessed on December 7, 2011].

Quarantelli, E.L., 1994. *Emergent Behaviors and Groups in the Crisis Time Periods of Disaster,* Disaster Research Center. Retrieved from http://udspace.udel.edu/handle/19716/591 [Accessed on June 29, 2014].

Quarantelli, E.L., 2005. *What is a Disaster?: A Dozen Perspectives on the Question,* Routledge.

Qu, Y., Huang, C., Zhang, P. & Zhang, J., 2011. Microblogging After a Major Disaster in China: A Case Study of the 2010 Yushu Earthquake. In *Proceedings of the 14th Conference on Computer Supported Cooperative Work.* CSCW '11. New York, NY, USA: ACM, pp. 25–34. doi:10.1145/1958824.1958830.

Raffelsberger, C. & Hellwagner, H., 2013. A hybrid MANET-DTN routing scheme for emergency response scenarios. In *2013 IEEE International Conference on Pervasive Computing and Communications Workshops.* PerCom Workshops '13. IEEE Computer Society, pp. 505–510. doi:10.1109/PerComW.2013.6529549.

Ramirez, L., Dyrks, T., Gerwinski, J., Betz, M., Scholz, M. & Wulf, V., 2012. Landmarke: an ad hoc deployable ubicomp infrastructure to support indoor navigation of firefighters. *Personal and Ubiquitous Computing,* 16(8), p.1025–1038. doi:10.1007/s00779-011-0462-5.

Randell, B., Lee, P. & Treleaven, P.C., 1978. Reliability Issues in Computing System Design. *ACM Computing Surveys,* 10(2), p.123–165. doi:10.1145/356725.356729.

Reuter, C., Heger, O. & Pipek, V., 2013. Combining Real and Virtual Volunteers through Social Media. In *Proceedings of the 10th International Conference on Information Systems for Crisis Response and Management*. ISCRAM'13. Baden-Baden, Germany.

Reuter, C. & Ludwig, T., 2013. Anforderungen Und Technische Konzepte Der Krisenkommunikation Bei Stromausfall. *Informatik 2013 - Informatik angepasst an Mensch, Organisation und Umwelt*, p.1604–1618.

Reuter, C., Ludwig, T. & Pipek, V., 2014. Ad Hoc Participation in Situation Assessment: Supporting Mobile Collaboration in Emergencies. *ACM Transactions on Computer-Human Interactions*, 21(5), p.26:1–26:26. doi:10.1145/2651365.

Reuter, C., Marx, A. & Pipek, V., 2012. Crisis Management 2.0: Towards a Systematization of Social Software Use in Crisis Situations. *International Journal of Information Systems for Crisis Response and Management*, 4(1), p.1–16. doi:10.4018/jiscrm.2012010101.

Rivera, J. & van der Meulen, R., 2014. Gartner Says Worldwide Tablet Sales Grew 68 Percent in 2013, With Android Capturing 62 Percent of the Market. *Garnter Inc.* Retrieved from http://www.gartner.com/newsroom/id/2674215 [Accessed on July 24, 2014].

Rivera, J. & van der Meulen, R., 2013. Worldwide Devices Shipments by Operating System. *Garnter Inc.* Retrieved from http://www.gartner.com/newsroom/id/2408515 [Accessed on January 3, 2014].

Rogers, R., Aberson, S., Aksoy, A., Annane, B., Black, M., Cione, J., Dorst, N., Dunion, J., Gamache, J., Goldenberg, S., Gopalakrishnan, S., Kaplan, J., Klotz, B., Lorsolo, S., Marks, F., Murillo, S., Powell, M., Reasor, P., Sellwood, K., Uhlhorn, E., Vukicevic, T., Zhang, J. & Zhang, X., 2013. NOAA'S Hurricane Intensity Forecasting Experiment: A Progress Report. *Bulletin of the American Meteorological Society*, 94(6), p.859–882. doi:10.1175/BAMS-D-12-00089.1.

Rosenberg, S., 2011. Norway massacre: How neighbour rescued five from island. *BBC News*. Retrieved from http://www.bbc.co.uk/news/world-europe-14266456 [Accessed on June 29, 2014].

Saavedra, J.L., 2010. Massive earthquake hits Chile, 214 dead. *Reuters*. Retrieved from http://www.reuters.com/article/2010/02/27/us-quake-chile-idUSTRE61Q0S920100227 [Accessed on December 16, 2014].

Sakurai, M., Watson, R.T., Abraham, C. & Kokuryo, J., 2014. Sustaining life during the early stages of disaster relief with a frugal information system: learning from the great east Japan earthquake. *IEEE Communications Magazine*, 52(1), p.176–185. doi:10.1109/MCOM.2014.6710081.

Samuel Burke, 2014. Protesters in Venezuela, Ukraine turn to peer-to-peer messaging app. *CNN International*. Retrieved from http://edition.cnn.com/2014/02/24/world/venezuela-ukraine-protests-apps/ [Accessed on July 23, 2014].

Sarcevic, A., Palen, L., White, J., Starbird, K., Bagdouri, M. & Anderson, K., 2012. "Beacons of Hope" in Decentralized Coordination: Learning from On-the-ground Medical Twitterers During the 2010 Haiti Earthquake. In *Proceedings of the 15th Conference on Computer Supported Cooperative Work*. CSCW '12. New York, NY, USA: ACM, pp. 47–56. doi:10.1145/2145204.2145217.

Savage, N., 2013. Backing creativity. *Communications of the ACM*, 56(7), p.20. doi:10.1145/2483852.2483860.

Scott, J., Crowcroft, P. & Diot, C., 2006. Haggle: a networking architecture designed around mobile users. In *Proceedings of the 3rd Annual IFIP Conference on Wireless On-Demand Network Systems and Services*. WONS'06. IEEE.

Seeburger, J., 2012. No Cure for Curiosity: Linking Physical and Digital Urban Layers. In *Proceedings of the 7th Nordic Conference on Human-Computer Interaction: Making Sense Through Design*. NordiCHI '12. New York, NY, USA: ACM, pp. 247–256. doi:10.1145/2399016.2399054.

Semaan, B. & Mark, G., 2011. Technology-mediated Social Arrangements to Resolve Breakdowns in Infrastructure During Ongoing Disruption. *ACM Transactions on Computer-Human Interactions*, 18(4), p.21:1–21:21. doi:10.1145/2063231.2063235.

Shklovski, I., Palen, L. & Sutton, J., 2008. Finding Community Through Information and Communication Technology in Disaster Response. In *Proceedings of the 12th Conference on Computer Supported Cooperative Work*. CSCW '08. New York, NY, USA: ACM, pp. 127–136. doi:10.1145/1460563.1460584.

Silva, A. de S. e & Frith, J., 2012. *Mobile Interfaces in Public Spaces: Locational Privacy, Control, and Urban Sociability*, New York: Routledge.

Simpson, P.V., 2010. Internet savvy Swedes launch "Angry note 2.0" - The Local. *The Local (Swedish News)*. Retrieved from http://www.thelocal.se/20101031/29934 [Accessed on August 1, 2014].

Smith, R.D., 2006. Responding to global infectious disease outbreaks: Lessons from SARS on the role of risk perception, communication and management. *Social*

Science & Medicine, 63(12), p.3113–3123. doi:10.1016/j.socscimed.2006.08.004.

Smith-Spark, L., 2014. *With more than 191,000 dead in Syria, U.N. rights chief slams global "paralysis,"* CNN International. Retrieved from http://www.cnn.com/2014/08/22/world/meast/syria-conflict/index.html [Accessed on December 16, 2014].

Souissi, S. & Meihofer, E.F., 2000. Performance evaluation of a Bluetooth network in the presence of adjacent and co-channel interference. In *Proceedings of the Emerging Technologies Symposium: Broadband, Wireless Internet Access.* IEEE, p. 6 pp.–. doi:10.1109/ETS.2000.916528.

Starbird, K. & Palen, L., 2012. (How) Will the Revolution Be Retweeted?: Information Diffusion and the 2011 Egyptian Uprising. In *Proceedings of the 15th Conference on Computer Supported Cooperative Work.* CSCW '12. New York, NY, USA: ACM, pp. 7–16. doi:10.1145/2145204.2145212.

Starbird, K. & Palen, L., 2011. "Voluntweeters": Self-organizing by Digital Volunteers in Times of Crisis. In *Proceedings of the 29th SIGCHI Conference on Human Factors in Computing Systems.* CHI '11. New York, NY, USA: ACM, pp. 1071–1080. doi:10.1145/1978942.1979102.

Starbird, K. & Stamberger, J., 2010. Tweak the Tweet: Leveraging Microblogging Proliferation with a Prescriptive Syntax to Support Citizen Reporting. In *Proceedings of the 7th International Conference on Information Systems for Crisis Response and Management.* ISCRAM'10. ISCRAM.

Star, S.L., 1999. The Ethnography of Infrastructure. *American Behavioral Scientist*, 43(3), p.377–391.

Star, S.L. & Ruhleder, K., 1996. Steps Toward an Ecology of Infrastructure: Design and Access for Large Information Spaces. *Information Systems Research*, 7(1), p.111–134.

Sterbenz, J.P.G., Hutchison, D., Çetinkaya, E.K., Jabbar, A., Rohrer, J.P., Schöller, M. & Smith, P., 2010. Resilience and Survivability in Communication Networks: Strategies, Principles, and Survey of Disciplines. *Elsevier Computer Networks*, 54(8), p.1245–1265. doi:10.1016/j.comnet.2010.03.005.

Stevens, G., Pipek, V. & Wulf, V., 2010. Appropriation Infrastructure: Mediating Appropriation and Production Work. In *Proceedings of the 2nd International Symposium on End-User Development.* IS-EUD '09. Siegen, Germany: Springer, pp. 58–81. doi:10.4018/joeuc.2010040104.

Storey, P. & Addley, E., 2010. 7/7 London attacks: the people who died. *The Guardian*. Retrieved from http://www.theguardian.com/uk/interactive/2010/oct/14/july7-london-attacks [Accessed on December 16, 2014].

Su, J., Scott, J., Hui, P., Crowcroft, J., De Lara, E., Diot, C., Goel, A., Lim, M.H. & Upton, E., 2007. Haggle: Seamless Networking for Mobile Applications. In *Proceedings of the 9th International Conference on Ubiquitous Computing*. UbiComp '07. Berlin, Heidelberg: Springer-Verlag, pp. 391–408.

Sutton, J., 2012. When Online is Off: Public Communications Following the February 2011 Christchurch, NZ Earthqauke. In *Proceedings of the 9th International Conference on Information Systems for Crisis Response and Management*. ISCRAM 2012. Vancouver, BC, Canada: ISCRAM.

Toups, Z.O., Kerne, A., Hamilton, W.A. & Shahzad, N., 2011. Zero-fidelity Simulation of Fire Emergency Response: Improving Team Coordination Learning. In *Proceedings of the 29th SIGCHI Conference on Human Factors in Computing Systems*. CHI '11. New York, NY, USA: ACM, pp. 1959–1968. doi:10.1145/1978942.1979226.

Trifunovic, S., Distl, B., Schatzmann, D. & Legendre, F., 2011. WiFi-Opp: Ad-hocless Opportunistic Networking. In *Proceedings of the 6th Workshop on Challenged Networks*. CHANTS '11. New York, NY, USA: ACM, pp. 37–42. doi:10.1145/2030652.2030664.

Trifunovic, S., Picu, A., Hossmann, T. & Hummel, K.A., 2013. Slicing the Battery Pie: Fair and Efficient Energy Usage in Device-to-device Communication via Role Switching. In *Proceedings of the 8th MobiCom Workshop on Challenged Networks*. CHANTS '13. New York, NY, USA: ACM, pp. 31–36. doi:10.1145/2505494.2505496.

Turoff, M., 2002. Past and Future Emergency Response Information Systems. *Communications of the ACM*, 45(4), p.29–32. doi:10.1145/505248.505265.

Urken, A.B., "Buck" Nimz, A. & Schuck, T.M., 2012. Designing evolvable systems in a framework of robust, resilient and sustainable engineering analysis. *Advanced Engineering Informatics*, 26(3), p.553–562. doi:10.1016/j.aei.2012.05.006.

Urry, J., 2002. Mobility and Proximity. *Sociology*, 36(2), p.255–274. doi:10.1177/0038038502036002002.

Vahdat, A. & Becker, D., 2000. *Epidemic Routing for Partially-Connected Ad Hoc Networks*, Technical Report CS-200006, Duke University.

Vieweg, S., Hughes, A.L., Starbird, K. & Palen, L., 2010. Microblogging During Two Natural Hazards Events: What Twitter May Contribute to Situational Awareness. In *Proceedings of the 28th SIGCHI Conference on Human Factors in Computing Systems*. CHI '10. New York, NY, USA: ACM, pp. 1079–1088. doi:10.1145/1753326.1753486.

Vieweg, S., Palen, L., Liu, S.B., Hughes, A.L. & Sutton, J., 2007. Collective intelligence in disaster: examination of the phenomenon in the aftermath of the 2007 Virginia Tech shooting. In *Proceedings of the 5th International Conference on Information Systems for Crisis Response and Management*. IS-CRAM'08.

Wachtendorf, T. & Kendra, J.M., 2004. *Considering Convergence, Coordination, and Social Capital in Disasters*, Disaster Research Center. Retrieved from http://udspace.udel.edu/handle/19716/737 [Accessed on June 29, 2014].

Wang, W., Joshi, R., Kulkarni, A., Leong, W.K. & Leong, B., 2013. Feasibility Study of Mobile Phone WiFi Detection in Aerial Search and Rescue Operations. In *Proceedings of the 4th Asia-Pacific Workshop on Systems*. APSys 2013. New York, NY, USA: ACM. doi:10.1145/2500727.2500729.

Wang, X.Y. & Ho, P.-H., 2011. Gossip-Enabled Stochastic Channel Negotiation for Cognitive Radio Ad Hoc Networks. *IEEE Transactions on Mobile Computing*, 10(11), p.1632–1645. doi:10.1109/TMC.2011.77.

Weick, K.E., 1998. Introductory Essay: Improvisation as a Mindset for Organizational Analysis. *Organization Science*, 9(5), p.543–555.

Weick, K.E., 1993. The Collapse of Sensemaking in Organizations: The Mann Gulch Disaster. *Administrative Science Quarterly*, 38, p.628–652.

Weiser, M., 1999. The Computer for the 21st Century. *Mobile Computing and Communications Review*, 3(3), p.3–11. doi:10.1145/329124.329126.

Whitbeck, J., Lopez, Y., Leguay, J., Conan, V. & De Amorim, M.D., 2012. Fast Track Article: Push-and-track: Saving Infrastructure Bandwidth Through Opportunistic Forwarding. *Pervasive and Mobile Computing*, 8(5), p.682–697. doi:10.1016/j.pmcj.2012.02.001.

WHO, 2003. Summary of probable SARS cases with onset of illness from 1 November 2002 to 31 July 2003. Retrieved from http://www.who.int/csr/sars/country/table2004_04_21/en/ [Accessed on December 16, 2014].

Wi-Fi Alliance, 2010. Wi-Fi Peer-to-Peer (P2P) Technical Specification, Version 1.1.

Wi-Fi Alliance, 2006. Wi-Fi Protected Setup Specification, Version 1.0.

Wildavsky, A., 1989. Searching for safety. In News Brunswick: Transactions.

Wilson, S., 2014. Syrian Medics Have So Little Medical Supplies That They Knock Out Patients With Metal Bars To Perform Surgery. *Business Insider Australia*. Retrieved from http://www.businessinsider.com.au/syrian-medics-must-knock-out-patients-with-metal-bars-to-perform-surgery-2014-3 [Accessed on June 29, 2014].

Wirtz, H., Backhaus, R., Hummen, R. & Wehrle, K., 2011. Establishing Mobile Ad-hoc Networks in 802.11 Infrastructure Mode. In *Proceedings of the 6th ACM International Workshop on Wireless Network Testbeds, Experimental Evaluation and Characterization*. WiNTECH '11. New York, NY, USA: ACM, pp. 89–90. doi:10.1145/2030718.2030737.

Wirz, M., Roggen, D. & Troster, G., 2010. User Acceptance Study of a Mobile System for Assistance during Emergency Situations at Large-Scale Events. In *Proceedings of the 3rd International Conference on Human-Centric Computing*. HumanCom'10. pp. 1–6. doi:10.1109/HUMANCOM.2010.5563347.

Wong, M., Powell, A. & Clement, A., 2007. Reading Service Set Identifiers (SSIDs): Marking and Locating for Public and Private Wireless Spaces. In *Proceedings of the International Conference, Internet Research 8.0, in Association of the Internet Researchers (A.o.I.R)*.

Wood, L.E., 1997. Semi-structured Interviewing for User-centered Design. *interactions*, 4(2), p.48–61. doi:10.1145/245129.245134.

Wulf, V., Aal, K., Abu Kteish, I., Atam, M., Schubert, K., Rohde, M., Yerousis, G.P. & Randall, D., 2013. Fighting Against the Wall: Social Media Use by Political Activists in a Palestinian Village. In *Proceedings of the 31st SIGCHI Conference on Human Factors in Computing Systems*. CHI '13. New York, NY, USA: ACM, pp. 1979–1988. doi:10.1145/2470654.2466262.

Wulf, V., Misaki, K., Atam, M., Randall, D. & Rohde, M., 2013. "On the Ground" in Sidi Bouzid: Investigating Social Media Use During the Tunisian Revolution. In *Proceedings of the 16th Conference on Computer Supported Cooperative Work*. CSCW '13. New York, NY, USA: ACM, pp. 1409–1418. doi:10.1145/2441776.2441935.

Wulf, V., Rohde, M., Pipek, V. & Stevens, G., 2011. Engaging with Practices: Design Case Studies As a Research Framework in CSCW. In *Proceedings of the 14th Conference on Computer Supported Cooperative Work*. CSCW '11. New York, NY, USA: ACM, pp. 505–512. doi:10.1145/1958824.1958902.

Wu, X., Mazurowski, M., Chen, Z. & Meratnia, N., 2011. Emergency message dissemination system for smartphones during natural disasters. In *Proceedings of the 11th International Conference on ITS Telecommunications*. ITST'11. pp. 258–263. doi:10.1109/ITST.2011.6060064.

Yanmaz, E., 2012. Connectivity versus area coverage in unmanned aerial vehicle networks. In *2012 IEEE International Conference on Communications (ICC)*. ICC 2012. pp. 719–723. doi:10.1109/ICC.2012.6364585.

Yau, N., 2012. Political allegiance via wireless network SSIDs, mapped. *FlowingData*. Retrieved from http://flowingdata.com/2012/06/05/political-allegiance-via-wireless-network-ssids-mapped/ [Accessed on August 1, 2014].

Yu, H., 2004. The power of thumbs: the politics of SMS in urban China. *Graduate Journal of Asia-Pacific Studies*, 2(2), p.30–43.

Appendix A: Own Publications

The research presented in this work has been presented and discussed in the field of human-computer-interaction and information systems for emergency response. The following list presents in reverse chronological order the papers published in the frame of this thesis.

I.   Al-Akkad, A. & Boden, A., 2014. Kreative Nutzung der verfügbaren Netzwerkinfrastruktur im Katastrophenfall / Creative usage of available network infrastructure in disaster situations. *i-com: Zeitschrift für interaktive und kooperative Medien*, 13(1), p.45–52. doi:10.1515/icom-2014-0007.

II.   Al-Akkad, A. & Raffelsberger, C., 2014. How Do I Get This App? A Discourse on Distributing Mobile Applications Despite Disrupted Infrastructure. *In Proceedings of the 11th International Conference on Information Systems for Crisis Response and Management*. ISCRAM'14. Penn State University, Pennsylvenia, USA: ISCRAM.

III. Al-Akkad, A., Raffelsberger, C., Boden, A., Ramirez, L. & Zimmermann, A., 2014. Tweeting "When Online is Off"? Opportunistically Creating Mobile Ad-hoc Networks in Response to Disrupted Infrastructure. *In Proceedings of the 11th International Conference on Information Systems for Crisis Response and Management*. ISCRAM'14. Penn State University, Pennsylvenia, USA: ISCRAM.

IV. Al-Akkad, A., Ramirez, L., Boden, A., Randall, D. & Zimmermann, A., 2014. Help Beacons: Design and Evaluation of an Ad-hoc Lightweight S.O.S. System for Smartphones. *In Proceedings of the 32nd SIGCHI Conference on Human Factors in Computing Systems*. CHI '14. New York, NY, USA: ACM, pp. 1485–1494. doi:10.1145/2556288.2557002. *Received an* **Honorable Mention Award** *(top 5% of all submissions)*

V.   Al-Akkad, A. & Vinkovits, M., 2014. Increasing Users' Autonomy in Obtaining Mobile Applications. In *Autonomy in Technology Design. Workshop at the SIGCHI Conference on Human Factors in Computing Systems*. CHI '14. New York, NY, USA: ACM.

VI. Al-Akkad, A., Ramirez, L., Denef, S., Boden, A., Wood, L., Büscher, M. & Zimmermann, A., 2013. "Reconstructing Normality": The Use of Infrastructure Leftovers in Crisis Situations As Inspiration for the Design of Resilient Technology. *In Proceedings of the 25th Australian Computer-Human Interaction Conference: Augmentation, Application, Innovation, Collaboration*. OzCHI '13. New York, NY, USA: ACM, pp. 457–466. doi:10.1145/2541016.2541051.

VII. Al-Akkad, A. & Zimmermann, A., 2012. Survey: ICT-supported Public Participation in Disasters. *In Proceedings of the 9th International Conference on Information Systems for Crisis Response and Management.* ISCRAM'12. Vancouver, BC, Canada: ISCRAM.

VIII. Al-Akkad, A. & Zimmermann, A., 2011. User Study: Involving civilians by
smart phones during emergency situations. *In Proceedings of the 8th International Conference on Information Systems for Crisis Response and Management.* ISCRAM'11. Lisbon, Portugal: ISCRAM.

IX. Perng, S.-Y., Buscher, M., Wood, L., Halvorsrud, R., Stiso, M., Ramirez, L. &
Al-Akkad, A., 2013. Peripheral response: microblogging during the 22/7/2011
Norway attacks. *International Journal of Information Systems for Crisis Re-
sponse and Management*, 5(1), p.41–57.

Table 29 displays how each publication has contributed to one or more chapter or
section of this thesis.

Publication	Type	Chapter
I	Overall	1-9
II	Help Beacons: second prototype	6, 7.3
III	Local Cloud: first prototype	6, 8.2
IV	Help Beacons: first prototype	3, 6, 7.2
V	Help Beacons: second prototype	7.3
VI	Empirical data, methodology and concept	2, 3, 4, 5
VII	Background	2, 6
VIII	Background	2, 3
IX	Background, empirical data	2, 4

Table 29 Publications contributing to this thesis

Moreover, this research resulted in the publishing of one patent application:

Al-Akkad, A., Ramirez, L. & Zimmermann, A., 2014. Method for organizing a wireless
network. European Patent Office, Application No. 13171881.9, Publication No.
2814299A1. Retrieved from
https://depatisnet.dpma.de/DepatisNet/depatisnet?docid=EP000002814299A1
[Accessed on December 20, 2014].

The author of this work contributed to further publications, which are out of the scope
of the thesis. In the following, these publications are listed in alphabetic order.

Al-Akkad, A., Jahn, M., Pramudianto, F. & Zimmermann, A., 2009. Middleware for building pervasive systems. In Proceedings of the International Conference Applied Computing, 2009, pp. 291-298. IADIS'09.

Al-Akkad, A., Reiners, R. & Jentsch, M., 2011. Where to draw the line? Approaching a scale to negotiate in-situ civil involvement for the inquiry of crisis information. In CSCWSmart? Workshop at the 12th European Conference on Computer-Supported Cooperative Work. ECSCW'11. Aarhus, Denmark: Springer.

Al-Akkad, A., Reiners, R. & Zimmermann, A., 2011. Utilizing Cell Phones for Bystander Intervention during Emergencies. In Communicating Disaster (2010-2011), Extended Jour Fixe, New Social Media and Crisis Workshop. Bielefeld, Germany.

Denef, S., Ramirez, L., Dyrks, T., Schwartz, T. & Al-Akkad, A.-A., 2008. Participatory Design Workshops to Evaluate Multimodal Applications. In Proceedings of the 5th Nordic Conference on Human-computer Interaction: Building Bridges. NordiCHI '08. New York, NY, USA: ACM, pp. 459–462. doi:10.1145/1463160.1463219.

Jahn, M., Jentsch, M., Prause, C.R., Pramudianto, F., Al-Akkad, A. & Reiners, R., 2010. The Energy Aware Smart Home. In 2010 5th International Conference on Future Information Technology (FutureTech). pp. 1–8. doi:10.1109/FUTURETECH.2010.5482712.

Jahn, M., Pramudianto, F. & Al-Akkad, A., 2009. Hydra middleware for developing pervasive systems: A case study in the e-Health domain. In Proceedings of the 1st International Workshop on Distributed Computing in Ambient Environments. DiComAe'09. Paderborn, Germany.

Jentsch, M., Jahn, M., Pramudianto, F., Simon, J. & Al-Akkad, A., 2011. An Energy-saving Support System for Office Environments. In Proceedings of the 2nd International Conference on Human Behavior Unterstanding. HBU'11. Berlin, Heidelberg: Springer-Verlag, pp. 83–92. doi:10.1007/978-3-642-25446-8_10.

Lawson, J.-Y.L., Al-Akkad, A.-A., Vanderdonckt, J. & Macq, B., 2009. An Open Source Workbench for Prototyping Multimodal Interactions Based on Off-the-shelf Heterogeneous Components. In Proceedings of the 1st ACM SIGCHI Symposium on Engineering Interactive Computing Systems. EICS '09. New York, NY, USA: ACM, pp. 245–254. doi:10.1145/1570433.1570480.

Simon, J., Jahn, M. & Al-Akkad, A., 2012. Saving Energy at Work: The Design of a Pervasive Game for Office Spaces. In Proceedings of the 11th International

Conference on Mobile and Ubiquitous Multimedia. MUM '12. New York, NY, USA: ACM, pp. 9:1–9:4. doi:10.1145/2406367.2406379.

Appendix B: Curriculum Vitae

Particulars

Family Name	Al-Akkad
First Name	Amro
Address	Mirecourtstr. 16, 53225 Bonn, Germany
E-Mail	amro.al-akkad@fit.fraunhofer.de
Date of Birth	7 January 1981
Birth Place	Ludwigsburg
Nationality	German
Marital Status:	Married

Academic Education

12 / 2008 – Current	RWTH Aachen University, Germany PhD in Computer Science, Degree: Dr. rer. nat. Focus: Mobile Computing
10 / 2002 – 09 / 2008	University of Siegen, Germany Graduation in Business Informatics, Degree: Dipl.-Wirt.-Inform., Focus: Software Engineering
07 / 2006 – 12 / 2006	QUT, Brisbane, Australia Study Abroad Semester

Military Service

11 / 2000 – 08 / 2001	German Air Force, Bayreuth and Haiger Burbach, Germany

Professional Experience

12 / 2008 – Current	Fraunhofer Institute for Applied Information Technology (FIT), Sankt Augustin, Germany Position: Research Associate Focus: Ubiquitous Computing
05 / 2007 – 09 / 2008	Fraunhofer Institute for Applied Information Technology (FIT), Sankt Augustin, Germany Position: Student Assistant Focus: User-oriented Software Development
09 / 2005 – 10 / 2005 and 03 / 2006 – 04 / 2006	Deutsche Bank, Frankfurt am Main, Germany Position: Intern Focus: IT-Security, Software Engineering

Skills

Languages	German (native), English (fluent), Arabic (basics)
Methods	SCRUM, Software Architectures, UML, UCD
Programming	Java, C++, C#, SQL
Markup Languages	MySQL, HTML, XML
Frameworks	Android, OSGi, REST, SOAP, .NET
Developer Tools	Atlassian Confluence and JIRA, Eclipse, Git, Subversion, Ant, Ivy, Visual Studio

Interests

Sports	Biking, Jogging
Hobbies	Music, Reading, Traveling

Printed in the United States
By Bookmasters